Human Growth And Development
The Childhood Years

John J. Mitchell

Detselig Enterprises Limited
Calgary, Alberta

Canadian Cataloguing in Publication Data

Mitchell, John J., 1941-
  Human growth and development

  Bibliography: p.
  Includes index.
  ISBN 1-55059-002-2

  1. Developmental psychology. 2. Child
development. I. Title.
BF721.M58 1989   155.4   C89-091201-7

© 1990 Detselig Enterprises Limited
P.O. Box G 399
Calgary, Alberta

Printed in Canada   SAN 115-0324   ISBN 1-55059-002-2

Dedication
This book is dedicated to Ilona and Stella whose
captivating charm rekindled afresh my love of children

Contents

Acknowledgments

Several People were of great assistance to me in the writing, researching and organizing of this book. My research assistants, Sara Yarwood and Sylvia Bowman were of great assistance in analyzing and classifying the current research in child psychology. My father, Robert Vincent Mitchell, who has edited each of my previous books, performed his usual word surgery with admirable precision. Loretta Moore carried out her secretarial responsibilities with good cheer and professional competence. And in this day of electronic word processing, Gene Romaniuk went well beyond the call of duty in helping me with computers, word processors, and other gadgets which the mechanically impaired, like myself, have so much difficulty negotiating.

To each of you I am indebted, and to each of you I say "Thank you."

John J. Mitchell

Detselig Enterprises Ltd. appreciates the financial
assistance for its 1990 publishing program from

Alberta Foundation of the Literary Arts
Canada Council
Department of Communications
Alberta Culture

1

Basic Concepts in Developmental Psychology

There is nothing permanent except change.
Heraclitus

This book is about children: their growth, their development, and their impact on the world in which they live. We will probe the significant domains of childhood, starting with the protoplasmic globule of fertilized egg which becomes the fetus, the infant, and finally the child. The part of the human saga this book is concerned with is short, ending just before the early adolescent years; nevertheless, it is the period in which virtually all foundations of human growth and development are laid.

The purpose of this book is to help you understand how children grow and develop. And, as well, to instill an understanding of the forces that mould children and, in turn, how children mould their world into greater harmony with themselves. The approach throughout this book is interdisciplinary, although it relies most heavily on data, research and theory from the field of developmental psychology. The emphasis is on *description and analysis of growth patterns, developmental sequences, and the range of abilities which typify childhood in North America.*

Major Concepts in the Study of Human Growth & Development

The Meaning of "Development"

All rising to a great place is by a winding stair.
Francis Bacon

Professionals who specialize in human development (pediatricians, edu-

1

cators, psychologists) use the term "development" in a more comprehensive manner than is typical of everyday usage. Development from the expert's point of view must be distinguished from mere change – acquiring a tooth is developmental change, acquiring additional head hair is not. *Development refers to the orderly sequence of change that takes place throughout the life cycle, with the developing person functioning in new ways at different ages* (Stone, 1984). Development has five central concepts which define its essential nature. They include the following:

1. *Time* – All development occurs over time. The amount of time involved is measured in terms of the stage of life being examined. For example, developmental changes during adolescence (puberty and formal thought, for example) take months, sometimes years, to be finalized, whereas developmental changes in prenatal development take place in days or weeks.

2. *Cumulativity* – A developmental change results in the addition of some new feature to the child. Each developmental change adds something new, which is added to what existed before. In other words, development *accumulates* with each change modifying, and adding to, the changes that went before. Cumulative changes may be dramatic (an infant acquiring laughter, or a toddler acquiring language) or incremental (progressing from walking with assistance to walking alone).

3. *Directionality* – Development has direction – it transports the child toward a final destination. Development progresses from general to specific, that is toward refinement and away from primitiveness; it progresses toward greater efficiency and parsimony.

   In embryology, we observe that development progressively moves toward an organism which, after nine months of development, we call the "newborn." Full-term newborns around the world are remarkably similar in every major feature. Since the earliest days after conception the embryo and the fetus have been developing toward the event of birth. From this perspective, development is directional and progresses toward a final "destination."

4. *New modes of organization* – As children mature they acquire new features and abilities which did not exist in earlier ages. These changes result in the "radical alteration or reorganization in the arrangement, constitution, or structure of the individual. In short, the rules of the system change." (Green, 1989, p. 17). A youngster who can solve a problem "in her head" possesses a new mode of organization she did not possess a few months earlier when she could solve problems only by experimentation or trial-and-error.

5. *Increased capacity for self-control* – As children develop they increase in their capacity for self-control. They accomplish this by monitoring their own behavior, by adjusting their behavior to suit their needs, and by inhibiting ineffective behavior.

This capacity for self-control is also known as *autoregulation.* "It implies some mechanism that anticipates the consequences of a particular activity, monitors the consequences of a particular activity, adjusts the activity to the expected outcome, initiates the activity, monitors the consequences as they unfold, and continuously readjusts the activity to achieve the planned consequences." (Green, 1989, p.18).

How change takes place is a vital issue for developmental psychologists. For example, how do emotions, language, affection, or moral beliefs change as an individual gets older? The developmental psychologist is also concerned with how the same behavior means different things at different ages. A two-year-old may throw a temper tantrum for different reasons, or have it triggered by different causes than an eight-year-old, just as four-year-old boys chase four-year-old girls for different reasons than 13-year-old boys chase 13-year-old girls. And, of course, developmental psychologists are very concerned with what *causes* development. Is development a product of the inborn forces of nature, of pre-determined genetic factors? Is development a product of our environment, our training, our socialization? Psychologists agree that development is nurtured by a mixture of forces, internal and external, genetic and social, but the *relative significance* of each ingredient in this mixture is a matter of considerable controversy.

The entire scope of human development is effectively summarized in the following passage:

> Developmental psychologists must try to distinguish development and more specifically, human development from all other kinds of change, like learning, forgetting, brain damage, and drug effects. "Development" implies that the change is systematic, not random; that it is permanent, not temporary, that it is progressive, not regressive – it goes forward not backward; that it is steady, not fluctuating; that it occurs over some period of time within a person's lifetime, not in an hour or over two generations; that it occurs for all people, not just a few; and perhaps most centrally, that it is related to a person's increasing age and experience. (Clarke-Stewart and Friedman, 1987).

Transformations and behavioral reorganization

Childhood development is a continuous series of changes in both physical and mental abilities. These changes are called *transformations* because they transform the child from a lower to a higher level of functioning. Mental transformations allow children to perceive subtle relationships not previously evident, and to solve problems which before were beyond them.

Physical transformations allow the child to make a vertical jump when before she could only strain, bend and flex. These breakthroughs (which occur by the dozen during every childhood year) produce a "transformed" and qualitatively more advanced individual.

An allied concept is *behavioral reorganization.* As youngsters mature they learn to coordinate memory with action, to match anticipation with outcome, and to gauge reaction from action. This ongoing process creates a more complex and more capable child. Behavioral reorganization of pre-existing skills comprise the building blocks of child growth.

The impact of transformations and behavioral reorganization on the overall functioning of the child has been compared, in a rather clever manner, to the organization of a business enterprise:

> Imagine an accounting firm years ago in which the employees did all their work using hand-held calculators. For a while the business grew simply by adding new accountants, each of whom did the same thing (quantitative change). But then a computer was installed. This new technology produced dramatic qualitative changes. Not only was the firm able to handle vastly more accounts, but tasks were performed in very different ways. Specialization occurred. Some staff members worked on designing new computer programs. Some actually worked on inputting information. Some primarily interpreted the output. A more elaborate organization hierarchy evolved. Granted, knowledge from the old systems was used in the new system, but it was now part of a totally different organization. So it seems to be with human development. (Sroufe and Cooper, 1988)

The Direction of Development

The genetic code which initiates and "oversees" child development follows several lawful precepts and the flow of development is channeled by these elementary principles.

The first principle is that *growth proceeds in a head-to-foot direction.* Areas near the head develop sooner and with greater priority than those of the lower body. This principle is readily evident during the stage of the embryo, when the head constitutes almost half of the total body volume. In the stage of the fetus the remainder of the body grows, hence the head assumes a progressively smaller portion of the entire body.

At birth the head is the most developed part of the body; the eyes and mouth are developmentally far more advanced than the fingers or the toes. Head-to-foot growth is known as *cephalocaudal development,* and its influence on physical growth is observed throughout the first years of life.

Growth also *proceeds outward from the central axis.* Internal organs mature earlier and begin to work efficiently before body parts away from the centre. Vital organs (heart, liver, kidneys) function with a precision not required of the hands, feet or shoulders. A child can survive with deformed or even missing extremities but may perish if vital organs are missing or deformed. *Proximodistal development* (centre-to-extremity) works in conjunction with cephalocaudal development (head-to-toe) to program many of the physical features of childhood.

The human body also develops *bilaterally,* with many parts appearing in pairs – one on each side. These pairs develop in synchrony, that is, they grow at nearly identical rates; they also begin their growth spurts, and settle into plateaus in almost total harmony.

These directional patterns (cephalocaudal, proximodistal, bilateral) provide the elementary blueprint within which far more complex and elaborate developments transpire.

Nothing in human development emerges fully flowered; everything begins with primitive outlines and gradually matures into more refined and streamlined patterns. This progression from primitive to sophisticated is known as *general-to-specific growth.*

It is the most easily recognized feature of directionality since it affects every phase of development. The baby crawls then walks, speaks one-word sentences, grasps with the entire hand then with only thumb and index finger. Every childhood development proceeds from general to specific.

Prehensile (grasping) development demonstrates general-to-specific growth and also provides a few clues as to how physical growth influences social behavior. Children begin making letters with a pencil at about age five, playing ball sports at about age eight, and playing cards with peers (rather than parents) at about age nine or ten. These activities parallel the fact that the fingers become dexterous enough to manipulate a pencil somewhere near the fifth year; near the eighth year the wrist can pivot with enough precision to clutch a ball thrown through the air, and near the tenth birthday manual dexterity is refined enough to allow shuffling a deck of cards. Thus, developmental groundplans cast their influence not only on the abilities but also on the games of children.

The general-to-specific growth pattern is dramatized by the child's reaction to pain. If the chubby rear end of a six-month infant is accidentally pricked by a safety pin, the baby will cry, and flail his entire body; at six years a pin prick will cause the child to cry, flail his arms, and rub the spot that was hurt; at ten years the child may or may not cry, may or may not flail, but will rub. The point is that the infant responds to pain with global (general) reactions, but with advancing age the reaction becomes more specific.

The Rhythm of Development

The work of developmentalists would be far easier if human development were linear and consistent. It is not. Development has its own tempo and pace. Like the sprawling metropolis in which so many of us live, it has moments of frenzied pace, districts of vitality and urgency, and zones of stable consistency.

Rhythm, like direction, originates in the genetic code which maps the unique features of our species. Every species has its own unique developmental sequence which time unfolds. Human development, in great measure, is the science of that rhythm.

Asynchronous growth – The principle of asynchronous growth assures that development is not uniform; rather, it undergoes periods in which one specific body system receives growth priority, and therefore, develops aggressively. After these irregular periods of aggressive growth, a more settled pace predominates.

It is obvious to even the casual observer that the human body does not mature at a uniform rate; otherwise, the legs would always have the meagre portion of the total body that they have at birth, and the head would be grotesquely enlarged.

During the first year after birth little development of higher brain centres occurs; during the preschool years, however, rapid growth erupts in the higher brain centres. Puberty is another example of an asynchronous growth manifestation. Genital development, which during the first 12 years or so has no growth priority attains prominence during puberty. During a 12-month period (usually around the age of 13), genitals, body contours, facial features, interests, and even fantasies undergo radical transformations. For this brief time span development is "dominated" by the body's effort to assure that it will be able to reproduce.

Specific organs also respond to asynchronous patterns. During the first two months after conception, for example, the heart grows so rapidly that by 45 days it is about nine times larger in proportion to body size than it will be in adolescence.

Growth stabilization – After a period of either fast or slow growth, developmental rhythm returns to its normal pace. Growth stabilization acts as a regulator of developmental rhythm. After growth has been slowed by normal lulls, or after abnormal events such as starvation or disease, stabilization prompts the body to develop at a faster pace. Stabilization also works in the opposite direction, causing the body to slow its pace after it has undergone a burst of accelerated growth.

Tanner (1963) investigated the growth of children following disease and malnutrition and discovered that during the recuperation period the child's body grows faster – sometimes as much as three times its normal rate – until the body reaches the approximate size it would have reached had adversity not struck. Tanner hypothesized that a genetic mechanism in the central nervous system regulates growth in accordance with a hereditary guideline, and, unless an exceptionally serious condition afflicts the child, the size dictated by this guideline will eventually be achieved. Growth destiny is not "carved in stone," and it can be altered by a seemingly endless array of obstacles, but most assuredly, it affects both the rhythm and direction in childhood growth.

This aspect of growth stabilization is known as "catch-up-growth." In essence, it is a period of rapid growth among children who have experienced some kind of deficit in order to get them back on the growth trajectory they are genetically programmed to follow.

This catch-up tendency, part of the body's developmental rhythm, is observed among some premature infants with low birth weight. These babies come into the world with significantly reduced body weight. Despite this deficit, by their first birthday these babies typically have attained nearly the same height and weight as babies of normal birth weight. Thus, during the first calender year the premature child, prompted by the catch-up mechanism, grows faster than the full-term child developing on a normal timetable. The catch-up tendency is observed most frequently among infants three to five weeks premature. Exceptionally premature infants (seven or more weeks) are at increased risk for central nervous system deficits which do not respond to normal developmental rhythms such as catch-up.

In addition to possessing the built-in mechanisms of stabilization, children possess a remarkable *capacity for self-repair.* Minor jolts to the system such as bruises and cuts tend to heal quickly. Few injuries create irreversible damage, and few psychological traumas leave permanent emotional scars. Irreversible damage sometimes occurs during childhood, but not typically. The developing child heals efficiently, recuperates briskly, and keeps in a state of rather good repair, all things considered.

The remarkable range of stabilizing mechanisms within the human organism has prompted some psychologists to proclaim the body has its own built-in "wisdom". The expression "wisdom of the body" is attributed to Walter B. Cannon, the renowned physiologist. He observed that the body is sensitive to nutrients it is lacking, and chooses food items which will satisfy deficiencies. An example of body wisdom is when patients with Addison's disease, which impedes salt metabolism, "naturally" increase their salt intake to counter the effects of the disease. It has been informally observed in many settings that given choice over a period of time, most individuals will consume a balanced diet. Cannon's viewpoint is that while individuals do not demonstrate perfect choices, they manifest a certain wisdom in self-regulation.

Ages and Stages

The term "stage" refers to a level of development in which traits emerge which did not exist (or were not observable) in previous levels of development. Each stage is different from, and more mature than, the preceding stage; each stage is universal in that everyone passes through it; and, each stage is part of a fixed sequence of stages – thus we grow through them in specific order.

The most famous developmental theorists to support the stage theory were Sigmund Freud, Jean Piaget and Hans Werner. They each viewed human development as a series of different stages, each depending on the previous stage, with no stage being skipped.

Each stage has its own unique features and identifiable ingredients. In biology the division of growth from an egg into a caterpillar into a butterfly is an example of clear-cut stage development. Humans are a bit more complicated because development is slower, less controlled by heredity, and attains a greater range of individual differences than is true for most species.

As far as child development is concerned, it is generally agreed that the following conditions characterize a "stage:"

1. A stage is characterized by *structure;* that is, within each stage abilities are linked by some kind of cohesive pattern.
2. A stage is characterized by *qualitative changes.* In a stage a child is not simply a bigger and better version of the previous stage; a stage must be characterized by traits qualitatively different from the previous stage.
3. A stage is characterized by *abruptness.* The transition from one stage to another should be rather brief (the most dramatic being the transition from fetus to newborn). The transformation in the young person's body brought about by puberty, for example, fulfils this requirement.
4. A stage is characterized by *concurrence.* That is, the various achievements of a particular stage occur with a certain amount of harmony and concurrence. Development is, so to speak, orchestrated.

Life Stage	Approximate Ages
prenatal period	conception to birth
infancy	birth to 1 year
toddler period	1 year to 3 years
preschool years	3 to 5 years of age (up to 6th birthday)
middle childhood	6 to 12 years (until onset of puberty)
early adolescence	from onset of puberty until about 16 or 17
late adolescence	17-18 until early adulthood

There is, of course, some disagreement among experts as to the precise ages at when specific stages begin or end. For the most part, however, these stages and their corresponding ages are quite appropriate for the study of North American children.

In this book we shall proceed from the assumption that developmental stages are real, that they are bound to age for the majority of individuals, and that by studying the traits which distinguish one developmental stage from another we vastly expand our knowledge of children.

Professionals who work with youngsters on an age-graded basis, especially school teachers, find their understanding of child behavior greatly enhanced by the "stage" approach to human growth and development.

The rubber-band hypothesis

Virtually all modern developmentalists accept that enriched environments "stretch" a child's hereditary potential. This belief has come to be known as the "rubber-band hypothesis." The formulator of the concept, Curt Stern (1956) describes the most significant dimensions to this viewpoint:

> The genetic endowment with respect to any one trait can be compared to a rubber band, and the trait itself to the length which the rubber band assumes when it is stretched by environmental forces. Different people may initially have been given different lengths of unstretched genetic endowment, but the natural forces of the environment may have stretched their expression to equal lengths, or led to differences in attained length sometimes corresponding in their innate differences, and at other times in reverse of these innate predispositions. (p. 56)

In short, according to the rubber-band hypothesis, an enriched environment can stretch a rich genetic endowment to considerable lengths, but an average genetic endowment to a lesser length. As well, a poor environment is unable to stretch either rich genetic endowment or average genetic endowments very far.

Maturation

Nature is often hidden, sometimes overcome, but never extinguished.
Francis Bacon

Every species has its own distinctive growth patterns, behavioral traits and age-related characteristics. The patterns of growth that characterize humans (or elephants for that matter) come from "within" the organism, that is, they are *endogenous*.

Human maturation is development through our genetically programmed sequence which evolves on a timetable that varies somewhat from person to person but nevertheless demonstrates remarkable consistency among all peoples of the globe. Although all developmentalists recognize the central role played by maturation in human growth and development, there is a difference of opinion as to whether the body matures in a continuous, fluid style, or in well-defined stages.

Some psychologists believe that maturation is *continuous* in that it involves overlapping growth of all body subsystems in a perpetual blend. That is, development is linear and cumulative, and proceeds in gradual, continuous increments. (A bit like an empty swimming pool being filled with water released in continuous, but varying quantities.) Differences between younger and older children are merely a matter of amount or complexity of behavior (Berk, 1989). These psychologists do not think of a child as being in a *specific* stage at any given moment, because maturation is so fluid that it is not contained by one specific stage. In essence, a child could be in several stages at any developmental moment.

Other psychologists (most notably Jean Piaget) argue that maturation is *discrete*, with definite steps, plateaus, and inclines. Although these two viewpoints are linked by their agreement concerning the powerful impact maturation exerts on the growth process, the "continuous" approach to human development does not place nearly as much emphasis on specific stages as does the "discrete" viewpoint.

The viewpoint among developmentalists who see growth as characterized by discrete stages is that the child experiences the world and acts upon the world in wholly different ways at different developmental levels. For example, infants are sensitive to the sounds of language, but once they actually begin to produce language (during toddlerhood) the way they learn about the world, and interact with it, changes in fundamental and qualitatively superior ways.

Maturational unfolding

Maturational unfolding refers to the timing and direction with which genetically programmed patterns present themselves. These patterns are regulated by hereditary instructions programmed in the genetic code at the moment (or very close to it) of conception. The basic progressions of human development are determined by inherent, maturational mechanisms.

Some "unfolding" occurs with very little practice or training. Children don't learn from imitation or observation to cut their teeth, to roll over, to begin to crawl. These developmental events simply "unfold." However, most maturation is not wholly self-generating because it is influenced by environmental factors which stimulate the maturation process. Speech, for example, cannot occur without considerable interaction with, and stimulation from, the environment. However, no matter how rich the stimulation from the environment, a child cannot speak until the brain centres have undergone sufficient maturation to permit speech.

Children are raised by parents but in a very real biological sense maturational unfolding is as instrumental in creating the physical child as the parent is in creating the social child. Maturational unfolding is most noticeable (and predictable) during early childhood, and developmentalists who specialize in this time frame are among its strongest advocates:

> Children have a sort of built-in "self-starter" for growing and thrive in an atmosphere that supports and facilitates that growth. They do not require a "trainer." Parents can trust their children's capacity to grow *in the right direction* without their pushing or pulling. In fact, parental intrusion on their children's *natural course of growth,* in order to teach or demand of them things the parents deem important at the time, can only interfere with children's optimal development. (Caplan & Caplan, 1977, p. 363)

The law of readiness

The *law of readiness* states that a child will engage in behavior governed by maturation only when "ready." Practice and coaching do not accelarate the onset behavior governed by readiness because it derives more from internal programming than from external stimulation. One cannot teach children to cut their molars any more than one can teach their parents to cut their wisdom teeth because they proceed at their own pace.

For most children the first production of words begins sometime near the twelfth month; as far as we presently know, word production cannot be induced at an earlier age. (In an interesting overview on the topic, Malina (1979) claims that as far as can be determined by the available data, children in ancient Greece and Rome, and children in the middle ages matured at the same rate as children do today.)

The principle of readiness is softened by an elementary, yet important, fact: no one knows for certain when a particular child is "ready" for a particular behavior. Some children are "ready" to walk at nine months and "ready" to talk at 18 months; other kids don't walk until 18 months and use words only in emergencies. To complicate matters, the precision with which readiness can be predicted is reduced as the child ages. It is possible to predict (often within hours) when the fetus will be born, to predict within a few days when the infant will first lift the head or reach for a distant object, and to predict within a month or so when the baby will begin to crawl. But, when it comes to walking, the child may be maturationally ready any time between 9 and 18 months – an error factor almost equal to the life span of the child. Imprecision continues as the child gets older; this is one reason why child psychology is a more precise discipline than adolescent psychology, and why adolescent psychology is more precise than "adult" psychology.

The law of practice

When children acquire new skills they practice with relentless persistence. This *law of practice* affects not only motor skills, such as crawling, walking, and running, but also verbal and intellectual skills. Development automatically triggers practice, and the child's inborn drive for mastery perpetuates it. A significant portion of every child's day is spent practicing, rehearsing and perfecting newly emerging skills and abilities.

Critical Periods

A *critical period* is a period of time in growth during which specific environmental or biological events must occur for development to proceed normally. Critical periods occur in the development of all animals, including humans. For example, if the newly formed sex glands do not produce male hormones near the seventh week after conception the development of female genitalia is irreversibly set in the human embryo. Likewise, if children are not exposed to language before age seven, they may never acquire it (Cole, 1989).

Some psychologists and pediatricians (perhaps the most notable being John Bowlby) believe that between 6 and 12 months the infant is in a critical period for emotional development, and if insufficient contact comfort is received during this period the chances are considerable that the child will suffer emotional damage.

Negative critical periods are periods in growth during which specific environmental or biological events cause permanent or irreversible damage. Perhaps the most notorious example of this is the impact of thalidomide on the human embryo. Thalidomide has become something of a classic example in critical period theory because of its precise, time-bound consequences. Research has shown that if the mother consumed thalidomide between the 34th and 38th day after her last menstrual period her child was born with no ears. If she took the drug between the 38th and 47th day the child had missing or deformed arms; if she took the drug between the 40th and 45th day, the child had defects in the intestines or the gall bladder. If mother took thalidomide between the 43rd and 47th day the child had missing or deformed legs (Schardein, 1976). Very few teratogens have been researched with the rigor of thalidomide, and as a result we have gained a considerable amount of knowledge about the degree to which some critical periods are specifically time-bound.

Finally, an *optimal period* is similar to a critical period in that it is a period in which a particular behavior develops most successfully as a result of the interaction between maturation and environment. At approximately 24 months, for example, an optimal period occurs for toddlers to become toilet trained. Maturational timing predisposes youngsters to learn sphincter control during this optimal learning period. An optimal period does not have the all-or-nothing quality of a critical period, and is not characterized by irreversibility. Therefore, age five or six might be an optimal time to teach a youngster to print letters with a pencil (primarily because prerequisite wrist development has occurred) but if he does not learn to print at this age it does not mean he will not pick it up quickly at a later age.

Several negative critical periods occur during prenatal development. Between the fourth and sixth week the embryo is extremely susceptible to disfigurement by the drug thalidomide. During this time frame thalidomide has the capacity to destroy and deform the barely visible stubs that would normally mature into sturdy arms and legs. However, *after* the seventh week and *before* the third week this drug exerts no negative influence on the developing fetus. (Thalidomide is no longer prescribed for pregnant women.) Another negative critical period occurs during the third month of pregnancy, when German measles in the mother may prove fatal to the fetus; however, if the mother contracts German measles during the eighth month the fetus usually is not adversely affected because *timing* is the crucial factor in all critical periods.

The critical periods of most animals are more precise in their time frame and more specific in their outcome than the critical periods of humans. Baby ducks, for example, become imprinted on (attached to) any moving object around 15 hours after birth. If nothing is moving during this specific time frame, the duckling will not develop typical following behavior. Such exact time periods (as far as we know) do not exist for human infants.

Most developmentalists believe that people undergo sensitive periods during which they are particularly responsive to certain experiences, or the absence of certain experiences. It is in this context that psychologists claim that the first five years of life, for example, are a sensitive period in the formation of personality and basic trust.

Developmental Tasks

At each developmental level several new skills and competencies must be achieved if the child is to master the social and biological requirements inherent to that stage. These bio-social demands are known as *developmental tasks*. They might be motor tasks (learning to crawl during the first year, or to walk during toddlerhood), they may be intellectual tasks (mastering representational thought during toddlerhood), they may be social tasks (establishing an attachment during the first year). The basic assumptions underlying the concept of developmental tasks include the following:

1. successful completion of developmental tasks is necessary for effective progression through the developmental stage in which it occurs,
2. unsuccessful completion of developmental tasks hinders mastery of future developmental requirements, and
3. developmental tasks are both social and biological.

By taking note of the developmental tasks required of different ages and stages we can better isolate the growth requirements of the developing child.

Women Scholars in the Field of Developmental Psychology

Women have been prominent in developmental research since the 1890s. Significant early contributions in the 1920s and 30s were made by Nancy Bayley in the area of intellectual assessment. Charlotte Buhler conducted research in several disciplines including social development and adolescent personality. Other prominent women developmentalists include Anna Freud, who pioneered the psychoanalytic investigation of children and adolescents; Florence Goodenough, who constructed the Draw-a-Person test which remains in wide use in diagnostic work with children. The scientific investigation of language and thought were the specializations of Dorothy McCarthy. Mary Shirley investigated infant development, while Lois Stolz played an important role in early parent education programs while serving as Director of the Columbia University Child Development Institute. Myrtle McGraw researched the significance of environmental enrichment and its effects on development during the 40s, while Martha Muchow was among the very first researchers to examine the "life space" of the urban child. Lois Murphy documented infant emotions; and Mary Ainsworth produced perhaps the most significant work to this date on infant attachment.

These women scholars contributed in significant and innovative ways to our understanding of child development. Contemporary women in developmental psychology continue to be a major force in the advancement of our knowledge and understanding. Their influence is felt throughout the field as women currently hold prominent positions as journal editors, administrators in professional organizations and as active, innovative researchers.

Egocentrism

Egocentrism, in its most general usage, refers to the child's limited ability to see the world from another person's perspective. It is, unquestionably, one of the most profound influences on the child's intellectual, social, and perceptual world. It affects every domain of adult-child interaction.

Childhood development is one long journey away from egocentric narrowness. In time the ability to obtain perspective upon one's personal thoughts and emotions gradually takes hold and as it does the child is progressively liberated from the inherent "self-ish-ness" which is the inevitable childhood by-product of egocentrism.

Children usually assume that their perception of a situation is the only possible perception of that situation. Generally they do not comprehend that other people perceive, feel, and think differently than they do. And most assuredly, children do not easily embrace the fact that others see the world from completely different frames of reference. As children lose their egocentrism they are better equipped to view the world from perspectives other than their own.

During the first weeks of life the newborn responds only to physical stimuli that impinge directly on the body; nothing else registers. By 12 months the baby has learned to distinguish self from non-self. During toddlerhood the child learns that what "I" want does not always jibe with what others want, and during the preschool years the child learns that the reasons for a person's actions are as important as the actions themselves. Finally, during middle childhood the child comes to understand that rules governing social life exist not only because authorities say so but because the rules possess some defensibility in themselves. In these ways egocentrism becomes less dominant as time passes; but even as it weakens it remains an important influence on how children perceive their world.

Some Concluding Observations about Child Growth & Development

In our attempt to understand the lawful and systematic aspects of child growth and development we cannot lose sight of the most significant reality: the child. It is, after all, the child who grows, who develops, and who eventually becomes the adult. Thus, a few additional comments before bringing this chapter to its end.

1. *Children are social beings.* Like all creatures, children must satisfy their needs for nutrition, elimination, basic elements, and shelter if they are to grow and develop. All needs, however, are met within a human framework and it is this very framework which ultimately exerts the greatest influence on the child. The rewards that assume the greatest priority, the goals most earnestly sought after, and the experiences that register the deepest emotions are interwoven with social life, with mother and father, brother and sister, teacher and coach. The most painful punishments and the wounds that inflict the deepest hurt are likewise social. Childhood needs and childhood behavior *must be understood within their human context.*

2. *Each child is unique yet at the same time possesses traits which characterize every member of our species.* Children must be understood and respected in their own right. Even identical twins, the most similar of all humans, are different from each other in important and noticeable ways. It is also true, however, that all children are somewhat similar because they share the characteristics which define and distinguish our species and which, in a scientific sense, define our humanness. Developmental psychology investigates similarities and differences among children; to focus excessively on one blurs the other.

3. *Children are motivated by psychological needs.* Despite their significance in the lives of every person, psychological needs are not well understood. Experts do not agree about which needs are learned (acquired) and which are part of the child's "natural" makeup. In this book we will not enter the debate concerning the *origins* of psychological needs; however, we will time and again remind the reader of the important role they play in the lives of children. We here assume that all children possess, in varying degrees, the following psychological needs:

1. the need for affection, for contact, and for embrace,
2. the need for security, predictability, and continuity,
3. the need for acceptance, belonging, and affiliation,
4. the need for competence, mastery, and a certain measure of control over the environment,
5. the need for recognition, approval and priority,
6. the need for independence, and self-reliance, and
7. the need to actualize their potential, to practice skills and abilities.

These needs manifest themselves differently at different stages in the growth cycle, and most assuredly, they manifest themselves differently among different children. Nevertheless, their impact on child behavior is monumental, and in each developmental period we shall illustrate the extent to which these needs impel the growing child.

4. *Child development is best understood from an interdisciplinary perspective.* When we remain too much within the clutch of a single academic discipline (even developmental psychology!) we run the risk of artificially narrowing our understanding of children. It is simply impossible to comprehend the human growth cycle without taking into account data from such varied disciplines as medicine (especially pediatrics); sociology (especially socialization theory); anthropology (especially crosscultural studies and comparative child-rearing); psychology (especially perception and motivation); genetics (a discipline that, with each passing decade, is becoming more integrally linked with developmental psychology, especially prenatal development and pediatrics); physiology; and nutrition.

The necessity for interdisciplinary investigation has prompted the formation of the discipline known as Developmental Pediatrics, which combines medicine and psychological development. In 1982, the Society for Behavioral Pediatrics was founded, which sponsors cooperative interdisciplinary research among pediatricians, developmental psychologists, and academics (Gottleib & Williams, 1987). These trends underscore the central role of interdisciplinary investigations in human growth and development.

In this text data from all of the above disciplines will be presented in our attempt to gather a comprehensive and honest assessment of child growth and development.

5. *The study of children must be both academic and humanistic.* Understanding children requires a subtle blend of scientific rigor, humanistic appreciation and philosophical dedication. All academic disciplines which employ the scientific method are rigorous in research and thorough in theoretical analyses. However, research, no matter how rigorous, and theory, no matter how thorough, are not sufficient to explain the lives of children. Theory and research must be tempered with a humane appreciation for children. In this text, every attempt will be made to keep the living child an integral part of child development.

6. *Behavior is increasingly influenced by environment as children age.* The younger a child the greater the influence of heredity and maturation on their skills and abilities. All behavior takes place within an environment, which imposes restrictions and limitations. We cannot understand the role of heredity except within the environmental context. For all intents and purposes, this environmental context exerts greater influence on the developing child with the passage of time.

If the environment fails to provide the minimum requirements needed for hereditary ground plans to manifest their design, the child simply cannot grow to hereditary potential. This interdependence of environment and heredity holds true for all living creatures, and most assuredly, for young humans. In the hundreds of human societies around the globe where the basic necessities are not provided, children simply never attain the potential which is inherently theirs. On the other hand, when the environment provides for basic human needs, then and only then, are the hereditary forces which regulate and monitor development freed to exert their influence.

In this book children are discussed within the context of the important ages and stages. We begin with the fetus, and end with the child readying for adolescence. In each stage of human development the reader will notice that the previous stage was governed more by the ground plans of maturation (which, of course, are regulated by heredity) than the present stage. Conversely, at each successive stage the effects of environment, culture, and interpersonal relationships become increasingly more significant in the lives of children.

The Major Concepts of this Chapter

1. Developmental psychology studies the orderly sequence of change that takes place throughout the life cycle in which the developing person functions in new ways at different ages.

2. Five concepts define the essential nature of development. These include: change over time, cumulativity of development, directionality, new modes of organization and increased capacity for self-control. Developmental psychologists are interested in how development occurs, the meaning of behavior at different ages, and the causes of development.

3. The direction of development is influenced by several principles. These include: cephalocaudal development (head-to-foot), proxi-modistal development (centre-to-extremity), bilateral development (synchronous development on either side of the body), and general-to-specific development (evolution from primitive to sophisticated).

4. The rhythm of development is influenced by: asynchronous growth (not all development is uniform), growth stabilization (the balance mechanism of developmental rhythm), and the capacity for self-repair (rebuilding after de-stabilization).

5. Stage theories describe episodes of development through which most humans grow in a fixed sequence. Stages are characterized by new structures, qualitative changes, abruptness of transition, and concurrence of the development of aspects of the stage.

6. While psychologists agree that maturation plays a major role in development there is less agreement regarding the degree of continuity. Some developmentalists argue that maturation is continuous, whereas others, that it is discrete. Unfolding refers to the timing and direction with which genetically programmed patterns present themselves.

7. The law of readiness states that a child will engage in behavior governed by maturation only when ready. The law of practice impels the child to master skills once they have emerged.

8. Critical periods are times when development is most likely to be hindered by specific trauma. Optimal periods are when a particular behavior develops most successfully.

9. Developmental tasks coincide with the various ages and stages. Successful completion of these tasks enhances development, whereas unsuccessful completion hinders it.

2

Prenatal Development

Before I was born out of my mother generations guided me
Walt Whitman

The great American humorist Mark Twain suggested that the biography of every person should begin with a comment on the quality of the wine shared by the mother and father on the evening of conception. Just what information would accrue from such an investigation is uncertain, and although offering interesting possibilities, it is well beyond the scope of this text. Conventional as it may seem, this chapter is restricted to describing development between conception and birth. Special attention will be paid to patterns that reflect the developmental growth principles established in Chapter one. This chapter will catalogue prenatal growth month-by-month, and it will also overview the vital components of fetal survival.

Most people think of life as beginning at birth rather than thinking of birth as one event in the total growth cycle. This habit leads students of child development to overlook the critical events that take place during the ten lunar (28 day) months prior to birth, when the unborn human grows from a fertilized egg (called a zygote) to a multibillion-celled newborn infant. The journey is one of the most miraculous in nature and worthy of attention, not only because of the instruction it provides concerning human development but also for the sense of appreciation, even awe, it injects into our knowledge of how humans grow and develop.

The systematic study of fetal development is not an easy undertaking because the fetus is not readily accessible to observation, and because direct investigation of the intra-uterine world may damage the fetus or the mother.

Prenatal life is divided into three stages by embryologists: (1) the germinal period, (2) the embryonic period, and (3) the fetal period.

The Germinal Period

The male sperm displays great determination in its struggle against gravity, time, and fellow sperm to fertilize the female egg. The microscopic spermatozoon, meagre in size though it may be, when coupled with the ovum (itself only about 1/7 millimetre in diameter) forms the humble beginning of human life. The egg is fertilized in the Fallopian tube and then journeys to the uterus – a three day trip if nothing interferes. (Sometimes the fertilized egg becomes lodged in the Fallopian tube, resulting in a *tubal pregnancy,* which may prove harmful to the mother and usually must be surgically terminated.) Upon reaching the uterus the fertilized egg attaches itself to the uterine wall, thus marking the end of the germinal period. The entire process takes from 7 to 14 days, and the mother usually is not aware that it is taking place. Only women extremely sensitive to their internal changes are able to detect the hormonal and chemical changes that have been occurring daily since conception.

In Vitro Fertilization

For many couples the normal route of fertilization is not possible due to factors such as occluded fallopian tubes, hostile cervical mucus or immunity to sperm. For these people, a process known as *in vitro fertilization* may provide a solution. In this process oocytes (eggs) are recovered from ovarian follicles and are placed in a culture medium where they are fertilized and cultured until they reach the 8-cell stage. These oocytes can be either the mother's own or can be from a donor. At this time conceptus (fertilized oocyte) is implanted in the mother's uterus to develop to term. Unfortunately the success rate for this procedure is low. Generally four to five fertilized eggs are cultured and implanted to increase the likelihood of a successful pregnancy. This, of course, may lead to multiple births.

An extension of the "donor-egg" process is the surrogate mother. This controversial process involves the impregnation of a woman, usually by artificial insemination, with a prospective father's sperm. The surrogate mother carries the baby to term and then turns the baby over to the father. Since the surrogate mother is paid a fee, plus medical expenses, critics claim that this is a form of child buying. In addition, there have been instances where the surrogate mother, after giving birth, decides not to turn the baby over to the father. This has resulted in highly publicized legal battles, (Baby "M", 1986).

The Embryonic and Fetal Periods

Between the second and eighth week of pregnancy the human organism is referred to as an *embryo,* from the Greek "to swell." After the eighth week it is known as a *fetus* – a Latin word meaning "young one." Because development during the embryonic and fetal stages is extremely complex, I will break them up into shorter periods. Therefore, I will review prenatal development month by month. In preface, however, I must stress that human embryology is a comparatively imprecise science; even though growth patterns are predictable, we also observe that the fetus is an individualized form of life. For this reason one must guard against thinking that norms represent all individuals, that sequences are always perfectly sequential, or that observations made in one setting will be perfectly replicated in another.

The Stage of the Embryo (First and Second Months)

The first month

Unlike the first month after birth, when growth is slow and uneventful, the first month following conception is a spectacular growth period unequalled in the remainder of the human growth cycle. At 30 days the embryo is ten thousand times larger than the fertilized egg but still no more than six millimetres (a quarter inch) from head to heel. The tiny embryo bears some resemblance to the form into which it will evolve but could easily be mistaken for a fish or monkey embryo. The body is formed of a gelatinous substance and affords little indication of the skeletal sturdiness shortly to come.

Despite the embryo's unseemly appearance, evidence of humanness is discernible. Tiny bulges, barely observable, are the first indications of four emerging limbs; the head has begun to form, and the two halves of the forebrain can be distinguished; and the kidneys, liver, digestive tract, bloodstream, and heart are partially formed and in some instances functioning. Body tissue has begun to divide into three major categories: ectoderm; which will become skin and nerve tissue; mesoderm, from which the heart, blood vessels, muscle, and bone tissue emerge; and endoderm, which gives rise to the digestive and alimentary tracts as well as the respiratory organs.

Growth during the first 30 days is remarkably coordinated; cells develop in relation to each other, and all organs function in such a manner as to complement one another. No part of the organism, when functioning properly, interferes with the growth of any other part of the organism. Organismic unity is the key to embryonic development and will continue to be a guiding principle throughout childhood. The growth process during the first weeks of life is riddled with hazards, and some authorities estimate that a third of all fertilized ova do not live until birth, with most of the attrition occurring during the first month.

Whether a child will be male or female is determined at the moment of conception. Every egg produced by the mother carries an X (female) sex chromosome; however, the sperm provided by the father may carry either an X (female) or a Y (male) sex chromosome. If the egg is fertilized by an X sperm the result is an XX baby – a girl; if the egg is fertilized by a Y sperm the result is an XY baby – a boy. Thus, the male sperm determines the sex of the infant.

While most pregnant women, if asked the question "Which are you hoping for, a boy or a girl?" respond with "It doesn't matter as long as it's healthy," others have a very strong desire for a child of a particular sex. Techniques have been developed which can increase the likelihood of producing offspring of a desired sex. These processes involve the filtration of sperm to enhance the concentration of either X or Y sperm and then the use of artificial insemination. At present this procedure is far from perfected. Often no pregnancy occurs and sex selection, while enhanced, is not guaranteed.

The second month

Growth during this period results in the embryo's taking on noticeable human features. The head, which now constitutes about a third of the body volume, has definite features, including the dark, circular beginnings of eyes and a mouth with lips. The eyes move closer together, causing the embryo to look a little less like a reptile as the facial area assumes more infant-like contours. Early development of the cerebellum and cerebral hemispheres is now taking place, and the internal ear has already undergone considerable development. At this stage of its career the embryo is about eight millimetres (just over a quarter inch) long and has a mass of only a few grams (less than a half ounce), an incredibly small organism for such complex and intricate growth. The limbs continue to mature and are much more visible; a slight elbow bend appears in the arm. In keeping with cephalocaudal growth, the legs are less developed than the arms (as they will be throughout prenatal life and for the first several years of postnatal life), although knee, ankle, and toe differentiations are noticeable. During the second month, sexual differentiation of the gonads becomes clear, and on close visual inspection it is sometimes possible to recognize the sex of the embryo. The miniature "tail" that extends from the tip of the spine is at its maximum length; in time this feature will disappear altogether, stripping the embryo of one observable reminder of human beings' evolutionary heritage.

By the eighth week virtually all major organ systems are differentiated and functioning. A fascinating discovery made in the course of intra-uterine investigation is that the embryo at this stage has a giant heart, seven times larger in proportion to its body than the adult heart, whose rhythmic, although sporadic, beat is already serving a role in the survival of the embryo. Although the heart is not yet structurally equivalent to the neonatal heart, significant partitioning has already begun and will be completed shortly after the newborn infant takes the first gasp of air. According to the principle of *asynchronous growth,* the heart is disproportionately large because of its central role in embryonic survival.

Sometime during the second month (from the 28th to the 42nd day, approximately) the embryo is vulnerable to permanent damage if the mother ingests the drug thalidomide, (which is no longer prescribed) because during this *critical period* arm and leg buds are highly susceptible to disfiguration and aberration. Limbs disfigured by thalidomide usually have a stumplike appearance similar to that during the embryonic period in which exposure to the drug occurred.

The Stage of the Fetus (8 Weeks to Birth)

The third month

After the eighth week the growing human is technically referred to as a *fetus*. The maturational signal for this name change is the formation of the first real bone cells, which replace the gelatinous cartilage. Before this process the human embryo has the structural firmness of the adult ear, because the skeleton is made of cartilage rather than bone.

Between the eighth and twelfth weeks the fetus attains numerous infant features. When shown photographs of a 12-week fetus, first-grade children invariably report that they are looking at a human baby. The head is not yet infant-like but is rapidly approaching that description. The eyelids are sealed tightly shut, because at this age exposure to the amniotic fluid would cause aberrations in retinal development. The lips exhibit the first sucking motions, and several parts of the body respond reflexively if stroked or stimulated. The kidneys begin to secrete urine, although most fetal waste material is removed through the placenta and, eventually, through the elimination system of the mother.

The fetus is enveloped in a warm, salty, pellucid liquid called *amniotic fluid,* which is confined by the transparent amnion sac. The water in the amniotic fluid is produced partially from amniotic cells but mainly from the mother's blood stream (Sadler, 1985). The water in the amniotic fluid is changed every three hours. This shows the significant exchange potential between mother and fetal environment. At 10 weeks the sac measures about 5 centimetres (2 inches) and houses an organism half as long; however, by 14 weeks the fetus may be 7.5 centimetres (3 inches) long. The liquid environment provides room in which the fetus can move and stretch. Fetal movements have been taking place for several weeks, but they now become more global, involving arm waving, neck flexing, and trunk rotating. Also present is a crude *tonic neck reflex,* which causes one side of the body to flex when the other side extends. The fetus is now architecturally sound and will increase in strength and durability as time progresses.

The mother does not yet feel the growing fetus, the womb has not begun to stretch, and there is no way an untrained bystander could determine that the woman is pregnant. Women who do not experience morning sickness, or who have irregular menstrual periods, may be quite shocked when informed by a doctor that they are pregnant and serving as the lifeline for a fetus sufficiently mature to have unique sleeping positions and facial features.

Most women, however, do not experience the first months of pregnancy with such ease. Continual fatigue and an incessant need to sleep or rest typify the early stages of pregnancy. Frequent urination is another sign, because during the first few months the uterus swells and places increased pressure on the bladder. During the middle months this problem tends to subside, as the uterus moves upward toward the abdomen; however, frequent urination may reappear in the later months, when the head of the fetus descends and again exerts pressure on the bladder.

During the first eight weeks of pregnancy many women experience considerable discomfort because of nausea. Upon awakening in the morning they have a queasy feeling that may result in vomiting. Usually the sight or smell of food creates sufficient irritation to keep the expectant mother away from food until noon. Most women experience *morning sickness* in a mild form; however, vomiting is sometimes severe enough to require brief hospitalization. "Morning sickness" most frequently occurs in the morning, but it can occur in the evening, or at any other time of the day or night.

The fourth month

The first trimester of development is now complete. The second trimester, starting with the fourth lunar month, is characterized by sensational growth. In one month the fetus increases in mass sixfold and in length by 12 centimetres (5 inches), to a full 20 centimetres (8 inches) long. Despite this prodigious growth, however, the fetus still has a mass of less than two hundred grams. The mother is noticeably with child; the womb expands to accommodate the burgeoning baby, the breasts begin to enlarge, and the pelvic girdle also must adjust. The tremendous amount of nutrients required for the growth spurt of the four-month-old fetus depletes the mother's reserves, making it necessary for her to take in surplus vitamins and calcium to keep up with the demands of her unborn child. A fair, although loose, generalization is that, as the mother's health goes, so goes the health of the baby.

Surrounding the fetus, and attached to it by the umbilical cord, is the *placenta* – a vascular organ through which all essentials are supplied to the fetus and through which waste materials are delivered from the fetus to the circulatory system of the mother. The circulatory system of the fetus is not directly connected with that of the mother: *all exchanges between mother and fetus take place by diffusion through the permeable placenta.* Passing through the placenta to the fetus are nourishment, oxygen, antibodies, and other life essentials. Passing from the fetus to the mother are potentially life-damaging waste materials, such as nitrogen and urine which are eventually eliminated by the mother. At birth the placenta will be expelled in the final stage of labor, and the umbilical cord will be severed.

Because the placenta is permeable, materials in the mother's blood stream work their way to the fetus. The placenta possesses a screening device that filters out many harmful materials, but most drugs ingested by the mother eventually make their way into the fetal system, and some of them can damage the fetus. Conversely, the health-enhancing nutrients in the mother's system diffuse through the placenta and contribute to overall fetal health. Healthy mothers with sound diets and a minimum of harmful agents in their bodies are much more likely to produce healthy children than are mothers whose nourishment is impoverished or whose systems are polluted with harmful drugs or viruses.

The fourth fetal month is the last month during which medical abortions are performed, under normal circumstances. Although possible to perform at a later date, owing to the danger late abortion holds for the mother, as well as the reluctance of some doctors to surgically abort after the twelfth week, medical termination of the fetus is rare beyond this month.

Abortion. Not all pregnancies are carried to full term. The termination of a pregnancy is either spontaneous or induced.

Spontaneous abortion (also known as miscarriage) occurs when the developing organism is expelled from the uterus because of factors internal to the mother. This is most likely to occur when the embryo is malformed or in some way defective; examinations of spontaneously aborted embryos indicate a much higher rate of developmental abnormalities than is found among full term infants. Medical examination also confirms that a greater number of males are aborted, which is in accord with the fact that a greater number of males than females die during birth and in the first few months of birth. Female infants demonstrate greater resistance to infection and avoid serious tissue trauma better than males. Females also are generally sturdier and more resistant to major ailments from the very earliest weeks of life. Although about 103 boys are born for every 100 girls, some geneticists believe that about 130 males are conceived for every 100 females. If this belief is correct (there is virtually no way to prove this hypothesis in human pregnancies), the susceptibility of males to spontaneous abortion is considerable.

Induced abortion results from intentional interference from an outside agent. Medical abortions performed by a doctor during the early weeks of pregnancy usually involve dilation of the cervix and gentle scraping or suctioning of the walls of the uterus. For abortions after 12 weeks two methods are commonly employed. The first is very similar to the procedure prior to 12 weeks but requires more dilation of the cervix due to the increased size of the fetus. The second method involves the use of an "abortificant," a chemical or drug which causes uterine contractions, death of the fetus, and expulsion of the uterine contents (Hacker and Moore, 1985).

Other methods of induced abortion that have been practiced through the centuries, such as cinching a belt tightly around the waist or inserting foreign objects through the cervix, are extremely hazardous because they cause infection, internal organ damage, and sometimes death for the expectant mother.

Some women experience negative emotional reactions after undergoing a medical abortion. However, most women do not experience psychological trauma if the abortion was the result of choice and conducted in a safe environment. The research on this matter is not totally consistent; Newman and Newman, however, conclude that "the available evidence suggests that women do not experience negative emotional reactions to abortions," and, furthermore, "for most women an abortion represents a successful close to an undesired pregnancy" (1978, p. 95).

Considerable controversy surrounds the abortion issue. One point of view is that the woman should have complete say about whether she carries a pregnancy to full term, and that pregnancy is a personal matter, the outcome of which is to be decided by the expectant mother – perhaps and perhaps not in consultation with the expectant father. Another point of view is that the unborn fetus has both civil and natural rights that are violated when its life is terminated and that even though the woman is the carrier of the child she does not have the right to terminate the life of the embryo or fetus. A compromise viewpoint is that medical abortion should be permitted when the health of the mother is jeopardized by pregnancy or when medical data suggest that the fetus will be born with a major deformity or malfunction.

North Americans presently maintain something of a middle-of-the-road outlook on abortion, compared with other people throughout the world, being more tolerant of it than most Latin Americans, the Spanish, and the Italians, but less tolerant than most Eastern Europeans, the Japanese, and Chinese, who accept abortion as a legitimate method of regulating family size.

The fifth month

The fetus is preparing systematically for birth. The activities required for post-uterine existence – sucking and breathing – are now part of the growing behavioral repertoire of the fetus. The swallowing reflex is well developed, the lips move as though the fetus were feeding; and the fetus occasionally sucks its thumb. Breathing has begun, although it is liquid, not air, that is passed in and out of the lungs. The digestive tract is mechanically as well as chemically functional, as is the liver. (Many pediatricians believe that an enlarged liver partially accounts for the potbelly of the newborn.) The heart is strong and regular, pulsing along at about 160 beats per minute (twice the adult pace), and can be heard through a stethoscope placed on the mother's abdomen. Just before birth the fetal heartbeat will slow to about 140 beats per minute.

Most bones are now formed, although *ossification* (bone formation) will continue for several years (complete ossification does not occur until early adulthood). Connections between neurons (nerve cells) and between neurons and muscle fibres are processing; one visible consequence is the increased smoothness of motion displayed by the five-month fetus. The legs are still scrawny and underdeveloped in comparison with the upper body; the hands, designed by nature to manipulate, are flexing, bending, and pinching in preparation for their future tasks. The fetus is swiftly becoming infantlike.

The fetus is now 30 centimetres (12.5 inches) long, has a mass of half a kilogram (1.1 pounds), and is beginning to find that living quarters are getting cramped. Flexing and stretching are gymnastic, and the mother may now experience the sensation of fetal movement. The fetus sleeps and wakes much as a newborn does and can be incited to movement by sudden sounds from the extra-uterine environment. The mother, usually over morning sickness by now (some mothers never experience it), is rapidly learning that pregnancy restricts her mobility, reduces her stamina, and shortens her temper. Her present discomfort is mild, however, compared to what she will experience in the final weeks of pregnancy, when heavy work and unnecessary social engagements will often be dropped altogether. The fetus gives fair warning that soon it will be a dominant factor in the lives of those who share its world.

The fetus possesses functions that serve little immediate purpose but will be important later. For example, although the fetus has little need for taste, this sense exists during the second trimester. This has been demonstrated in experiments in which the amniotic fluid is sweetened by an injection of saccharine; the fetus responds to the sweetened fluid by drinking more of it than usual.

The fetus is not yet *viable,* meaning it could not survive if born. To become viable the fetus must await the necessary developments that unfold during the sixth and seventh fetal months.

The sixth month

The fetus becomes progressively more sturdy during the sixth month. Its total action system shows refinement, and the organ system is well coordinated. If born, the fetus has only a very slight chance of survival if medical attention is good, if an incubator is available, and if the fetus has unusual respiratory development. The youngest human known to survive was born between 23 and 25 weeks and had a mass of less than half a kilogram. At this stage the birth process is rather easy, requiring no labor, and sometimes the baby is born still encased in the amnion sac (in full-term babies the sac ruptures shortly before birth). The baby born during the sixth fetal month is characterized by extreme fragility, and almost invariably the lungs and respiratory tract are too immature to sustain life. At six months the skin is so transparent that veins, arteries, and some of their tributaries are clearly visible, leading an observer to marvel at the intricate complexity of the human circulatory system.

Near the end of the second trimester of intra-uterine life the eyelids reopen and the eye demonstrates some response to light. Buds for permanent teeth appear; a fine, woolly substance, which will usually disappear before birth, covers part of the arms, legs, and back; blood cells are being formed in the marrow cavities of the bones; and the grasping reflex is of sufficient strength that the fetus can grasp and hold tightly to a rod placed in its palm.

Three major events take place during the sixth month that are essential for development of air-breathing capacities: (1) the nostrils reopen, (2) the air cells of the lungs (pulmonary alveoli) develop, and (3) the respiratory centre in the brain undergoes prefunctional organization. In the absence of these events the fetus has no chance for extra-uterine survival, because the human cell, having no capacity to store oxygen, requires a smoothly operating respiratory network to provide this life-giving element.

The fetus now awaits the last third of uterine life. During the next three months it will increase in mass, length, and strength and receive many finishing touches before being delivered into the world. These last three months of uterine life witness the refinement of the developing fetus; during this period the fetus begins genuinely to resemble the newborn both in internal mechanics and external appearance. The growth and maturity gained in the last trimester prepare the baby to survive its first major life shock: birth.

The seventh month

Approaching the 28th week of life the fetus may have a mass of more than a kilogram, an increase of half a kilogram over the previous month. Overall body strength and organ development now make the fetus increasingly able to survive birth if for some reason it is born prematurely. Although the mortality rate is high for infants born only 28 weeks after conception, this is the age at which some expectation of survival is medically justified. Because the layer of fat that insulates the baby has not yet fully developed, the fetus is extremely sensitive to temperature change. Premature babies lose body heat so rapidly that some doctors wrap them in cotton blankets even before the umbilical cord has been severed. An *isolette* (formerly known as an *incubator*) is often required to prevent the infant from literally freezing to death.

During this four-week period (25 to 28 weeks after conception) the baby begins to receive from the mother the special disease-combating proteins called antibodies. The mother carries in her blood antibodies against diseases she has had, and the antibodies provide her with a certain degree of immunity against those diseases. These usually include, among others, measles, mumps, the common cold, and, if she has received a vaccine, polio. The immunities transmitted from the mother to the fetus will wear off by the time the child is six months old, and the baby's system will have to cope with infectious adversaries on its own. Because it cannot do this completely, the baby must acquire immunity by going through sickness. However, the mother's antibodies have served their critical survival function by granting amnesty from illness during the first few months of extra-uterine life, when the infant is fragile and recuperating from birth shock. By toddlerhood most children are so strong that they take illness, as well as injury, in stride, with only a minimal recuperation period necessary before they are back at full speed.

As far as survival is concerned, perhaps the most significant development during the seventh month is increased maturation of the lung tissue, which makes it capable of absorbing inhaled oxygen. Without this capacity, life outside the uterus is impossible.

Along with physical maturation of the fetal lungs and the development of terminal air sacs is the development of cells which produce *surfactant*. Surfactant is a chemical which helps to reduce surface tension within the lungs thus enabling them to expand more easily. In instances of premature labor one of the criteria used to assess the viability of the infant is her level of surfactant production. When premature labor does occur and surfactant production is low it is possible to administer corticosteroids to hasten lung maturation and surfactant production. This treatment only proves useful if the drug can be administered at least 24 hours prior to delivery. (Avery, 1985).

Prematurity

We should distinguish between two kinds of premature infants. The first kind (termed Intrauterine Growth Retardation – IUGR) is the child of low weight at birth who is full term. The second kind is the low birth weight infant who is not full term. Tanner (1963) claims that the first kind of prematurity is the more serious because these babies have not developed normally during nine months, and their low weight at birth is the result of faulty development. On the other hand, the second example of low weight at birth is due to the shortened fetal growth period (remember that the last six weeks of the prenatal period is a time of tremendous increase in weight), and the child is likely to grow normally after a "catch-up" period. Tanner claims that the first kind of premature infant is likely to encounter difficulties throughout the growth cycle because of the developmental defects that caused the low mass at birth; therefore, the prognosis for these infants is considerably less optimistic than the prognosis for babies who are simply early.

The problems facing the premature infant are directly related to how premature the baby is. Babies born 25 to 29 weeks after conception have extreme difficulty merely surviving, and their mortality rate is high. Because their lung tissue is poorly developed, the ability to take oxygen into the lungs and transmit it to the circulatory system is impoverished. Their immature respiratory system also makes them highly susceptible to respiratory ailments, some of which are fatal. Babies born 30 to 35 weeks after conception usually survive if good medical treatment is available. Their sucking reflex is not sufficiently strong to permit self-feeding, so they are force-fed by a tube inserted down the throat into the stomach. As is the trend throughout childhood, males have more troubles with prematurity than females. If two babies are born at 30 weeks, one a boy and the other a girl, the girl is more likely to survive than the boy, and if the boy survives he will be more likely than the girl to experience developmental irregularities. Premature infants have two to three times as many physical defects and about 50 percent more illness than full-term infants. About a third of all children with cerebral palsy were born prematurely.

The causes of prematurity are diverse, but factors over which the mother has control include cigarette smoking, diet, general health habits, and prenatal medical care. Mothers who do not smoke, who follow sound nutritional policies, and who consult a physician often during their pregnancy greatly reduce the probability that their baby will be born prematurely.

Behavioral Progressions during Prenatal Development	
Age (weeks)	Behavior
8	Stroking mouth region produces flexion of upper torso and neck and extension of arms at the shoulder.
9	Some spontaneous movements. Most of the whole body responds when mouth is stroked.
10	Stroking palms of hands leads to partial closing of the fingers.
11	Other parts of face and arms become sensitive.
13	Specific reflexes appear: lip closing, swallowing, Babinski reflex, squinting.
14	Entire body is sensitive, with more specific reflexes such as rooting, grasping, finger closing.
15	Can maintain closure of the fingers with muscle tightening, muscle strengthening.
16 to 18	Defined periods of activity and rest begin; sucking reflex.
19	Grasping with hand appears.
25	Respiration is sustained for up to 24 hours. Eyelids open spontaneously, rapid eye movements occur, and Moro reflex appears.
27 to birth	Blink response to sound at 28 weeks. Rhythmic brain waves appear. After this age, it becomes less easy to elicit reflexes in the fetus until the time of birth. Habituation begins at 30 weeks. After 36 weeks, eyes are inactive, as in deep sleep.

(Adapted from Fogel & Melson, 1988).

The eighth month

The eight-month fetus is somewhat akin to the 13-year-old preadolescent, in that it has outgrown one environment but is of insufficient skill and maturity to live well in another. There is nothing to do except wait for time to bestow growth and strength.

The 30-week fetus can cope with birth, but it will tax the baby's entire system to its limit. During the eighth month a layer of fat encases the fetus, adding about one kilogram of weight. Housing becomes even more crowded, and somersaults and other such activities, which have been going on for the past few months, are restricted by lack of space. The fetus is now biding time until it has sufficient stamina and organ efficiency to make the great transition to extra-uterine life, which will occur sometime during the next 30 days.

A question of enduring interest is whether the emotions of the mother affect the developing fetus. No direct connections exist between the nervous system of the mother and the nervous system of the fetus; therefore, it is not precisely understood *how* the emotions of the mother could affect the fetus. On the other hand, we know that chemical changes in the mother's circulatory system can be transmitted to the fetus and thereby influence its behavior. A few general tidbits spice our knowledge on this topic.

Mothers with active autonomic indicators (such as high heart rate or high respiratory rate) are more likely to produce active infants. Also, infants of emotionally disturbed mothers tend to exhibit highly active autonomic nervous functions at birth. Thus, we have reason to believe that under certain circumstances the emotionality of the mother may influence the activity level or the temperament of the fetus. The nature of this link, however, remains unclear even though it has been the object of scientific investigation since the 50s.

The ninth month

When the uterus cannot expand any farther, soon the infant is born. Hormone production in the mother as well as the fetus triggers the labor process. The pituitary gland of the mother releases the hormone oxytocin, which sets in motion a series of reactions resulting in contraction of the uterus. When the fetus reaches full term its adrenal gland produces cortisol, and its pituitary also produces oxytocin. Fetal production of oxytocin is believed to be the final indicator that the birth process is ready to begin. For about 75 percent of all babies this production occurs within 11 days of the 266th day after conception. The baby now has a mass of between two and four kilograms (4.4 to 8.8 pounds), a substantial layer of fat to assist in the maintenance of thermal constancy, and, if development has been normal, all biological mechanisms required for survival outside the womb will be in working order. We should point out, however, that determination of the exact age of the fetus at birth is problematic because it is difficult to pinpoint the exact date of conception.

Obstetricians usually estimate fetal age by adding 15 days to the date of onset of the mother's last menstrual period, assuming that conception took place during the next ovulation cycle. However, both the menstrual cycle and the ovulation cycle show variation from woman to woman, because the cycles are influenced by stress and many other variables; therefore, this method of age dating leaves some room for error. This uncertainty is one reason the maturity of the newborn infant is determined by weight at birth. Generally, any baby with a mass of less than two kilograms at birth is considered premature.

The activities that characterized the 36-week fetus also characterize the 36-hour infant, with a few minor exceptions: the infant's breathing involves oxygen, not liquid; food enters the infant body by way of the mouth, not the umbilical cord; infant crying is vocal now that air can vibrate the vocal cords. From a humanistic perspective, at birth the mother ceases to be only a carrier and impersonal provider and begins to assume her role as the child's first source of love and contact.

Table 2-1 Differences between Prenatal and Postnatal Life

Condition	Prenatal	Postnatal
Environment	Amniotic fluid	Air
Temperature	Relatively constant	Fluctuates with atmosphere
Stimulation	Minimal	All senses stimulated by various stimuli
Nutrition	Provided directly from mother's blood	Dependent on outside source and proper functioning of digestive system
Oxygen supply	Provided from maternal bloodstream via placenta	Inhaled and then passed from neonate's lungs to pulmonary blood vessels
Metabolic elimination	Passed into maternal bloodstream via placenta	Discharged by kidneys, lungs and gastrointestinal tract
Emotional experience	Bland, nonexistent	Active with distress and relaxation

Labor and birth

During the last week of uterine life the placenta loses most of its nutritional efficiency, presumably because of old age, triggering a chemical reaction that facilitates the onset of labor.

There are three stages of labor. The first stage, which requires the greatest time, is the period when the cervix is dilated to allow passage of the infant head. The second stage involves passage of the baby through the vagina, or birth canal, into the extra-uterine world . The final stage involves the expulsion of the placenta, the amniotic and chorionic membranes, and the remainder of the umbilical cord, together usually referred to as the *afterbirth*. Occasionally the labor process is severely strained by the baby's attempt to exit buttocks first, in what is known as a *breech birth*. In some circumstances the doctor will remedy this dangerous situation by realigning the fetus so that a more normal delivery is possible; however, often the most feasible solution is to remove the child surgically by *Caesarean section*.

Child delivery via Caesarean section requires that an incision be made through the mother's abdominal and uterine walls for removal of the fetus. This surgery is most often performed when the mother's cervix has not dilated sufficiently, when the baby is too large to exit through the birth passage, when the fetus is thought to be too frail to survive prolonged labor, when the birth process is too lengthy, and when the placenta is not functioning properly. It also is used in cases of pelvic deformity or death of the mother in labor. Although Caesarean section is a delicate operation, it is performed routinely in modern hospitals and results in few complications; therefore, it is considered a low-risk operation.

Venereal disease and the fetus

A matter of practical consequence to many expectant mothers is the effect of gonorrhea and syphilis on the developing fetus. Syphilis is a chronic contagious venereal disease that, if untreated, may be fatal. Although the placenta is a fairly effective screening device, the organisms that cause syphilis frequently make their way from the mother to the fetus. If a pregnant woman is in the first or second stages of syphilis and has received medical treatment, the chances are good that the baby will be born without ill effects. However, if the expectant mother does not receive treatment, or is in a more advanced stage of syphilis, the child may be born with congenital syphilis and suffer from a wide variety of defects and abnormalities.

An expectant mother with gonorrhea poses special problems as well because as the child moves down through the birth canal during delivery the bacterium that causes gonorrhea (gonococcus) may infect the child's eyes and cause blindness. Because a woman may have gonorrhea and not be aware of it, drops of silver nitrate or penicillin are put in the eyes of all babies, immediately after birth. This procedure has virtually eradicated blindness caused by maternal gonorrhea.

Because venereal disease is fairly widespread (especially in the 17-to-25 age group) expectant mothers and fathers must be aware of the damage it can do to the developing fetus.

Although syphilis and gonorrhea cause major birth complications, in North America *chlamydia, herpes, and AIDS (Acquired Immune Deficiency Syndrome)* are more significant because of their widespread prevalence and their serious consequences.

Blackman (1985) reports that 5-20 percent of pregnant women have cervical chlamydial infections, with higher rates seen in adolescents and lower socio-economic women. As many as 67 percent of infants born to infected mothers show signs of infection arising during the birthing process. Maternal chlamydial infections also increase the likelihood of stillbirths, neonatal deaths and premature deliveries.

About seven percent of AIDS cases in the United States have occurred in women, with the primary routes of infection being intravenous drug use or heterosexual contact with males in a high risk group (Guinan and Hardy, 1987). Infected women have a high probability of transmitting the virus to their fetuses, with transmissions usually occurring during the first trimester (Kaplan, 1988). The virus may also be passed on during the birthing process or possibly through breast feeding (Rudd and Peckham, 1988). The afflicted children show increased susceptibility to infections and may exhibit neurological impairment.

Assessment of Prenatal Well-Being

Of significant concern to the pregnant woman is whether the child she is carrying is healthy. In recent years a number of techniques have been developed to assess this very question. These techniques usually are reserved for pregnancies considered "high-risk," including maternal diabetes, previous history of problem pregnancy, pre-term labor, maternal age (less than 20 or greater than 35).

Ultrasound – This is one of the most commonly used prenatal assessment devices. It is non-invasive (nothing is placed inside the mother's body) and safe to use even for multiple examinations during a single pregnancy. It uses high frequency, low intensity ultrasonic waves which are reflected differently by tissues of varying density. The image thus produced is viewed on an oscilloscope screen. Ultrasound imaging can be used to determine fetal age by cranial, femur, or crown/rump length measurement. This is sometimes necessary when the mother is unsure of her last menstrual period dates or when a problem is suspected with regard to the size of the fetus (e.g., Intrauterine Growth Retardation, IUGR). Ultrasound can detect various structural abnormalities, and it can determine fetal sex; it is used as an adjunct to several other assessment techniques such as biophysical profile monitoring, amnioscentesis, fetoscopy and chorionic villus sampling.

Biophysical Profile Monitoring – Here the fetus is observed via ultrasound and assessed on four variables over a ten-minute period: (1) appearance of fetal breathing movements, (2) appearance of body movement, (3) normal fetal tone, and (4) normal amniotic fluid levels.

This test is an extension of the ultrasound technique, and as such it is non-invasive and can be repeated many times over the course of a pregnancy to ensure that a high-risk infant continues to progress normally. If there is evidence of deterioration (i.e., decreased levels of amniotic fluid) consideration can be given to early delivery.

Nonstress Test – This test is used to determine if the fetus is reacting normally to stimuli – an indicator of its well being. Using an external heart rate monitor the mother reports when she feels fetal movements and this is compared to a chart recording of the fetal heart rate. In a normal fetus, movement will correspond to an increased heart rate.

Amniocentesis – This procedure involves the withdrawal of amniotic fluid from the amniotic sac. With the aid of ultrasound (to insure that the needle is aimed at a sufficient pocket of amniotic fluid) a needle is inserted through the mother's abdomen into the uterus. Both the amniotic fluid and shed fetal cells floating in the amniotic fluid can be used for analysis. The fluid can be tested for elevated levels of alpha-fetoprotein (AFP) which is indicative of open neural tube defects such as spina-bifida. Cells can be cultured and chromosomal studies performed to detect disorders such as Down's Syndrome or Turner's Syndrome. These cultured cells can be tested for certain inborn errors of metabolism such as Tay-Sachs disease or phenylketonuria. Amniocentesis also reveals blood group and fetal sex.

The major drawback of amniocentesis is that it cannot be performed until adequate levels of fetal cells have been produced, generally not until the second trimester. The test also requires several days to culture and analyze cells.

Fetoscopy – This is an invasive procedure where, under the guidance of ultrasound, a fibre optic instrument is inserted surgically through the abdomen into the uterus and into the amniotic sac. This procedure allows for direct viewing of the fetus and can also be used to take fetal blood and tissue such as skin and liver for direct biopsy. Fetoscopy is rarely used as it poses a fairly significant risk of miscarriage and many of its applications can be performed using other less risky procedures.

Chorionic Villus Biopsy – This involves the extraction of a sample of chorionic villus material through the vagina and the neck of the uterus. The analyses performed are similar to those obtained through amniocentesis. The advantage of this technique is that it can be performed as early as eight weeks, allowing for much earlier results. AFP determination cannot be made using this method so if neural tube defects are suspected, amniocentesis would be the method of choice.

Recombinant DNA Technology – This very recent technology can be applied to cell cultures obtained through amniocentesis or chorionic villus biopsy for rapid detection of a number of inherited disorders such as sickle cell anemia and Huntington's Chorea.

The results of tests such as Amniocentesis, Fetoscopy, and Chorionic Villus Biopsy are often used in the decision to medically abort. These decisions are difficult and not based solely on test results, but also on the moral and ethical beliefs of the mother, father, and their doctor.

Twins

Identical twins, more than any other combination of human siblings, are of special interest to psychologists, because they provide a unique opportunity to observe how children with identical history grow and develop. The two general types of twins are identical and fraternal.

Fraternal twins are the products of two different eggs fertilized by two different sperm, and they develop as two individuals with completely different hereditary determinants. The mother, instead of releasing one egg, for some reason releases two eggs, both of which are fertilized, but by different sperm. Even though they are born at the same time, fraternal twins are not, in terms of heredity, any more alike than two children born separately of the same parents. Fraternal twins may be of the same sex or one of each sex, because the chromosome that determines sex is carried within the sperm; because two different sperm were involved, the chances are about 50/50 that the twins will be of the same sex. The incidence of fraternal twins increases with advancing maternal age and a family history of twin births. No such observations occur with identical twins (Hacker and Moore, 1985).

Identical twins are of even greater interest because they represent two separate humans that originate from exactly the same hereditary materials. Identical twins are products of a single egg and a single sperm that produce one embryo that at a very early stage divides in half. The separate halves grow into two separate individuals; however, having come from the same egg and the same sperm, they carry the same chromosomes and genes.

Identical twins have much more in common than the mere fact that they look alike (which they do because facial features and formations are governed by heredity). Identical twins are extremely similar in height, even when reared apart. Identical twin girls begin to menstruate about one or two months apart, whereas fraternal twin sisters begin about a year apart. Identical twins are more alike than any other siblings in their pulse rates and perspiration rates. In addition, they are more similar than fraternal twins in complex and incompletely understood phenomena such as autism, sleep-walking, and bed-wetting.

The characteristics of twins have been investigated for decades, not only by psychologists but also by geneticists, sociologists, and pediatricians.

Favorite subjects of investigation are identical twins who for, whatever reason, were separated at birth and raised in different environments. By studying these particular twins, researchers hope to learn more about the relative mixture of heredity and environment in the human brew. These studies have yielded mixed results, but they confirm that heredity regulates certain human traits (such as height, body type, and facial features) and that the environment, to a significant extent, determines others (such as personality, educational achievement, and personal values).

Abnormalities in Prenatal Development

The genetic rules that regulate fetal development are not perfect; the fetus may incur growth deficits because of the genetic limitations of the parents or because of faulty environmental conditions within the uterus. To complicate matters, a genetically sound fetus living in a healthy uterine environment may be adversely affected by foreign agents introduced into its system from the mother. In this section I shall discuss four basic factors that contribute to fetal abnormality: (1) teratogenic agents, (2) chromosomal abnormalities, (3) multiple births, and (4) maternal characteristics and habits. Two additional factors significantly related to fetal damage – prematurity and abortion – have been discussed and will not be treated again here.

Teratogenic Agents

An agent that produces a malformation in the fetus or even increases the probability of a malformation is known as a *teratogen*. The most widely known human teratogens are drugs, viruses, and radiation. These teratogens adversely affect metabolic processes and thereby distort normal growth blueprints within the fetus. Their destructive power is directly related to critical growth periods of the fetus. Rubella (German measles) is a severe teratogenic agent during the first three months of pregnancy but usually has no negative effects during the final three months of pregnancy. Likewise, the drug thalidomide does not harm the fetus during the second or third trimester but grossly distorts limb development during the first trimester.

The following principles are crucial to understanding the effects of teratogens on the fetus:

1. The age of the embryo or fetus determines which tissues are most susceptible to damage.
2. Teratogenic agents interfere with phases of metabolic development; therefore, these agents produce fairly consistent patterns of malformation.
3. The greater the extent of malformation, the greater the chance the fetus will die before birth.
4. Agents that are damaging to the fetus may be relatively harmless to the mother.

Sometimes a specific agent is clearly teratogenic, as with rubella or thalidomide; in other instances we are uncertain whether a substance (such as cigarette smoke) is genuinely teratogenic – that is, whether negative effects that correlate with it are actually caused by it. Three agents that are known to be teratogens and to have greatly influenced the prenatal development of millions of children are rubella, certain drugs, and the Rh factor.

Rubella – Also known as German measles, rubella is a contagious disease characterized by a slight fever, a sore throat, and small skin eruptions. It is less severe than measles, although similar in its symptoms. Rubella poses no serious threat to the mother (as is the case with many teratogenic agents), but, depending on the stage of pregnancy in which it occurs, it may be hazardous to the fetus. If the expectant mother is infected with rubella during the first three months of pregnancy, the parts of the fetus undergoing a critical phase of development may be damaged, especially the eyes, ears and heart. The main abnormalities that result are deafness, congenital heart disease, and eye defects. Medical research indicates that the chance of an infant's incurring a major defect if the mother contracts rubella during the first month of pregnancy is about 50 percent; about 20 percent if she contracts it during the third month; and virtually nil if rubella is contracted during the fifth through ninth months of pregnancy. In recent years the incidence of congenital Rubella infection has been declining due in large measure to wide scale vaccination programs (Rudd and Peckham, 1988).

When a medical doctor confirms a pregnancy, the expectant mother is routinely examined for resistence to rubella. If she does not have antibodies to protect her against rubella, she may receive immunization with gammaglobulin injections. If her susceptibility to rubella is not discovered until after she contracts the disease, nothing can be done to protect the fetus. (Using fetoscopy it is possible to obtain a fetal blood sample to determine whether or not the fetus has been exposed).

Drugs – Medical opinion is divided on how effectively the placental barrier prevents harmful agents from entering the fetal system. Some specialists claim that only a very few damaging agents ever permeate the placental barrier and enter the fetus. Others believe that the barrier is not an effective defense against drugs and that most drugs which enter the system of the mother eventually make their way into the system of the fetus. During the 60s and 70s, the former viewpoint was widely accepted; in the 80s and 90s, however, after numerous technical advances in the field of embryology, most experts accept the latter viewpoint.

Whatever the case, certain harmful agents definitely do pass through the barrier and cause considerable damage to the fetus. Mothers who are consistent morphine users give birth to babies addicted to morphine, and heroin-addicted mothers may miscarry or give birth to infants addicted to heroin. Deafness may be caused by the mother's use of quinine, and heavy sedation of the mother may result in fetal asphyxiation. Some investigators have concluded that LSD may cause chromosomal damage, although the data on this are not nearly as conclusive as those related to the other drugs mentioned.

Less conspicuous examples of the impact of drugs on the development of the fetus are to be found. For example, the possibility of damage to the fetus has been linked with excessive use of eye drops, because vasospastic drugs (drugs that cause spastic contraction of blood vessels) may adversely affect the blood vessels of the placenta. The use of contraceptive jellies after conception may also be injurious to the embryo.

Fetal Alcohol Syndrome (FAS)– Over the past few years, alcohol has been recognized as a potent teratogen. Studies indicate that alcoholic mothers have an increased risk of producing offspring with a pattern of birth defects referred to as "fetal alcohol syndrome." The most commonly occurring features include: (1) prenatal growth deficiency for weight, height and head circumference. (2) distinct craniofacial (skull-face) anomolies, and (3) mild to moderate mental retardation. Other features such as heart defects, behavioral disorders, and abnormal muscular or skeletal formation have also been noted but are not as consistently observed.

As with all teratogens, timing of consumption is of critical importance in determining which disorders will be observed. Some contend (Ernhart et al, 1987) that craniofacial abnormalities result from early first trimester consumption (period when head and facial features are developing) and that growth deficiency is more closely related to alcohol abuse during the third trimester.

At the present time scientists have not been able to determine safe levels of alcohol consumption. Some research indicates that a pregnant woman who daily consumes between 2 and 4 ounces of 100 proof whiskey or 1 to 2 glasses of wine has a 10 percent chance of producing a child with FAS. One who daily consumes 6 glasses of wine or a six-pack of beer has a 50 percent chance. Even a single binge drinking episode may be sufficient. Based on this information, prudent counsel for prospective mothers is to reduce or abstain from alcohol use prior to conception and throughout pregnancy.

The Rh Factor – Blood composition of the fetus can clash with the blood composition of the mother, causing damage or even death to the fetus. Such blood incompatibility occurs, for example, when the red blood cells of the fetus contain the protein "Rh factor" and the blood of the mother does not. If the blood of the fetus "leaks" into the mother's bloodstream (because of poor filtration in the placental membrane), the mother's blood becomes contaminated with the Rh factor protein. As a defense against this invasion of foreign protein, antibodies are formed in the mother's bloodstream. These antibodies work their way into the fetal bloodstream and destroy blood cells and reduce oxygen supply, which may cause brain damage or death from oxygen starvation. An Rh positive fetus in an Rh negative mother can be spontaneously aborted during the early stages of pregnancy.

Sometimes the baby can be saved by purging its bloodstream with transfusions. However, for some infants the reaction to the antibodies received from the mother is so severe that higher brain functions are permanently impaired.

About 85 percent of the population is Rh positive and about 15 percent Rh negative. Whenever an Rh negative woman becomes pregnant, tests are conducted to determine the presence of antibodies in her blood. Rh disease occurs in the babies of about five percent of Rh negative women and usually during a third or later pregnancy. Some evidence indicates that the mother's blood becomes contaminated with Rh positive protein during the birth process, when the baby's blood leaks into the mother's system. Therefore, during later pregnancies the fetus receives the bulk of the antibodies built up in the mother.

Recent breakthroughs in immunization have greatly reduced the incidence of Rh disease. A vaccine is administered to the Rh negative mother upon delivery of her first Rh positive baby – a vaccine that "blinds" her immune system to the presence of the Rh factor. The mother does not produce antibodies against the blood factor, and the fetus in future pregnancies is not exposed to the antibodies' destructive influence. Women who receive this immunization are much less likely to produce a child with Rh disease.

Chromosomal Abnormalities

Down's Syndrome – Chromosomes are small, dark-staining, rodshaped bodies that appear in the nucleus of a cell at the time of cell division. They contain the genes, or hereditary factors, and are constant in number in each species. The normal number in humans is 46. However, sometimes in the reproductive process specific chromosomes may be defective and cause developmental abnormalities. Among the most significant of the chromosome-related abnormalities is Down's syndrome (also known as mongolism).

Down's syndrome is a serious disorder characterized by slanting eyes, a flat, broad face, and usually, mental retardation. It is caused by a defective pair of chromosomes that appear as a triple chromosome. Thus, in Down's syndrome there are 47 chromosomes rather than the usual 46.

The risk of giving birth to a Down's syndrome child is greater for older women than for women in their 20s. The chance that a woman in her 20s will give birth to a Down's-syndrome child is about one in three thousand. For a woman in her early 30s the chance is about one in six hundred. And for a woman in her late 40s the chance is about one in 40.

Why an extra chromosome is produced is unknown, but the fact that this syndrome is associated with increased age is undeniable. Once this chromosomal abnormality has occurred it creates a nonreversible aberration that persists throughout the life of the Down's syndrome person.

Identical twins exhibit a predictable consistency with regard to Down's syndrome. Research conducted by A. Smith (1960) demonstrated that in the overwhelming majority of cases, when one identical twin is affected by Down's syndrome, so is the other. However, if one child from a set of fraternal twins is affected by Down's syndrome, the other twin is virtually never affected.

"Fragile" X Syndrome – Recent evidence suggests that the so called "Fragile" X Syndrome may be the second leading cause of mental retardation (next to Down' Syndrome). Its discovery has helped to explain a high proportion of the previously uncharacterized incidents of mental retardation. In this disorder, the X chromosome has a tendency to break. The condition produces varying degrees of mental retardation. In addition to mental retardation, males frequently exhibit large ears, long faces and, after puberty, enlarged testicles (Persaud, 1985).

Like all X-linked disorders, males are predominantly affected. Since they have a single X chromosome (XY) any genetic defects found on the X chromosome are generally expressed, as they have no corresponding genes on the Y chromosome to counteract the effect. Among females, these X-linked traits are generally masked because they have two X chromosomes (XX) and one of these is likely to be normal.

Genetic Counselling – In order to reduce the risk of producing genetically defective children, many prospective parents choose genetic counselling. This process examines the family genetic background of both parents to determine the odds of subsequent children being defective. Generally this service is used by families with a history of genetic defects, a history of spontaneous abortions or stillbirths, or for women over 35 years, who are at increased risk for chromosomal abnormalities (e.g., Down's Syndrome).

The genetic counsellor determines an estimate of risk and also discusses ways of dealing with the risk. For severe anomalies with a high risk of occurrence, the parents might opt for adoption or alternative conception methods such as the use of donor eggs or sperm. The potential exists in many cases to detect genetic disorders early in pregnancy through procedures such as amniocentesis or chorionic villus biopsy.

The genetic counsellor's role is primarily as an information source. Decisions, of course, are made by the prospective parents, based on their own ethical and moral principles. The counsellor then provides guidance and support to the family in dealing with their decision.

Multiple Births

Multiple-birth children (twins, triplets, and so on) are more likely than singleton children to suffer birth defects or deficits. The chance of premature birth is greater with multiple fetuses and, as noted elsewhere in this chapter, prematurity is associated with numerous developmental abnormalities. When twins share a placenta, there is a chance that one twin will have a more favorable position and receive better nutrition. The less fortunate twin may suffer adverse effects from this unfair division of natural resources.

Twins and triplets tend to have slightly slower than average motor development and slightly lower IQs than singletons. Interestingly, twins incur more problems than singletons, triplets more than twins, and quadruplets more than triplets. In conclusion, even though multiple-birth children may be average or above average with regard to any particular trait, the probability that they will possess developmental handicaps is slightly greater than for the general population.

Mother's Impact on the Unborn Baby

Maternal Characteristics and Habits

In recent years considerable evidence has accumulated to indicate that the age of the mother, her dietary habits, and the kinds of drugs she ingests have significant influence on the development of the unborn child. Increased knowledge of how the placental barrier works and how substances (whether teratogenic or health-promoting) are transmitted from the mother to the fetus has increased sophistication in this area. So also have technological advances that permit observation of the fetus and its reactions to foreign substances introduced into its system.

Diet – Pediatricians generally agree that the single most important factor in the production of healthy children is the soundness of the expectant mother's diet. Malnutrition (and its corollary defects, such as vitamin shortage) is the pre-eminent cause of defects among the children of the world.

Nutritional deficiency in the mother increases the chance that the fetus will be spontaneously aborted, be born dead, suffer brain damage, have perceptual disabilities, or be lower than normal in intelligence. Malnutrition (like most teratogenic conditions) does the greatest damage during the earlier stages of pregnancy.

Nutritional soundness does not improve the fetus by raising IQ or accelerating perceptual development; rather, it permits normal maturation to occur, and it prevents defects associated with malnutrition. Teratogenic agents such as drugs or a virus may deform the child even when the mother's nutrition is excellent. In North American culture, however, the single most important factor in the health of the newborn is the nutritional health of the expectant mother.

Social Class – The incidence of defects and abnormalities among newborns is not equal among social classes in North America. Low-income parents have a considerably higher percentage of children who are defective at birth and a greater percentage of children whose birth abnormalities continue throughout childhood rather than disappearing in the first year. Low-income families also report a higher incidence of defects among children of low birth weight.

Problems associated with pregnancy and delivery are three to four times more frequent among lower-class families than among middle-class families. Toxemias, infections, prematurity, and anoxia are all more likely to occur in the lower-class mother and her infant than in a middle-class mother and her infant. The risk of infant damage or death is between 50 and 100 percent higher in the lower socioeconomic classes than in the middle and upper-middle classes. This may be accounted for by factors such as an impoverished environment (involving greater likelihood of maternal malnutrition and poorer health and greater exposure to disease), parental ignorance about child care, and failure to seek professional help.

Maternal Age – The age of the mother is an important factor in the general health of the baby because several growth defects are associated with increased maternal age. Down's syndrome is significantly correlated with maternal age: every increase of five years after the age of 25 doubles the probability that the child will be born with Down's syndrome.

Mothers under 20 or over 30 produce a greater percentage of defective children than mothers in their 20s. In particular, very young and over 35 mothers are more likely to produce children with anancephaly (lack of cortex) or hydrocephalus (enlarged brain with mental deficiency) and are more likely to suffer miscarriage, stillbirth, or the death of the infant. Middle-aged mothers are apt to have muscle degeneration, which adversely influences the reproductive apparatus. Some researchers believe that Down's syndrome is caused by a defective ovum that contains an extra chromosome and that this defect is more likely to occur as the mother ages.

Very young mothers (early and middle adolescents) tend to be physically immature and this immaturity increases the chance of fetal abnormality and birth complications. Whether physical immaturity or poor prenatal care is the primary cause of these abnormalities has not been determined. Much of the current data however, suggest that lack of adequate prenatal care is as significant as the age factor. Factors such as nutrition, smoking, alcohol consumption, and sexually transmitted diseases (STDs) have major impacts on fetal well-being no matter what the mother's age and these may be particularly significant for pregnant teenagers. Often teens ignore the need for medical care until their pregnancies are far advanced, their eating habits are frequently poor, and STDs are common in the sexually active teen. One study (Smith et al, 1985) showed that most obstetric complications could be significantly reduced by providing improved prenatal care.

Smoking – Women who smoke increase the likelihood of premature delivery and they also are likely to produce babies with significantly reduced body weights, and with an increased risk of spontaneous abortion. The risk of low birth weight increases with the number of cigarettes smoked but returns to levels of non-smokers if smoking is given up early in pregnancy.

Paton and Yacoub (1987) have shown that nicotine in the maternal circulation produces reduced blood flow to the placenta for up to 15 minutes after smoking a single cigarette. As well, carbon monoxide inhaled by the mother reduces the oxygen available to the fetus.

Summary Comments on the Prenatal Growth Period

For nine months the fetus has developed in systematic fashion from a circular speck smaller than the period at the end of this sentence into a three-kilogram (6.6 pounds), multibillion-celled, organismically sound human infant. Its growth has been cephalocaudal, unfolding in a head-to-toe direction, and proximodistal, developing from centre to periphery.

The fetal journey began with gross, global, and undifferentiated behavior and concludes with refined and complex activity. All body members and organs have progressively differentiated; the hand has been converted from a shovel-like stub to a five-digit instrument capable of prehension; and the froglike, bulbous head has acquired childlike facial contours, functional brain hemispheres, and the cortical foundations for higher thought processes. Not all body parts mature at the same rate; thus, the underdeveloped legs of the fetus will remain so through infancy and toddlerhood, although by middle adolescence they will constitute half of the body length. Conversely, the fetal head is disproportionately large and will gradually lose prominence, until by adulthood it will constitute only a tenth of total body volume.

The fetus has prepared for infancy by sucking, breathing, swallowing, digesting, crying, and eliminating, all of which will be required for neonatal survival. The parasite fetus has depended completely on the mother for nourishment, disease immunity, and shelter and has thereby established itself as a socially dependent creature.

The fetus is remarkable for its mixture of complexity and simplicity, durability and fragility, predictability and individuality, inability and potentiality. These polarities, far from disappearing at birth, in many respects will be magnified in the new infant.

The fetus is now ready to be born, never again to know the nameless isolation and experiential void that until the moment of birth made up its world.

Major Concepts of this Chapter

1. The germinal period refers to the time from conception to implantation of the fertilized egg in the uterine wall. The egg is fertilized by the male sperm in the Fallopian tube and then travels to the uterus. The time from the beginning of the sperm's journey toward the egg to the attachment of the fertilized egg to the uterine wall is 7 to 14 days.

2. Once the egg is attached to the uterine wall the embryonic period begins. Major body systems and organs begin to form. Tissue differentiates into ectoderm, mesoderm, and endoderm.

3. In the second month the embryo attains some infant characteristics. Features of the head become recognizable, the brain is developing, limbs mature and by the eighth week all major organs are differentiated and functioning.

4. After eight weeks the growing human is referred to as a fetus. At this point bone cells begin to develop.

5. The first months of pregnancy are often accompanied by morning sickness and tiredness. Frequent urination is also typical of the first months of pregnancy.

6. The second trimester (starting with the fourth month) brings about tremendous fetal growth. By the end of the fourth month the fetus may have reached a length of 20 centimetres (8 inches). The fetus is nourished by the placenta and attached to it by the umbilical cord. Exchanges from mother to child take place through the placenta but the blood of the fetus never mixes with that of the mother.

7. In the fifth month some reflexes develop and organs begin to function more efficiently. Most bones are formed and the fetus has reached approximately 30 centimetres (12 inches) in length.

8. In the sixth month the fetus becomes sturdier and the organ system is well coordinated, however, the fetus rarely survives birth at this age because lungs and respiratory system are too immature to sustain life.

9. Infants born after 28 weeks of gestation have some chance of survival. From 28 to 32 weeks gestation the mother passes immunity to the infant in preparation for the first few weeks after birth. Lung tissue matures, increasing the chances of survival.

10. The first stage of labor, during which the cervix is dilated to allow for the passage of the infant, usually takes the greatest amount of time. The second stage consists of the actual delivery of the infant and the third stage expels the afterbirth.

11. The well-being of the fetus can be monitored during the pregnancy using a number of techniques. These include ultrasound, nonstress test, chorionic villus biopsy, amniocentesis, fetoscopy, and recombinant DNA technology.

12. Twins are produced either through the fertilization of two separate eggs (fraternal twins) or through the early splitting of a single fertilized egg (identical twins). Since identical twins have exactly the same genetic endowment their maturational unfolding is remarkably similar.

13. Teratogenic agents can exert severe impact on the fetus. Thalidomide, rubella, and Rh factor incompatibility have caused a wide range of congenital defects.

14. Down's syndrome and the fragile "X" Syndrome are chromosomal abnormalities which cause mental retardation and other defects.

15. Maternal characteristics and habits such as diet, social class, age and cigarette smoking are correlates of abnormal fetal development.

3

Nature's Child: Birth to Four Months

*When I approach a child, he inspires
two sentiments; tenderness for what he
is and respect for what he may become*

Louis Pasteur

The first year of life begins with a reflexive gasp of air at birth and ends with a misdirected burst of air caused by an excited parent's coaxing to blow out a birthday candle. Between these two events incredible growth takes place.

Newborn infants have no voluntary control over their limbs and no ability to move themselves. They cannot perceive the world except by means of underdeveloped eyes, insensitive ears, and an imprecise sense of touch; newborns do not even recognize their own mother. Newborns do almost nothing of their own volition, relying instead on primitive reflexes and random flexing. They have no emotions as adults experience them; they experience only various states of distress and excitement. Except for a piercing and persistent cry, they are incapable of oral communication. Not one of the abilities that distinguish humans from other animals is present in the newborn. They are proficient at nothing, and would die within days if left unattended. From this meagerly equipped package of incomplete humanity will develop the most complex, intelligent, and creative animal on earth, and the foundations for this development are established during the first year of life.

In this chapter the significant milestones and developmental events of the first four months after birth are described and analyzed. The time periods of most significance are: (1) birth to six weeks, when life is dominated by reflexes, recuperation from birth, and gaining the necessary strength required for the infant to interact with the environment; and, (2) six to 16 weeks, when the infant greatly expands in awareness and comes to interact with the physical and social environment. In Chapter Four the focus will be upon infant development from four months to 12 months.

The Great Transition: From Mother to Outside World

The First Six Weeks after Birth

Birth shock is the biological stress experienced by the infant during the transition from intra-uterine to extra-uterine life. Although newborns shortly are engaged in meeting the requirements of a new environment, some parts of their system require several days of recuperation. Birth shock should be distinguished from "birth trauma," a concept used by several psychologists – most notably, Otto Rank. Rank suggests that the trauma of birth is a significant factor in the emotional development of the child. This is not my contention, because most evidence suggests that the birth process, although severe, does not leave a lasting psychological imprint on the normal child. Despite the infant's remarkable ability to recuperate, birth does impose considerable strain on the infant (and the mother).

A difference of opinion among experts surrounds the question of what life inside the womb is like – if it is like anything. On the one hand is the group of experts who claim that some features of intra-uterine life are somehow impressed on the psyche of the child. On the other hand is the group of experts who insist that the fetus cannot experience sensation or perception, therefore intra-uterine experiences do not influence them to any appreciable degree. Bower (1979) has this to say about life in the womb:

> The world inside the womb is as uniform and neutral as any environment could be. There are no rewards or punishments, so the fetus's actions have no real consequences. There can be very, very little sensory input in the womb. Since the newborn has no exposure history, no history of reinforcements of any sort, any capacities demonstrated at birth must have been formed under genetic control. Because the psychological environment prior to birth is so bland as to be nonexistent, it is to the expression of genetic information that we must look for an explanation of the capacities of the newborn. (p. 47)

Let us briefly reconstruct the environment of the full-term fetus. Softly cushioned in the mother's uterus, protected from bumps and jostles by a liquid shock-absorbing system, the fetus is partially free from the effects of gravity and can move without being restricted by it. Nutrition is funnelled directly into the fetus's system via the placenta and umbilical cord. The temperature of the amniotic fluid (37.8 degrees Celsius) is subject to minimal variation. There is no competition for basic goods (except in the case of twins, triplets, and so on) or hassles of any other sort. The fetus never experiences punishment or encounters demands to be anything other than what it is.

The fetal environment is not at all like the buzzing, changing environment of the newborn, and eventually the shock of changing from one to the other must be experienced. The transition from tranquil intra-uterine to hectic extra-uterine existence takes place during a very brief yet highly critical 20-minute period.

Labor and Birth

During labor the fetal head is forced through the mother's cervix. If the delivery is normal, the balance of the baby's body will follow shortly thereafter. To deliver the baby, a force equal to almost 100 pounds is required; the infant's head receives the brunt of this pressure and is able to withstand it because five major bone plates in the skull are pliable. The process of forcing the child out of the womb, taxing to the mother as well as to the infant, constitutes only one phase of birth shock. The infant's first gasp of air requires five times the effort of ordinary breathing, because air must be taken in to expand the uninflated air sacs of the lungs. Breathing passages are not cleared of mucus for several days, making breathing irregular. Almost all of the newborn's body cavities are filled with fluid or mucous that must be removed. (This is one reason for yawning, coughing, and sneezing during the first hours of extra-uterine life.) Still reeling from the shock of birth and breathing, the newborn experiences the thermal shock of a drop in temperature of 11 to 14 degrees Celsius when first exposed to outside air. The eyes are instantly assaulted with brightness, and hearing is exposed to stimuli of greater intensity than ever experienced before (although the shock is lessened by the fluid that fills the ears for about 48 hours). The neonate must rapidly adjust to consuming food via the mouth, throat, and stomach – a completely new experience. The heart is subject to new pressures, as it must now pump blood to the lungs to pick up oxygen. A major valve inside the heart must close if oxygenated blood and deoxygenated blood are to be kept separate.

In addition to these jolts to the system, the newborn must undergo administration of silver nitrate to the eyes (a preventative against gonorrheal opthalmia), a brisk cleansing, and a lively handling by as many as five adults during the first 30 minutes of life.

Reducing birth shock – In recent years there has been an increased preference for "natural" childbirth, especially from young mothers delivering their first child. Usually this involves the mother's receiving as little anesthesia as sound medical practice warrants. One birth method that has achieved considerable popularity is the Lamaze method – a procedure in which the mother learns to control her pain responses to birth by concentrating on breathing and by learning new reactions to labor pain. This method also encourages the father to join the mother in the delivery room in order to provide emotional support in the birthing process. As a result of the popularity of this method many hospital delivery rooms have abandoned their traditionally inflexible practices in favor of more personal and intimate birthing methods.

The Leboyer Method – Frederic Leboyer (1975), has focused public attention on a birth procedure that reduces birth shock. Leboyer claims that the sudden contrast between the warm, tranquil world of the fetus and the hustle-bustle pace of the first few minutes following birth is painful to the child and psychologically defeating to the mother. He makes the following suggestions for bettering the birth process. First, the delivery room should be rid of glaring lights that assault the newborn's eyes; a dimly lit room serves just as well (although extra lights must be available in case they are suddenly needed). Unnecessary noise should be eliminated; soft voices are reassuring and less harsh than the chatter that ordinarily fills hospital delivery rooms. In the Leboyer method, when the newborn is expelled in the final stages of birth, rather than being carried off for cleaning and testing, and before the umbilical cord is severed, the baby is placed gently on the mother's stomach. The infant is thus given time to adjust to the new environment, and the mother is the first person to caress and hold her infant, a gesture some psychologists believe contributes to mother-child bonding. In a few seconds the newborn begins to breathe, and the umbilical cord ceases to function; when this happens the cord is cut. Next, the baby is placed in a small tub of water preheated to body temperature (to which the newborn in accustomed); then the baby is cleansed. Eventually the eyes open, limb movement begins, and normal infant activity commences. Some doctors (and parents) claim that babies delivered by the Leboyer method do not cry at all during the birth process and may even smile during the early hours of life. Although these claims may somewhat glamourize the Leboyer method, the technique certainly appears to be more congenial to the infant than traditional delivery procedures.

Several factors contribute to the interest of parents and obstetricians in the Leboyer method. First, is the common sense aspect. All things considered, it makes sense that being born into a quiet, soft, warm, sheltered environment is more pleasant than being born into a noisy, bright, "hospital sterile" environment. Second, is the social trend of the past two decades for the mother to be more actively involved in birth rather than leaving everything to specialists attending her. Mothers now demand (and receive) less anesthetic, and as a result, they and their newborns are more alert and responsive immediately after delivery. Third, is the increased popularity of the viewpoint that the birth process directly affects the *emotional* well-being of the child. Advocates of this viewpoint claim that a "violent" birth creates negative reactions, whereas a "violence-free" birth enhances the child's emotional strength. In fact, Leboyer's book, which brought worldwide attention to this birthing method is titled *Birth Without Violence*.

The evidence is inconclusive as to whether children delivered via the Leboyer method encounter fewer problems during childhood than babies delivered via traditional methods. A thorough longitudinal study of these children would be necessary for a scientific assessment of Leboyer's method. Presently, however, it simply is not known what, if any, positive effects the method has on the newborn.

As difficult and strenuous as the birth process may be, it is only the first of many shocks each child endures in the course of normal development and maturation. Shortly after birth the infant must adjust to a less intense, but still critical shock – social living. This is a major task for which the infant has only minimal reflexes. He must learn to cope with a mother who, no matter how loving and caring, is unique and not totally predictable. The infant must adjust to the shock of an environment which constantly changes (auditory, visual, tactile and temperature stimuli vary tremendously in the course of a routine day). Before the shock of social living has subsided the infant will encounter the transition from an exclusively horizontal to a partially vertical position. This remarkable achievement, made by few other animals, requires fundamental adjustments in social as well as physical development. Each of these changes requires adaptability. All normal children make these transitions, although some have more difficulty than others.

Full-term infants are usually durable specimens both resilient and sturdy. If they are born into a loving and providing environment, only a major obstacle such as illness or accident will prevent their growing strong and straight. Thus, birth shock is the infant's introduction to a world that will continue to present shocks. It is the price of admission into the human milieu.

Obstetric Drugs and the Newborn

Pain-relieving herbs and drugs have been used during labor for centuries. The 20th century has witnessed a dramatic increase in the use of medical drugs during delivery. Among some researchers there is a growing concern that the impact of these drugs on the newborn is stronger (and more negative) than previously thought. Mothers who receive medication during labor deliver babies who perform less well on measures of perception, attentiveness, and motor skills (at least during the first hours after birth). A wide variety of drugs, including tranquilizers, local anesthetics, and general anesthetics, impede the baby's ability to respond to stimulation and also seems to reduce their cuddliness.

Some researchers (and most medical doctors) claim that even though the baby is influenced by drugs ingested by the mother, the effects are short term, and when they have run their course the infant is back to normal. These researchers claim that the effects of drugs on the baby are similar to their effects on the mother, who also is "back to normal" after the grogginess wears off. It is well to keep in mind, however, that knowledge of the newborn's susceptibility to drugs is skimpy and that recent findings indicate that the fetus may experience more adverse effects than heretofore believed. We also know that most teratogens are relatively harmless to the mother yet devastating to the fetus; therefore, it is possible that drugs that exert only minor effect on the mother may have serious effect on the soon-to-be-born fetus.

The impact of obstetric drugs on the newborn is one of many topics about which it is extremely difficult to obtain rigorous scientific data. It is not possible to conduct controlled studies in which all variables are held constant and then measure the differential effects of the manipulation of the drug. As frequently is the case, students of human infancy must rely on observation, logical inference, and animal studies when formulating their judgments.

"Soothing" Children in the Nineteenth Century

Robert Sunley, in an informative essay on American child-rearing customs during the 19th century, reports that many practices that were then common, including the drugging of children, are now not only obsolete but also illegal. Concerning the chemical "soothing" of children, he makes the following observations: "Drugs were given to infants to stop their crying and put them to sleep. In the form of patent medicines, drugs were given to remedy a variety of illnesses, major and minor, including gripes, flatulence, and irregular bowels" (p. 7). Sunley quotes a writer of the times as saying "The bane of infants and young children is laudanum [a form of opium. . . which is the basis of all quack medicine and given almost indiscriminately in this country to infants, from the moment they are born – till, I may say – the day of their death." Another writer comments, regarding a patent medicine based on laudanum: "If improper food has slain its hundreds, Godfrey's Cordial has slain its thousands."

Alcohol was similarly used to quiet a child both in home-made and in patent medicines. Servants, it was believed, often resorted to such drugging to be quit for a time of a troublesome infant or to make sure the child slept while the servant took time off. Laudanum was used by some working mothers to make sure their children slept while they were away, but evidence indicates that mothers of the upper classes also used such drugs. So often is this practice mentioned and so often condemned by medical writers that it may be inferred that the practice was widespread. A number of infant deaths were officially attributed to opium. In 1837-38, for example, inquests showed 52 infants were included in the total of 186 deaths due to opium.

Caesarean Section

Caesarean sections are occurring with greater frequency than in the past. In the United States in 1970 the rate of Caesarean section deliveries was about 5 in 100 births; in 1980 this increased to about 18 in 100 births. This has met with mixed reaction. In defense of the increase are doctors who claim it has resulted in lower mortality rates, and superior care for premature babies. Antagonists claim that disadvantages also exist. A "C" section is major abdominal surgery, and mother's recuperation time is often longer than from normal childbirth. It is also argued that some doctors encourage this operation because it is easier on them because it takes considerably less time than a delivery in which the mother undergoes a lengthy labor. Hospitals and medical doctors reject this criticism. The three most prevalent reasons for caesarean section, according to hospital records, are: (1) failure to achieve normal progress in labor; (2) repeat caesarean delivery (it is a recommended practice that when a mother delivers by caesarean that her next baby should also be delivered this way), and (3) breech position of the fetus. Thus, it is the well-being of the infant or the mother that necessitates delivery by Caesarean section.

The Appearance of the Newborn

How parents manage to perceive the newborn as beautiful is one of nature's unsolved mysteries. The infant head, elongated by the birth process, takes up a fourth to a third of the total body length and rests precariously on a scrawny neck that provides minimal support and no direction. Usually the baby has a weight of three to four kilograms, (about 6 to 8 pounds) although mass commonly varies half a kilogram (a pound) or so in either direction. The head is partially covered by thin, fine-textured hair that eventually develops a "monk spot" at the back.

Two greyish eyes, when not hidden by squinted lids, the wrinkles of which spread diagonally to the cheek bones, are wandering randomly because of their temporary inability to fixate. These multidirectional eyes are separated by a ski-run nose frequently scathed by scratch marks from unclipped fingernails. (One of the first chores of the attending nurse is to clip the nails before they do further damage). The mouth moves unpredictably, depending on the position of the jaw and the intensity of sucking action, and frequently has a tongue protruding from it. The chin is insignificant and the forehead, adorned with sparse eyebrows, is slanted. During the first hours of life, the ears are filled with amniotic fluid and therefore do not work effectively. Jaundice, and the slightly yellow skin appearance that accompanies it, is not uncommon during the first week or two of life; however, the condition tends to disappear as the liver becomes more efficient. Newborns frequently develop a variety of rashes, which tend to disappear with normal hygiene and time.

Aesthetic quality does not significantly improve as one moves downward. The chest is overshadowed by an extended potbelly, a sort of distant relative of the "beer paunch" found in adult males, and is connected to a meagre set of shoulders not much wider than the widest part of the head. Located directly on the centre of the stomach is the stub of the umbilical cord, which remains about 14 days before falling off to leave a scar usually called a "belly button." Affixed to the shoulders are arms perpetually folded upward, with clenched fingers that always seem to be nearer the clavicle than the waist. The fingers cannot be voluntarily controlled, and it will be months before the thumb has any value whatsoever. The genitals are exposed, unprotected, between two bowed legs to which feet are appended so that the soles face each other and can easily be tucked under the buttocks. The entire body is encased in marginally transparent skin that issues blotchy color configurations and strawberry-colored pressure markings; the skin is frequently dry or flakey. In general, the newborn is a rather disconcerting sight to everyone except the adoring mother and proud father (and often even to them) and a few other assorted types who consider a newborn's assemblage of disproportionate limbs and partly functioning parts to be beautiful – or at least "natural."

The appearance of the newborn tells us a good deal about their abilities and their potential. Eyes that do not fixate precisely will obviously impose restrictions on the visual world; bowed legs with turned-under feet prevent locomotion; and a large, bulky head, which houses the most advanced cortex in the animal kingdom, makes movement difficult. Human infants, although they will develop into one of nature's most sophisticated animals, are the least well adapted to survival of all animal offspring.

Reflexes and Responses of the Newborn

Newborns come into the world with several reflexes and responses, which as a rule, disappear during the first year of life. This cluster of genetically determined reflexes is the newborns' link with an evolutional past, as well as the initial behavior upon which they will build their future. Without a repertoire of reflexes, infant behavior would be (at least for the first few months) much more restricted and much less predictable than it is. At no other stage of the postbirth growth cycle will the child be as restricted to reactive behavior and reflexive responsiveness as during the first few weeks after birth.

Like the rest of us, infants must have food. Usually it comes from the mother's breast or a bottle, but in either case infants must do their share of work if they are to eat. When the child is cradled in a breast-feeding position, the mother's nipple may graze the newborn's cheek; on receiving this stimulus she will reflexively turn toward the source of stimulation, thus locating the nipple and nourishment. This elementary behavior pattern is called the *rooting reflex* and can be elicited in most newborns with a stroke of their cheek. Once the nipple has been reached, the infant's job has just begun, because she must also suck to receive nourishment. The newborn demonstrates some proficiency at this task, having practiced it during the last months of fetal development. The baby tends to suck in short bursts, rest for a few seconds, then continue. Because newborns have difficulty coordinating two different activities they usually shut their eyes while sucking; by three months, however, this restrictive division of labor is outgrown, and visual exploration during feeding occurs. Most newborns are inefficient at feeding, but they improve with practice. Feeding is more complex than one might suspect, involving coordination of breathing, sucking, and swallowing; there is some discomfort if this sequence is not properly adhered to. Interestingly, the sucking reflex can be elicited by a wide variety of stimuli, such as a loud noise or stroking of the arm. As infants mature they acquire greater voluntary control of sucking behavior, until it leaves the realm of reflex and enters the larger domain of voluntary behavior.

Table 3-1   Reflexes of the Newborn

Reflex	Stimulus that Elicits Reflex	Response
rooting reflex	light touch to cheek	head movement in direction of to sometimes accompanied by sucking action
pupillary reflex	weak or bright light	dilation or contraction of pupils
doll-eye movement	tilting head forward: tilting head backward	eyes move upward eyes move downward
startle reflex	sudden noise	extension of arms head thrown back extension of legs
creeping reflex	feet pushed against a surface	arms and legs drawn under, head lifted up
grasping reflex	pressure on palm	making a fist, closing of fingers
walking reflex	being held over a flat surface	"stepping" leg motion
abdominal reflex	stroke stomach	stomach muscles contract
achilles-tendon reflex	stimulation of achilles tendon	contraction of calf muscles
Babinski reflex	stroke sole of foot	outward fanning of toes
tonic neck reflex	turning head to one side while on back	flexion of arm and leg on other side

When infants turn their head, they trigger a flexion reaction on the opposite side of their body; thus, when babies lie on their back, facing right, the left arm and leg will flex, resulting in a pose not unlike "cheesecake" poses. This *tonic neck reflex* is seen in premature babies and is also observed during the first week of life in about 60 percent of all normal infants. Like several other infant reflexes, if it persists more than 12 months or does not weaken with the passage of time, it may indicate brain damage or neurological malfunction.

When a loud noise interrupts the tranquility of the newborn, he will exhibit a *startle reflex*. This consists of extending the arms and legs simultaneously outward and suddenly retracting them; it is usually accompanied by crying shouts of disapproval. To the naive observer the startle reflex appears to be nothing more than a chaotic thrashing of limbs. Investigation of this reflex by slow-motion film, however, reveals a rhythmic symmetry. The arms invariably follow a narrow pattern, with little variation, and the same is true of the legs. The startle reflex is induced by such varied stimuli as loud noises, bright light flashes, and sudden exposure to a cold object. After recuperation from the startle response, the infant may return to the more customary tonic neck position. The startle reflex has been observed during the fourth month of fetal development and seems to be universally present during the first three months after birth, but if it continues after the twelfth month it may suggest retardation or some other organically based deficiency.

Several other reflexes are worthy of mention. The *grasping reflex* permits babies to hold tightly to anything placed in their palm, sometimes with sufficient strength to support their own weight. This reflex also disappears before the first birthday for most infants.

Shortly before the acquisition of voluntary eye movement, the infant displays what Cratty (1970) calls *doll-eye movements*. When the infant's head is tilted forward the eyes turn upward, but when the head is tipped backward the eyes roll downward. This is most commonly observed in premature infants, and only during the first few days of life for normal infants. The *pupillary reflex* begins within two or three hours after birth. It involves contraction of the pupil in response to strong light and dilation of the pupil in response to weak light, thus serving a protective as well as an adaptive function. This reflex has a much greater longevity than others, lasting through adulthood. A reflex with a much less clearly understood function is the *Babinski reflex,* which causes infants to fan their toes up and outward when the sole of the foot is stimulated. Once this reflex is lost, the human responds to stroking of the sole of the foot with a downward curl of the toes. The only exception to this generalization occurs among braindamaged individuals.

Many infants manifest a *walking reflex* if held upright with their feet lightly touching the floor. Some also display what overly eager parents interpret as a *swimming reflex*. These rhythmic movements, strikingly similar to those employed by a swimmer, have been filmed in infants 11 days old. The reflexive arm and leg movements that make up the swimming motion disappear approximately five or six months after birth, but even at full strength they could never permit the infant to swim. Swimming requires conscious control of breathing as well as the ability to keep the head above water, neither of which can be mastered by the young infant. Thus, the swimming reflex no more results in swimming than the walking reflex results in walking.

Reflexes are vital to the day-to-day life of the newborn and provide the trained observer with information concerning the infant's maturity and health. When reflexes are uneven in strength, when they are stronger on one side of the body than on the other, or when they are nonexistent, there is good reason to suspect some sort of neurological dysfunction in the baby. It is not known how the infant would learn to grasp, reach, feed, or avoid pain without the rudimentary beginnings that reflexes provide, but it is known that babies who show highly irregular reflexes have a much greater probability of physical or mental defectiveness than infants whose reflexes are normal.

The Behavior of the Newborn

To the uninitiated observer, behavior during the first few weeks of life appears singularly uninteresting; however, for the individual schooled in the ways of early infancy, there is an abundance of activity to observe, most of which is preparing the infant for growth into a more sophisticated being. One reason for the apparent monotony of infant behavior is that the most essential developments are internal rather than external.

The Apgar Score: Baby's First Exam

Immediately after birth the status of the infant is evaluated by the Apgar scoring method. Five important indicators of vitality are scored on a scale from 0 to 2 and then totalled. A score of 7 to 10 means that the infant is in good condition; a score of 4 to 6 indicates that the infant is in fair condition and would probably benefit from supplemental oxygen; and a score of 0 to 3 indicates extremely poor condition requiring immediate attention, including resuscitation. The life signs measured by the Apgar method are heart rate, respiratory effort, muscle tone, reflex irritability, and body color.

A child's score on this chart alerts attending doctors and nurses (as well as the parents) to the general strength and maturity of the child. The chart is sufficiently accurate that infants who score as high as 7 or 8 (in the "good condition" range) have less power of attention than infants who score 9 or 10. The Apgar chart usually provides the first formal information on the health and vitality of the infant.

Table 3-2   The Apgar Scoring Chart

| | Score | | |
Sign	0	1	2
Heart rate	absent	slow (less than 100)	over 100
respiratory effort	absent	slow irregular	good, crying
muscle tone	flacid	some flexion of extremities	active motion
reflex irritability	no response	cry	vigorous cry
color	blue, pale	body pink. extremities blue	completely pink

From "Proposal for a New Method of Evaluating the Newborn Infant." by V. Apgar. *Anesthesia and Analgesia.* 1953, 32. 260-267. Copyright 1953 by the International Anesthesia Research Society. Reprinted by permission.

Behavior

The greatest restriction on observing infant behavior is that infants sleep from 18 to 22 hours per day. This in itself will dampen the enthusiasm of most students of infant behavior. However, a good deal is transpiring during sleep. The body musculature, the skeleton, the sensory modalities, and the central organs all develop during sleep hours. During sleep infants periodically manifest a startle reflex for no apparent reason, they suck a good deal, and they wave their arms a bit if lying on their back. Most pediatricians recommend that infants become accustomed (if possible) to sleeping in a rather noisy environment, so that they can tolerate disruption and distraction. By toddlerhood, children who have attained this tolerance amaze adults with their capacity to sleep in the noisiest surroundings. Children who fail to acquire this tolerance may become "light" sleepers and sleep neither as deeply nor restfully as their growing bodies require.

Some newborns are wide awake at meal time and show interest and responsiveness to their environment. Others seem half awake at best and doze off during feeding, content to feed when they reawaken. These individual variations during the first weeks are not in themselves of particular significance as far as growth is concerned. However, they are of concern to parents, who have their own sleeping and waking patterns and prefer that their baby get into sync with them. By the end of the first year the child usually has acquired sleep patterns that coincide with the rest of the household, even though the 12-month-old requires considerably more sleep each day than the older members of the family.

Newborns feed regularly, although now and then, they refuse a regular feeding. Normal infants have an efficient digestive system. Solids may be eaten for the first time near the second week, but opinions differ among doctors, parents, and infants concerning exactly when this practice can effectively begin. As with other topics in pediatric care, the issue of solid feeding has changed over the past 30 years. In the 50s, it was thought best to start baby on solids quite early, even during the second week. In the 80s, especially among mother's milk enthusiasts, it was thought best to wait until the fourth or fifth month.

At birth the infant is well supplied with taste receptors, which are located in taste buds on the tongue. Infants the world over prefer sweet-tasting items; sucking increases considerably in response to a sweet solution and it decreases in response to salty or bitter solutions. Judging by these reactions, one could say that the sense of taste is well developed in the newborn, certainly well enough to handle their limited diet.

Newborn infants possess only meagre limb control and rarely are able to hold their head up for a length of time before the third week, and the thrill of doing so is tempered by the head's sudden collapse after a few brief seconds. Many parents report that their infant begins to "play" energetically during the second and third week – a welcome addition to an otherwise dull routine.

The infant complains when held or dressed in such a way that limb movement is restricted. However, this aversion to being swaddled too tightly can be overcome, because certain peoples, such as the Hopi Indians, bundle their infants very tightly, allowing virtually no limb movement, and their babies adjust to this confinement.

The hallmark of the infant is an ability to cry prodigiously. Pediatricians report that normal infants may cry full tilt for 10 to 20 minutes under normal circumstances without serious side effects, even though their angry face may turn beet red. During the second month, crying may stop when mother comes into view (indicating that the child associates mother with comfort and pleasure) or when the child is picked up and caressed. Children compensate for the agony their crying causes by giving parents a smile sometime around the third week. By six weeks a gibbering father may elicit genuine social smiles and perhaps even a gasping giggle. When the baby reaches this age, an inexplicable instinct compels the parents to buy cameras and take dozens of pictures, which are spontaneously shown without warning to blood relatives and innocent visitors.

Habituation

At three weeks the infant may concentrate on a mobile for as long as 20 minutes without distraction. Of equal importance to developmentalists, however, is the infants' ability to *not* pay attention to certain stimuli that do not affect them. For example, when a feeding infant is suddenly distracted by a novel sound, she will stop feeding, look around, pause from routine for a few seconds, and then resume eating. If the sound occurs again, the baby will follow the same procedure, but with less energy and enthusiasm. Eventually, if the sound has no direct relationship to her immediate needs, the infant will stop responding to it altogether. This process is called *habituation,* and infants are rather good at it, considering their limited equipment.

And without doubt, the intellectual ability of the infant is limited. Burton White (1971), one of North America's foremost authorities on infant behavior, provides a brief summary of their general mental functioning:

> In the area of intellectual or pre-intellectual function, two facts seem clear. Infants less than six weeks old are not easily conditioned, and their primitive behavior repertoire consists of a series of reflex-like functions which appear to operate independently of each other . . . . It is not until the end of the infant's second month of life that researchers routinely report consistent success in establishing conditioned responses and more than very short-lived learning effects.(p. 12)

The infant's growth from helplessness at two months to adventurousness at 12 months is both eventful and exhilarating. Inevitably, it entails progress on four basic fronts.

First, infants gradually acquire the *ability to voluntarily control* their behavior. This requires anticipating an outcome, choosing means to achieve it, and starting and sustaining a chosen series of acts. Second, infants learn to *control their attention* so that it can be directed toward problem solving rather than determined by external stimuli. Third, infants *learn to execute two or more activities at the same time.* And finally, infants *learn to establish codes* that pave the way for speech and other forms of human exchange. The gradual, persistent unfolding of these abilities transforms the infant from a mere "reactor" to an "actor," from an object of creation to the creator of objects.

How does the Newborn Experience the World?

When investigating the experiences of a child who is old enough to speak, the psychologist can be told what a certain experience feels like or what sensations accompany it. Psychologists have no such good fortune in the study of the newborn's experience of the world. Researchers must infer from infant behavior and from their knowledge of the child's sensory equipment what he most likely feels or experiences. This is no easy task, because infants vary considerably in their activity level, their ways of responding to the environment, their degree of excitability, and their ability to tolerate stress. Understanding early experience is made more difficult by our inability to know what meaning, if any, infants attach to their perceptions. Parents sometimes attribute to infants states of mind that, in all probability, they are incapable of experiencing, such as envy, sorrow, or remorse. An exact understanding of infant experience will probably never be achieved, but gaining an understanding of the sensory equipment of the infant is a step in the right direction.

Sensory Equipment – None of the senses operate during the first six weeks with the efficiency they later acquire. The sense that researchers know the most about is vision. Although structurally complete at birth, the infant's eyes are by no means in full working order. Initially, infants have only pupillary reaction to various intensities of light, but they soon acquire the ability to fixate, focus, and track. Infants show an early preference for patterned rather than plain colors and also demonstrate greater interest in drawings that resemble a human face. Within a few hours after birth, infants are able to fixate their eyes – or at least one eye – on a light source. They also are able to respond to moving objects placed in their line of vision, if the objects are not moved too rapidly. Within four days after birth most infants are able to track moving objects with a fair degree of precision. The muscles that control the eyes are now in greater control, and thus the eyes are able to move upwards and sideways. (Earlier they moved more randomly, with one eye moving in one direction and the other eye in another direction). It takes about three months, however, for the eyes to work in consistent, coordinated fashion throughout the day. Research into infant vision is restricted by the fact that infants are nearsighted, highly distractible, limited in their attention span, and indifferent to the advancement of pediatric knowledge.

By eight weeks children play actively with their hands and diligently observe their own activity. By ten weeks they may gaze about the room (as long as it does not involve rotating the head more than 180 degrees), rapidly scanning one object after another. They investigate things that come into close view and may show frustration at not being able to grab tempting tidbits from the surrounding area.

At two weeks infants display a noticeable reaction to sound emanating from the radio or television. Hearing becomes coordinated with vision shortly after birth, as indicated by turning of the eyes toward an auditory stimulus. Sudden loud sounds invariably elicit a startle reflex. From the earliest days after birth, a calm, rhythmic chant exerts a soothing effect on the child. It has been reported that the magnified sound of the heart beat soothes the young infant, but this finding requires further investigation before its implications can be assessed.

Little is known about smell and taste during the first six weeks, chiefly because these are highly subjective experiences and it is difficult for the psychologist to know their significance to the infant. Parents and pediatricians agree that infants prefer sweet substances and show an aversion to solutions that are salty, bitter, or sour. When solids are eaten for the first time, most infants show a preference for certain vegetables over others, even though the infant has had no previous experience with them. Although children can be taught to eat almost anything, all foods are not equally pleasant initially. Infants quickly acquire idiosyncrasies with regard to what they will eat – a habit that reaches its zenith between the second and third year.

The Dawn of Awareness

Six weeks to Four Months

The fairly predictable and routine behavior of the early infant undergoes a remarkable transition between 6 and 16 weeks. The infant blossoms in all areas of development, but especially physical, social, and sensory.

The infant is now completely recovered from birth shock and smoothly making the transition to postnatal existence – although development is never perfectly smooth, no matter what the age. The period between 6 and 16 weeks is called "the dawn of awareness" because the child is now growing beyond the limited patterns of the first six weeks and is becoming aware of, and responsive to, things that before not only went unnoticed, did not really even exist as far as the primitive infant is concerned. The body is outgrowing its reflex-dominated simplicity, the mind begins to shine through its own cloud and in every regard the infant surges forward into an elevated awareness.

During this period the infant requires less sleep than before, and the experience gained during the waking hours promotes development. Children discover their hands and begin the manipulation activities essential to visually directed reaching. Of special concern to most adults, including developmental psychologists, is the tremendous *social* growth during this period. Smiling and laughing are common, and games such as peek-a-boo bring boundless joy. The average three-month-old greets visitors with a pleasant gurgle or a cordial grin (they are several months away from fear of strangers). To the enjoyment of nearly everyone, infants of this age are entertainable. They laugh at funny faces, incongruous sounds, and gestures such as waving one's finger with the thumbs inserted in the ears. They hold their head up for a sustained period of time, following closely the social action in their environment. By all standards the child is becoming a genuinely social creature. Parents complain that their baby is getting spoiled, because he has learned that crying is the most effective means of getting what he wants.

Hands are outgrowing the restrictions imposed by the palmar (grasping) reflex, and the tonic neck reflex has been outlived, allowing increased freedom of motion.

During this crucial growth spurt the infant's ability to concentrate on the environment is greatly facilitated by increased visual capacity. The infant can focus rather well on moving objects as long as they are fairly close; visual convergence is also achieved.

Infant Intelligence

The intelligence of infants is difficult to assess because of their limited ability to respond to stimuli, and because it is almost impossible to elicit their undivided attention. Most measures of infant intelligence are based on sensory-motor responses because these are easily observed by the psychologist, and because the infant provides so few other indicators. (Please note that an intelligence test which assessed only sensory-motor responses in an eight-year-old, for example, would be an extremely crude measure of intelligence.)

Most infant tests are reliable; that is, they yield consistent scores. Doubt arises, however, concerning their validity – their ability to measure what they are trying to measure (intelligence). The validity of an infant test is based on two factors: (1) its ability to differentiate infants by age and (2) its ability to predict the infant's future IQ. Most infant scales satisfy the first criterion rather well but are weak with regard to the second. They simply do not predict with a high degree of accuracy future IQ scores, therefore, their practical value is limited.

The greatest value of infant intelligence tests is they help psychologists diagnose sensory or motor deficits and they create a general picture of the young child's overall sensory-motor abilities. They are more helpful in diagnosing low abilities than high abilities and more accurately predict retardation than genius. A disappointment of infant testing is that during the first five years of life the best predictor of a child's intelligence is an average of the IQs of the biological parents (Munsinger, 1975).

Learning Capacity

There is no question that very young children are able to learn. The problem is that *how* they learn can be observed or manipulated (the essential ingredients of verifiable knowledge) only in a limited way. Psychologists use *classical conditioning* to demonstrate the infant's ability to learn. In this technique a condition that naturally causes a response, such as the stroke on the cheek that exhibit a rooting reflex, is paired with a stimulus that does not elicit any particular reaction, such as the sound of a mild buzzer. If this pairing takes place enough times, the young child will exhibit a rooting reflex at the mere sound of the buzzer, because she associates the buzzer with a stroke on the cheek. This experiment demonstrates that the newborn can learn but it does not tell us a great deal about learning, because even low animal forms (such as earthworms) can be conditioned with classical conditional techniques. Another technique is *operant conditioning,* wherein the psychologist waits until the child manifests a behavior the psychologist wants repeated and then reinforces the child for this behavior. When consistently rewarded in this manner, the child will repeat the behavior over and over, demonstrating that infants learn specific behavior when rewarded.

In one study the techniques of classical and operant conditioning were combined. Papousek (1967) placed infants in a crib with a special head cradle that measured how often, and in which direction, the infants turned their head. The experimenter used a tone, a stroke of the cheek, and the reward of milk. When at the sound of the tone the infant turned his head in the desired direction, a reward of milk was given. It took newborns an average of 177 trials to learn to respond as the experimenter preferred. There was considerable variability in the time it took newborns to master this learning experiment: the fastest was seven days and the slowest 30 days. It is revealing about the growth that takes place during the early months that three-month-olds mastered the task in 42 trials and five-month-olds in only 28 trials.

Other studies indicate that infants suck more vigorously if by doing so they can create a change in the external environment, such as an increase in the amount of light in the room. Infants also will move one part of their body more than they normally would if it will create a change to which they can respond. Rovee and Rovee (1969) found that, when a cord was tied to an infant's foot and connected with a mobile hanging over the crib, the baby would kick the leg up to three times more than usual.

These mini-experiments on mini-humans indicate that infants learn at a very primitive level, that they respond in a limited way to changes in their environment, and that they can somewhat modify their own behavior in order to bring about change or stimulation. These studies, however, tell us very little about *how* learning takes place, and thus far they have not provided many clues as to how learning in infancy relates to learning in future developmental stages.

Although the abilities described thus far may not seem impressive, some psychologists believe that infants possess a substantial range of competencies. Bower (1979), for example, notes,

> In one of the most striking examples of a learning task that newborns can solve, babies were required to discriminate between two stimuli and to respond to only one . . When a bell sounded the head was to be turned right to obtain reinforcement (sugar solution); when a buzzer sounded the head was not to be turned. The experimenters then reversed the contingencies, so that the bell sound meant no head turn and the buzzer a right turn. The babies were able to cope with this discrimination reversal very easily, more easily than most other organisms would.

Bower continues with the following observation concerning the learning ability of the newborn:

> Contrary to common belief, then, the human newborn is an extremely competent organism. He is built to take in information about the world, he has a few motor behaviors, and he can learn. He is sensitive to success and failure, reward and punishment. (p. 71)

Thus, it seems that developmental psychologists, like the administrators who run their universities, and the officials who run their governments, do not see eye-to-eye on what is an apparently straight-forward topic – in this case, the learning abilities of human infants.

Infant Emotions

During the 1920s most experts believed that infants are born with three general emotions – fear, anger, and love – and that these emotions are elicited very early in life. This viewpoint was based on research conducted at John Hopkins University Hospital by the famous American behaviorist J.B. Watson. Watson believed that all adult emotions, such as sorrow, grief, hatred, and elation, derived from the original three inherited emotions by a process of learning and conditioning.

Subsequent research has not treated Watson's concepts kindly. Studies in the recognition of infant emotions reveal that adults are influenced by the child's environment when they judge what emotion the baby is experiencing. (If adults know the infant was spanked recently, they interpret the emotion as anger.) Many observers in the experiments on infant emotion failed to distinguish physical pain from hunger pangs. Still other adults, when shown photographs of infants, would attribute different emotions to the same picture on different days.

For the most part, there is little current acceptance of Watson's interpretation of infant emotion. The theory most widely subscribed to in the 90s is that during the first few weeks of life there are no specific emotions, only generalized states of excitement. The infant's state of excitement is characterized by periods of pleasantness or unpleasantness, withdrawl or approach, and sometimes distress (although this could be defined as a form of unpleasantness).

Table 3-3   The Emergence of Infant Emotions

Progression First 2 Years	Approximate Age of Emergence
attentiveness-awareness	present at birth
neonatal smile (semi-smile, not social, accidental)	present at birth
startle response	present at birth
distress	present at birth
disgust (in response to unpleasant taste or smell)	present at birth
social smile (in response to human situations)	4-6 weeks
delight	3-4 months
anger	3-4 months
surprise	3-4 months
fear	5-7 months
shyness, self-awareness	6-8 months
uncertainty, apprehension	10-12 months
jealousy	second year of life
contempt	second year of life
guilt	second year of life

Before the third month definite signals of delight and enjoyment come from the infant, as well as indications of fear, relief, and anger, although it must be noted that considerable disagreement exists over which emotion is being signalled at any given moment. Of great significance to the student of child development, however, is the fact that before their third birthday most children experience a wide spectrum of adult emotions, including elation, sorrow, joy, jealousy, fear, disgust, love, distress, and affection. (Table 3-3 shows the ages at which various emotions are differentiated from the generalized excitement state). Thus, the transformation from generalized states of excitement to adult-like emotion takes place during the first 36 months of life.

Sudden Infant Death Syndrome (SIDS)

Sudden Infant Death Syndrome is a disorder which occurs while infants are asleep and results in their death. It is especially tragic because it frequently occurs without any warning. About 10,000-12,000 infant deaths per year are attributed to SIDS in North America, approximately 1,000 of which occur in Canada.

In many instances the baby appeared healthy at bedtime, and frequently an autopsy cannot discern the cause of death. SIDS first appears in infants 2 to 3 weeks old; it peaks in frequency in the vicinity of the third month. About 90 percent of all deaths occur before babies are six months old, after which it occurs progressively less frequently until the first birthday. It rarely occurs after the first birthday.

Babies who succumb to SIDS are not always in perfect health. Naeye's research (1980) indicates that the majority of SIDS victims in the United States had a premature birth, and were born to lower socio-economic class parents. Remarkably, the SIDS rate for babies of adolescent mothers is five times greater than that of babies of older mothers. Babies whose mothers smoked cigarettes are also at slightly greater risk. Of considerable significance is the fact that the lower the birth weight of a baby the greater the likelihood that they periodically stop breathing during sleep.

The cause of SIDS is uncertain. Perhaps the most widely accepted explanation is that death is caused by failure of the breathing mechanism. All infants experience periods of breathing interruption known as *sleep apnea*. A small organ in the neck monitors the oxygen content of the blood, and re-ignites breathing when sleep apnea occurs. Some evidence indicates this organ is underdeveloped in infants who have died of SIDS. In essence, they stop breathing, but unlike other babies, the mechanism to re-start breathing does not act.

Parents who suspect (or know) that their child periodically stops breathing may obtain a *home apnea monitor* which sounds an alarm when the baby stops breathing for more than 20 seconds. The parents then jostle the baby, the stimulation of which triggers renewed breathing. Other than this, we presently do not know how to prevent SIDS.

The following factors place babies at higher risk for SIDS:

male
black
younger than six months
birth weight of 5 pounds or less
Low Apgar score (7 or less) [see page 57 for more information]
severe respiratory problems at birth
mild upper respiratory infections
bottle fed rather than breast fed
adolescent mother
mother smokes
mother anemic at time of birth

Infant feeding

Shortly before the fifth month some infants begin eating three meals per day, although many perfectly healthy infants do not do so until nine or ten months. This is a matter for the mother and child to work out together, although sometimes the advice of a pediatrician is required, especially when digestive or elimination problems occur as a result of changes in the dietary schedule.

During the first year of life feeding is one of the infant's most significant social, emotional, and physical realities. Whereas during the prenatal period nutrition was introduced directly (and impersonally) into the system through the umbilical cord, after birth such simplicity vanishes. The newborn is equipped with a sucking reflex, the ability to swallow, and a fairly efficient digestive system; however, someone must provide nourishment.

Feeding time is not always pleasant for the infant. Sometimes the parent is rushed, tired, or simply not in the mood to be either patient or playful. On the other hand, it can be a time for closeness, contact, and playfulness. During the first year of life perhaps the most controversial feeding issue is whether the child should breast feed or bottle feed.

Breast feeding versus bottle feeding – For many mothers the decision to breast feed or bottle feed is not an easy one. Some research suggests that the type of feeding does not influence mother-child relationships one way or the other and whether baby is bottle fed or breast fed does not play an important role in later childhood development. Benjamin Spock (1957), who through his medical advice to mothers has exerted as much influence on child rearing as anyone in this century, suggests that the mother should decide how to feed her baby on the basis of what is most comfortable and natural for her.

In some cultures breast feeding is highly valued, and a woman who fails to do so is thought to be negligent as a mother and as a woman. Among the British working class, however, women traditionally have thought breast feeding a sign of poverty, unsightly and unfeminine, and they consider it an embarrassment to be seen breast feeding their child. Other cultures, such as middle-class North America, tend to go along with Dr. Spock and leave it up to the mother; whatever she decides is fine.

The decision to breast feed is also influenced by personal factors. Some mothers consider their shared moments of breast feeding relaxing and intimate and openly admit to its warm emotional sensation. Others view it as a nuisance and an inefficient way to feed a baby.

Mothers who breast feed believe that mother's milk is better for their baby than either formula or cow's milk. Some evidence supports this. Mother's milk contains more vitamins A and C and more iron than cow's milk. As well, it contains antibodies which protect against infant diseases. Most research also suggests that breast-fed babies have less digestive distress, and fewer allergies. On these issues mothers who nurse see eye-to-eye with the scientific research.

Many mothers believe, in addition to the above, that breast-feeding yields psychological benefits such as closer bonding between mother and baby, greater sense of well-being in the baby, and better sleep patterns. Research does not openly contradict these maternal sentiments, but neither does it clearly support them. Most of the long range studies which evaluate the differences between breast-fed and bottle-fed babies have not discovered important differences between them when they reach the preschool years – especially on psychological measures.

Mother's milk is unquestionably one of nature's most ideal nutrients. It has been described as the ultimate health food, and the perfect fast food. However, it is susceptible to contamination via the mother, therefore, a nursing mother who consumes excess alcohol, drugs, or toxic wastes such as PCBs (from drinking water) will pass these along to the baby.

The bottom line is that bottle-fed babies who are well loved and properly nourished tend to thrive – just as do equally treated breast-fed babies.

During the past 20 years or so, most baby specialists have taken a favorable attitude toward breast feeding. The American Academy of Pediatrics, for example, in 1978 stated that the best food for newborn infants is breast milk unless the mother or child has some specific condition that makes breast feeding extremely difficult. As of 1990 there has been no appreciable change in this viewpoint among pediatricians.

The disadvantages of breast feeding are also psychological and physical. Some mothers simply are not available when their baby needs to be fed – especially working mothers. Breast feeding is time consuming and requires that one person be responsible for every meal, which during the first six months, may take four to five hours out of every 24. Also with breast feeding it is difficult to know how much the baby has consumed, and underfeeding or overfeeding may therefore occur at any given sitting.

Bottle feeding serves as a practical alternative for many women. The bottle is more convenient in that it allows different people to share in the work and pleasure of infant feeding. Some mothers are not good milk producers; they may not produce sufficient volume for a hungry baby, they may incur breast infections that make feeding painful and occasionally, their milk may not taste good to the baby. Bottle feeding makes it easy to observe exactly how much the child has consumed, thereby allowing easy regulation of the diet. Also, some infants actively prefer the bottle and will reject the breast when it is offered as a substitute.

Bottle feeding does have limitations. Some mothers claim the emotional relationship is not as rich when the baby is bottle fed. Bottle feeding of powdered formulas is unhealthy when the local water supply is contaminated – a serious matter in most communities since purified water is available on a daily basis to only about 20 percent of the world's children. Likewise, it may be unhealthy if the cow's milk that the baby is fed has not been hygienically treated.

Adequate nourishment for the growing baby – Adequate nourishment is vital to proper growth and development during the first year of life. How do parents, pediatricians (and sometimes social workers) determine whether a baby is properly nourished? The first indicators are vitality, well-being and alertness – these are almost always associated with a well nourished child; on the other hand, a dull and listless expression, apathy, lack of energy, dark circles under the eyes, little smiling, are associated with poor nutrition. In addition, the following criteria are employed to determine the quality of a child's nourishment:

Adequate Nourishment	Less than Adequate Nourishment
Bright, clear eyes; smiling, happy expression; no dark circles under eyes	Sad-looking; prone to tears
Recovers quickly from fatigue; endurance during activity	Chronic fatigue; tires easily; takes excessive time to bounce back from physical activity
Full of energy; vigorous	Lack of energy; weakness
Smooth, glossy hair	Dry, brittle, easily "pluckable" hair
Good appetite	Poor appetite; unwilling to try new foods; may have many food dislikes
Skin is firm, resilient, and "feels alive"; subcutaneous fat layers	Skin is dry; has little or no subcutaneous fat
Interested in environment; curious; responsive	Irritable, nervous, slow to react; indifferent, passive, unresponsive

Different Ideas about Raising Infants in the 20th Century

Ideas about the best way to raise and nurture infants have fluctuated considerably in both pediatrics and child psychology. Not only has the prevailing outlook towards infant feeding changed over the past decades; so also have ideas about disciplining, expressing affection, and teaching the child. An investigation of child-rearing trends popular just before World War I, uncovered some startling (by current standards) ideas about the treatment of babies:

> In 1914 government pamphlets containing advice to American mothers instructed them to avoid all excessive stimulation of their child because babies had extremely sensitive nervous systems. In the 1960's these pamphlets instructed mothers to allow infants to experience as much stimulation as they wished, because that was the only way they would learn about their world. In 1914 the mother was told not to feed or play with the baby every time he or she cried, because such action would spoil the infant. Fifty years later the mother was told the child would feel secure if she nurtured the crying infant, and she should not be afraid of "spoiling" her baby.

> The 1914 pamphlet urged the mother to toilet train her child before the first year was over and to prevent thumbsucking and handling of the genitals. A half-century later she was told to wait until the child understood the purpose of toilet training (at least until the middle of the second year) and not to worry about thumb-sucking or genital touching. (Mussen, 1979 P. 154)

Obviously, there is historical basis for assuming that some of our current outlooks and practices will fall into disfavor in the coming decades. The question that intrigues experts in child psychology is which trends will slip by the wayside and which will endure the test of time.

Some Final Comments on "The Dawn of Awareness"

The infant is now on the verge of several breakthroughs. Soon she will begin to move, to reach with direction and precision, and to form lasting emotional attachments. She will acquire a host of new locomotor skills, thus moving closer to becoming captain of the body rather than merely a passenger within it. All parts of the body are growing, maturing, and developing (some more rapidly than others); in every significant domain the four-month-old gives conspicuous indications of growth. The achievements made between 6 and 16 weeks, significant as they are, will seem minor when compared with those yet to come.

At the age of four months the infant is ready to make the transition from an organism that responds only to those parts of the environment that come to her to one who ventures out to explore the world. This transition to an environment-exploring creature is perhaps the most significant event in the life of the young child, and upon it intellectual and physical growth greatly depend. Once the child begins to actively explore the environment an upward escalation into the world of people and things takes place with such a fury that child, parent and household are never again the same as before.

Major Concepts of this Chapter

1. Birth shock is the biological stress experienced by the infant during the transition to extra-uterine life. The shock is the result of pressure on the head, the extraordinary effort required for the first breath, thermal shock, and a sudden burst of sensory stimuli.

2. The infant is born with a repertoire of reflexes. The rooting reflex allows the infant to orient to a food source; the infant sucks by reflex. The grasping reflex allows infants to hold tightly objects placed in their palm. Pupillary reflexes begin within hours of birth allowing the infant to adjust to varying light intensities.

3. Between six weeks and four months remarkable social development occurs, as some smiling and laughing accompany social interaction. Increased head control, visual acuity, and freedom from reflexes facilitate interaction and the ability to concentrate.

4. Infant intelligence tests are useful for diagnosing sensory or motor deficits; although reliable, they have low predictive validity for future IQ scores.

5. Infants are capable of learning through techniques of classical and operant conditioning. Infants learn to respond to changes in the environment and to modify their own behavior (within a limited range) in order to bring about change.

6. At birth emotions are characterized by relative degrees of excitement. Periods of pleasantness and unpleasantness or withdrawal and approach are noticeable. Before the third month, however, definite signs of delight, fear, relief, and anger are exhibited.

7. The decision to breast feed or bottle feed is an individual one based on psychological, physical, social and economic factors.

8. At four months the infant has developed to an era of new abilities in movement, emotion, and thought.

4

Nature's Child: Four Months to One Year

The Journey Becomes Adventurous

Certain dazzling and explosive segments of human development are more akin to a shooting star than to a tranquil starry night. Such is the universe we are about to enter.

The structure that nature has been faithfully but ploddingly building since conception is now ready for another opening ceremony of sorts. It is not as dramatic as birth (what is?) but from it emerges a new infant, or at least, a greatly improved version.

Mother and father are by now well aware of the beauty and complexity of their child, partly because between them they spend about 24 hours per day within a few feet of their baby. Parents recognize subtle behavior not evident to the casual observer, and possess a sixth sense they themselves cannot explain. Except when things go wrong the young infant doesn't disclose much about herself. This is about to change. Nature now rewards the child with a range of charm and skill that excites and humbles the loving parents, and fascinates the developmental psychologist who is dedicated to understanding forces which, in all likelihood, are beyond his developmental abilities.

The Great Leap Forward

four to twelve months

The period from 6 to 16 weeks is referred to as the dawn of awareness because the young infant is coming out of a reflex dominated style and moving into a greater awareness of body, environment, and self. This period of expanded awareness is followed by an equally significant period of expanded action that constitutes a great leap forward in the baby's growth. During the eight remaining months in the first year of life the infant makes

73

definite headway in learning to think; becomes mobile as well as upright; begins to communicate orally (although not with words); develops impressive social skills; and evolves the beginnings of a sense of self. Because these major growth achievements can be categorized as intellectual, speech, motor, and social, my discussion of the last two-thirds of the first year of life is organized under these general headings.

Intellectual Development during the First Year

T.G.R. Bower has contributed as much to the scientific investigation of infant cognition as any single researcher in the 20th Century. He believes that infancy is the most significant stage in the cognitive development of human beings, and he has presented his ideas over the past decades with considerable art and force. He states: "I believe that infancy is the critical period in cognitive development – the period when the greatest gains and greatest losses occur. Further, the gains and losses that occur here become harder to offset with increasing age" (1979). As we shall note in the course of this chapter, not all experts on infancy or cognition go along with Bower's assessment of the importance of infancy in the formation of intelligence. His theory however, does provide us with a fascinating starting point for our investigation of the thought process in the first year of life.

Piaget's Stages of Infant Mental Development

Piaget (1952) claims that intellectual development of normal children goes through six stages during the first 18 months of life – five during the first year. These stages can be used as general guidelines by which to understand normal intellectual growth.

First stage (birth to one month) – Behavior is dominated by inborn reflexes such as sucking and grasping. The infant's primary tasks are to become more proficient in the use of reflexes and to recover from the physiological complications associated with birth shock.

Second stage (second and third months) – This stage is characterized by repetitive practice of simple acts, such as flexing of limbs, for no apparent ulterior purpose. It is practice for the sake of practice, and researchers generally believe that this cultivates neural pathways to and from the brain centres. The child rarely acts purposively, and does not recognize that actions create consequences. The child has no awareness of herself as a person or as a being separate from other environmental objects; and she is still too immature to recognize that her behavior effects change.

Third stage (fourth through sixth month) – Behavior becomes progressively more purposive as the child repeats responses that produce interesting or important results. The child will bang on the crib because of the sound that action creates, or slap at a mobile to make it move. The infant acquires some awareness that events do not occur randomly. This stage marks the beginning of the child's primitive awareness of causality, as she forms a hazy connection between cause and effect, and between action and reaction.

Fourth stage (seventh through tenth month) – The child now solves simple problems. She pulls up in order to acquire an object out of sitting reach, removes a barrier to get an object, and is not distracted by every new environmental stimulus. The child begins to recognize that objects have *permanence,* an insight that takes several months to completely evolve. Previously the infant has functioned on the "out of sight, out of existence" principle.

Fifth stage (eleventh to eighteenth month) – The child begins to systematically manipulate things, employing trial and error experimentation, and does not stop when thwarted in the first attempt to solve a problem, preferring instead to devise new solutions. When the child gauges the appropriateness of behavior by observing its consequences a significant breakthrough in cognitive ability has taken place; previously the child did not recognize how actions created specific consequences.

Sixth stage (eighteenth month on) – The child learns to think about the *probable* consequences of actions before they occur. (You will learn more about this stage of intellectual development in the next chapter. It is of such tremendous significance in the child's unfolding intellect that it requires special attention).

Conclusion – During the first year of life mental development is characterized by the following behaviors and abilities:

1. reflexive behavior,
2. practice of reflexes, arm movements, and eye movements,
3. repetition of actions that produce important results,
4. use of elementary skills to solve simple problems or achieve simple goals, and
5. trial and error experimentation.

The Recognition of Objects and the Understanding of Permanence

The object concept – At the most basic level, infant intelligence is impeded by an immature brain and an underdeveloped central nervous system. At the behavioral level (the domain of social science) the infant is restricted by the fact that he simply does not differentiate his environment, and does not understand that physical reality exists in its own right.

For example, to frustrate a child in Piaget's third stage of intellectual development by hiding a desired object is not easy because once the object is out of sight it ceases to exist to a mind that cannot remember it. Out of sight is, literally, out of mind.

The child eventually recognizes that objects continue to exist even when they cannot be seen (object permanence), and, in turn, eventually recognizes that specific objects maintain a unique identity from one moment in time to another. The crib is the same crib from day to day, toys remain the same, mother is the same mother.

Bower (1975) investigated this phenomenon in a rather ingenious manner. He arranged mirrors to create the image of several mothers standing in front of the baby. Infants of six months and younger did not take much note of this unusual event. Infants older than this, however, were bewildered and sometimes frightened by seeing so many mothers when there should only be one. Their reactions indicate an advanced understanding of object identity when compared with younger babies.

Object permanence – In our understanding of reality, we know that objects are external to ourselves, that they have an existence of their own, and that they continue to exist even when we cannot see them. This awareness of the world of objects is what Piaget called *object permanence*.

The child exhibits object permanence when he searches for an object that cannot be seen but is obviously nearby. A universal children's game aptly demonstrates this principle. An adult takes a ping-pong ball (or some such object) between thumb and index finger, in plain view of the intrigued child, and pretends to insert the ball into her mouth and, with difficulty, "swallow" it. The child will look again and again into the adult's mouth; that is where the ball should be. When the adult retrieves the ball from her palm, the child will innocently play the game again, not realizing he has been lured into a contest beyond his developmental level. Time works against the magician adult, however, because the next time she visits, the child may not be restricted to such limited awareness of permanence. The intellectual significance of object permanence is that the child knows that objects do not lose their existence merely because they are out of sight. The child understands that physical objects exist *independently* of his perception of them. Without this cognitive breakthrough, exploration required during toddlerhood could not occur.

Object permanence involves more than merely remembering the location of a hidden object. Piaget claims that a mature conception of objects demands that a group of sensations be seen as a separate whole and that the object be seen as separate from, and independent of, the activities that the child applies to the object. Under these conditions the child is aware that an object has an existence of its own that is durable and independent of the perceiver.

When infants under 24 weeks see their mother "disappear," they usually are not upset; nor do they seem to realize that mother is gone when she is gone. However, infants over 24 weeks react with distress when mother gets ready to leave and with searching behavior once she has left (Bower, 1979).

At eight months the infant typically looks down from her high chair when an object falls from it, but when she does not immediately locate the fallen object her attention shifts elsewhere. At 12 months, however, the child locates the object and, if it cannot be reached, points and yelps and demands assistance in retrieving it.

The child's limited comprehension of object permanence during the first year is demonstrated in experiments in which the child reaches behind a barrier to retrieve an object which has been hidden there several consecutive times. When the experimenter varies routine and hides the object elsewhere, the infant continues to look behind the original barrier. Some infants will continue to look behind the same barrier even when the desired object is in plain view a few inches to the right or left of where it previously had been hidden.

The relationship between Piaget's stages of mental development and the ability to solve object permanence problems is submitted in Table 4-1.

Table 4-1   Object Permanence and Mental Development

Stage	Age	Action on Object
reflex activity	birth-1 month	follows object over short distances (tracking)
primary circular reactions	1-4 months	attention remains when object disappears (seems unaware the object has vanished)
secondary circular reactions	4-10 months	can "find" partially hidden object (partially visible object)
coordinating secondary schema	10-12 months	uncovers hidden object
tertiary circular reactions	12-18 months	uncovers hidden object, but not when displaced (re-located)
symbolic representation	18-24 months	uncovers hidden object, even when displaced

Memory During the First Year

Investigating the memory of very young children is made difficult by the fact that they lack the vital skills that psychologists use to verify what is going on within their minds. First, they have only limited concentration span, and they do not focus for long on what we want them to focus. Second, prehensile skill and body control are so poorly developed they make it hard for us to test by physical means what children remember. Third, they do not speak, therefore they cannot tell us what they remember.

Despite these limitations, psychologists have shown remarkable ingenuity in uncovering the mystery of human memory during the first year of life. We now know that newborns can learn, that they can remember, but only in limited and primitive ways. Most researchers presently accept that newborns are not able to retain memories over a 24-hour period. However, some researchers believe that infants can retain a memory for 24-hours at 4 or 6 weeks of age. Infants 2-4 months old trained to kick their legs in order to make a mobile move, when placed in the experimental setting eight days later began to kick. This indicates they associated kicking with a specific environment – a form of memory. Research indicates that some 5-month-olds can recognize previously-seen faces even after an interval of two weeks (see Sroufe and Cooper, 1988, for a thorough overview of related research).

The ability to store information in *categories* (people, animals, machines) and, the ability to process *numerical information* into memory begins in the second half of the first year of life, but does not attain much proficiency. As with all forms of learning, memory proceeds from crude to refined (general to specific, as described in Chapter one); therefore, first manifestations are cumbersome and imprecise.

Because of the inherent non-communicativeness of the infant, research efforts have not been as fruitful as, for example, investigations of the memory of five-year-olds. In general, after one has digested what the numerous experts have to report, the nature of memory during the first year of life remains more obscure than clear. Most scientific research focuses on issues which are irrelevant to the infant and to those who nourish and love him. Nevertheless, from these modest achievements greater clarity will eventually emerge. As of now, our knowledge is limited.

Concluding Unscientific Postscript: Infant Intelligence

The study of infant behavior is itself in its infancy. Although great advances have been achieved in the past several decades, we remain night explorers in a murky lagoon. Virtually all of the instruments by which we evaluate intelligence are primitive and minimally predictive. As of now, it appears that the infant comes into the world something of a "blank slate," just as John Locke proclaimed 300 years ago. However, the infant is not completely blank because her equipment includes a repertoire of species traits which provides the basis for emotional expression, for imitative behavior, for social responsiveness, and for exploration and mastery. Thus, even if the infant's mind truly is "empty," the means by which nature permits it to be filled is embedded in developmental guidelines, maturational constraints and other mysteries of our era.

Speech During the First Year

Speech development is less dramatic than intellectual development during the first year of life because, by adult standards, so little is accomplished. The infant undergoes significant changes in "speech" during the first year but communication is far from word-oriented. At the end of the first year, only the very unusual child uses more than five or six understandable words with purpose. The median age at which children use their first word is about 13 months, but several additional months of development are required before a two-word message can be constructed. Toddlerhood brings spectacular speech growth which is discussed in greater depth in Chapter five. And even though this is an extremely intricate topic, in this segment we shall provide only a brief overview of speech during the first 12 months.

Earliest vocalizations, usually vowel sounds, are random and have little communication value. Newborns have no capacity for making the sounds that (in English) correspond with the letters p, b, m, w, v, t, and n, but they develop the capacity during the first year. Year-old children have about 19 phonemes (the most basic elements in a language system) in their repertoire.

Children of all cultures go through approximately the same sequence of speech development. Babbling occurs near the third month, followed in a few months by nonsensical chatter, which sometimes has intonations and inflections similar to adult speech. Although children are doing a great deal of imitating between the ages of 9 and 12 months, they are not yet ready to imitate complete words. Children must await further developmental maturity (especially within the speech centres of the brain) before they can do much with words; but, once words appear, children never return to exclusively nonverbal communication.

During the first two years, speech progresses from random vocalizing of vowels to consonants, from syllables to simple words, and, finally to two-word phrases. Table 4-2 indicates the months at which various speech developments generally occur.

Babies are not neutral toward words even though they do not use them. Babies respond to words both matter-of-factly (almost solemnly) and playfully. They love sing-song intonation, pleasant exclamation, and excited whispering. At 12-months a child can be tickled with excitement over words spoken with suspense and excitement. The actual words don't matter all that much – tone of voice, melody of expression and dramatic style are everything. At 12-months most infants understand dozens of words even if they don't speak a single word. Almost always they know their names, foods, mommy and daddy, and no. Nature has wired them in such a way that they sometimes don't hear "No" but always hear "food."

Table 4-2   General Trends in Language Development
During the First Two Years of Life

Average (in months) Age	Language Skill
2	vocalizes one syllable; responds to another person's voice
2-3	coos
4-6	babbles
5-6	clearly pronounces a few syllables; distinguishes friendly from angry speech
7-9	repeats syllables
10-14	utters first word; responds to simple commands
14-18	uses five or more words
19-20	understands simple questions
21-23	use two-word sentences; names pictures in a book
24-25	uses phrases and sentences; understand some prepositions – for example, under

(Data are from numerous research studies but especially Lenneberg, 1967, and Bayley, 1969.)

Manual Skills During the First Year

At about 16 weeks the infant's hands come together, signalling the first of several important developments in prehensile growth. If the child does not bring the hands together by the sixth month when grasping or reaching, concern about neurological dysfunction may be justified. At about six months a baby holds her bottle with modest proficiency, and at about this time begins to drop one object in favor of another. Soon she transfers objects from one hand to another, showing no preference for one hand over the other. Among the most significant achievements is *visually directed reaching*.

At about eight months finger-thumb opposition occurs, signalling another major triumph in prehensile development. The index finger, employed as an exploratory probe, searches openings, cracks, and holes, including nostrils and ears. At 40 weeks the child is reaching with even greater precision but still has little success in intercepting moving objects, such as a rolling ball. At about 44 weeks children may place one object after another into a box. They crave give-and-receive games, although they frequently give the impression that they engage in games such as this as much for motor-skill practice as for the social interplay the games afford.

Near the 12th month the ability to throw objects emerges, a significant event in the child's motor development. The child now understands the meaning of "No!," an exclamation that becomes more frequent with the emergence of throwing behavior. Children's obsession with mechanical devices at this age prompts them to remove lids, unscrew caps, and take apart things that they have no ability to reassemble. Manual dexterity is becoming increasingly sophisticated with each month. The child, however, is still almost six years away from efficient use of a pencil!

Locomotor Skills During The First Year

After four-month-olds lift their head to visually inspect the environment, they embark on a crash developmental campaign that eventually allows them to live in the environment rather than be restricted to one small part of it. Like manual skills, locomotion is regulated by maturation and progresses through a fairly predictable sequence. All infants do not go through every stage; sometimes they skip a stage altogether. But most infants attain their locomotion via the same general sequence.

**Table 4-3   Significant Motor Achievements
during the First Year of Life**

Average Age (in months)	Motor Skill
1	Lifts chin up while lying on stomach; looks around
2	Lifts chest off ground
3	Reaches for objects (usually misses)
4	Sits with support
5	Rolls over for first time; grasps objects
7	Sits alone, picks up objects with palm of hand
8	Stands with help; remains upright by holding furniture; Sits upright with ease
9	Stands without help for first time
10	Creeps on all fours
11	Takes steps when held by hand
12	Takes first steps independently pulls to a standing position on furniture

Sitting occurs when the brain centres that regulate upper body muscles have matured sufficiently to coordinate upper-body muscles with those in the lower trunk. Sitting is a major developmental achievement.

The first forms of horizontal locomotion (crawling, creeping, and hitching) usually begin between the 9th and 12th months. When crawling, the child drags her stomach along the floor while the arms and hands propel the body. Creeping, which occurs later, entails elevating the abdomen and locomoting with all four limbs. Hitching is a mixture of creeping and crawling wherein the child lies on the stomach and pushes the body forward with one foot while dragging the other. At ten months the child is primarily a quadruped, moving about on all four limbs. However some infants do not creep or crawl; they forego these preliminaries and wait until they are ready to walk. These children are rarities, however. Table 4-3 summarizes the most frequently observed sequence of motor achievements during the first year of life.

As we observed in Chapter one, growth is asynchronous; therefore, different systems (and abilities) develop at different rates. As a consequence of this basic principle the infant simultaneously operates at several different levels of proficiency. For example, forward crawling at nine months may be rather proficient, but if the child crawls into a corner he may not be able to get out of it because reverse locomotion requires a few additional weeks of maturation before it is executed effectively. For this reason mother is sometimes startled to find her child jammed into a corner with one shoulder helplessly pinned to the floor and the buttocks elevated above all other parts of the body. When infants first learn to pull themselves upright they cannot seat themselves without quite a plop. They crawl or climb into situations from which they cannot exit because almost all forms of reverse locomotion are developmentally more complex than forward movement. Though crawlers can stand upright when held by the hands it will be a month or two before they achieve independent standing. Although most children walk within a month of their first birthday many fail to do so until 16 months or later. Some experts claim that the age at which a child begins to walk can be predicted by doubling the age at which she first sits alone or by adding 50 percent to the age at which she begins to creep. Like most formulae for predicting developmental milestones, the ability of this one to predict accurately is limited at best.

Children who begin walking sooner than is average do not necessarily continue to develop at an accelerated pace. Highly intelligent children do not walk sooner than children of average intelligence, although severely retarded children begin to walk later than average children.

Social Development During the First Year

Social development during the first year of life (and all other childhood stages) is less governed by maturational guidelines than intellectual development or motor development. Nevertheless, a good deal of commonality is observed in the social skills of one-year-old children. As a rule, children of this age love to be the centre of attention; they enjoy themselves thoroughly when in pleasant company. Their egocentric nature impels them to seek praise and recognition from the adults in their world. One-year-olds experience fear, anger, sympathy, anxiety, and jealousy. They like music, have a sense of humor, and are making strides in the direction of independence and

---

Cradleboarding

The important role played by maturation in the emergence of locomotor skills is highlighted by a series of classic studies conducted by W. Dennis in the early 40s among the Hopi Indians. As part of the Hopi cultural tradition, the newborn is tightly swaddled in blankets and bound to a cradleboard. This custom severely restricts the infant's movement. During the first three months of life the Hopi child is unbound from the board for only a few moments at a time, and not until the last half of the first year is much freedom of movement allowed. Despite this constraint Hopi children go through the same general walking sequence as other children and begin to walk at about the same age as children who have never been cradleboarded. This unusual natural laboratory provided Dennis the opportunity to investigate a variation of infant development that is virtually impossible to replicate, and from it he concluded that walking in humans is determined primarily by maturation.

During recent years the practice of "cradleboarding" has been abandoned by some Hopi, making it possible to compare the walking age of infants reared in the old tradition with infants raised in the new way. The evidence indicates no significant difference in the age at which the two groups of Hopi children walk, suggesting that swaddling during the first six months of life has little effect on the onset of walking. This is generally thought by contemporary developmentalists to support Dennis' belief that maturation is the most significant determinant of walking skills during the first year of life.

---

autonomy. Whereas the four-month child is only marginally social (sometimes neglecting altogether a stranger in the room), the typical 12-month child is social in a very elaborate sense of the word.

Four-month-olds seem content with minimal social interaction as long as their biological needs are taken care of; 12-month-olds complain bitterly if deprived of human company and may become fearful or panicky when no one is nearby. Their feelings can be hurt by a sharp voice or even a facial grimace, indicating that their social responsiveness is becoming increasingly childlike and decreasingly infantlike.

The 12-month-old resorts to almost any measure to be held and fondled, because the need for contact and caress are powerful. By the end of the first year the child is unmistakably social not only in interpersonal style and sensitivity, but in emotion as well.

At 12 months the child repeats whatever is laughed at, turning into a creative, although inevitably boring, performer. Ownership sprouts and is evidenced by the child's objection to anyone playing with her special toy. The word "selfish," as commonly used by adults, is a fair description of the one-year-old. The process of learning about the rights and needs of others is slow and tedious. The one-year-old is reminiscent of the classic Hobbesian individual, but eventually loses global selfishness in favor of regional altruism.

Table 4-4   Social Development during the First Year

Average Age	Social Behavior
1 week	Shows excitement and distress.
1 month	Eyes fix on mother's face in response to her smile. Makes eye-to-eye. contact Looks at faces and quiets down. Responds positively to comfort and satisfaction.
2 months	Shows distress, excitement, delight. Smiles at some people other than mother. Quiets when held.
3 months	Smiles spontaneously. Crying decreases. May stop crying or start crying according to who holds him. Cries when mother leaves. Smiles, babbles; orients to mother's presence or voice.
4 months	Vocalizes moods, enjoyment, protest. Laughs. Wails if play is disrupted. Shows anticipation, breathes heavily. Is much more sociable. Interested in mirror images.
5 months	Shows fear and anger. Discriminates self and mother in mirror. Smiles to mirror image, human faces and voices. May distinguish familiar and unfamiliar adults. Stops crying when spoken to. Expresses protest – resists adult who tries to take toy. Frolics when played with. Raises arms to be picked up.
6 months	Smiles at other children. Distinguishes children from adults. Plays peek-a-boo, come-and-get-me, go-fetch. Tries to imitate facial expressions. Turns when hears name.
7 months	May fear strangers and cry at their presence. Shows humor, teases. Resists pressure to do something he doesn't want to. Distinguishes friendly and angry talking. Plays with toys.
8 months	Tries to kiss mirror image. Fears strangers, separation from mother or quiets to mothers voice. Shouts for attention. Pushes away what he doesn't want. Rejects confinement.
9 months	Performs for home audience; repeats act if applauded. Cries if other children cry, is interested in other people's play. Initiates play. Fights over toy. Begins to evaluate people's moods and motives.
10 months	Tries to alter mother's plans through persuasion or protest. Asserts self among siblings. Obeys commands. Seeks approval but is not always cooperative. Establishes meaning of "no." May test parental limits.
12 months	Expresses many emotions and recognizes them in others. Fears strangers and places. Reacts sharply to separation from mother. Develops sense of humor. Is affectionate to humans and objects. Negativism increases. Refuses eating; resists napping. May have tantrums. Play games with understanding; may give up toys on request. Prefers certain people to others.

One cannot precisely distinguish motor, intellectual, and social developments from one another. The child acts out social needs by grasping, holding, hitting, crying, and playing, all motor activities. The child cannot distinguish a pleasant reaction from a disapproving one without intellectual maturity, and cannot become anxious by mother's absence without object permanence. Every developmental category interacts with and influences every other. In this section distinctions have been drawn between motor, speech, intellectual, and social development, but the intent has been to point out the intricate manner in which they interrelate.

The Emergence of Self

The child's sense of self does not emerge full blown any more than does the ability to walk or the capacity to think. Unquestionably, however, the fundamental first steps in this remarkable venture take place during the first year of life. One-year-olds possess a genuine sense of self. They are mature enough to have their feelings hurt (which is not true of the four-month baby) they experience satisfaction upon accomplishing a task, they show off, they laugh, they experience sadness and they are possessive. (Identical twins at 12 months compete with one another for parental affection.) All in all, one-year-olds are attaining a self. A "primitive" self, to be sure, but a self upon which the future self is established.

During the first two or three months the baby has only minimal recognition of her body parts. Babies use their hands, for example, before they are aware that hands are apart of "me." At about six or seven months babies discover their feet, but may be startled at the pain they experience when they bite their own toes. Within a few weeks of this discovery, however, they use their feet purposely to reach and touch. Most babies learn *purposeful* screaming, to indicate they want something, at about eight or nine months. This is not merely the screaming of an unhappy baby; it is a signal that "I" want "you" to obtain "it." This is one elementary beginning of verbal communication, but it cannot take place until the child, however dimly, distinguishes self from not-self.

Self-awareness has two significant dimensions. First, the child differentiates herself from the environment. She learns that she is an agent within the environment, that she can act upon it, that she can change it. Second, the child acquires the ability to monitor herself, that is, to regulate her own behavior. Self-awareness is that mode of consciousness where the child interacts with the world while simultaneously interacting with herself. It is the building block of human personality.

The way babies respond to their reflections in a mirror provides us with a few clues about their unfolding self-awareness. Initially, infants are interested in their reflections but don't give any indication that they know who is in the mirror; later they recognize how their actions influence what happens in the mirror. Next they grasp the difference between mirror activity reflecting their own actions versus the actions of others. Eventually, they learn to recognize their own face no matter where it appears in a reflection; as well, they recognize photographs of themselves. Finally, they come to learn the parts of their faces and bodies, and the names used to describe them. Each of these adds increment upon increment to the gradual emergence of the self.

Eventually self-awareness leads to self-evaluation and self-criticism. During the first year of life, however, these exist as glimmers rather than as fully developed phenomena.

Self-awareness results in increased *self-direction* (the ability to generate action which leads to a desired outcome) and to *self-control* (the ability to monitor one's action, and to stifle one's actions). The outcome of all this: by the end of the first year the child becomes purposeful, self-directing, and self-governed. Conversely, she becomes less ruled by reflexes, less monopolized by reactivity, and less constrained by the narrowness inherent to non-awareness. Thus, in a brief 12 months, she has surpassed in self-awareness, and self-reflection the evolutional attainment of most other life forms on this planet.

Individual Differences During the First Year

Temperament Differences

Babies, like all children, demonstrate a considerable range in temperament and general arousal levels. Some babies are extremely active, fidgety, and persistent; others are reserved and low-key.

The temperament that characterizes the very young child remains somewhat constant throughout childhood. For example, high-energy infants who are easily irritated tend to retain this trait, and babies who in the earliest weeks are placid and nonexcitable tend to remain that way. Some authorities believe these predisposing tendencies become general traits within the older personality. Brophy, however, claims that "the causal events that determine the infants' later personality traits lie in their socialization and general experiences. Unreactive infants who are raised by introverted parents and/or who "turn off" the parents because of their unresponsiveness may develop into passive and introverted individuals. In contrast, the same infants would be likely to become sociable and person-oriented if raised by parents who modeled and reinforced this behavior" (1977, p. 107). Not all psychologists (or parents, for that matter) are as confident of the power of socialization as Brophy. Some youngsters have a remarkable capacity to resist attempts to change their basic temperament. Fast-paced youngsters are sometimes impervious to the hundreds of reprimands they receive for their behavior; likewise, slow-paced youngsters may never acquire a more accelerated pace, no matter how consistently the parents encourage them to behave more actively or more assertively.

Bee (1989) suggests six dimensions of temperament on which infants vary considerably. Older children vary along these same dimensions, and the relationship between infant temperament and later childhood temperament fascinates developmental psychologists.

1. *Vigor of responding* – Some babies respond with intensity and vigor to new stimuli and retain their interest with enthusiasm. Other babies are less intense, responding in a more detached manner and reacting less noticeably when a new stimulus is presented.

2. *General activity level* – Some babies simply are more active than others. They flail their limbs and twist their trunks and are forceful in resisting restraint. Others are more compliant, demonstrate less random behavior, and in general conserve their energy more than other infants do.

3. *Restlessness during sleep* – Some babies move a lot and even thrash about during sleep; others sleep soundly and with comparative motionlessness.

4. *Irritability* – Some babies are difficult to soothe, are easily irritated, and, when discontented, remain so for considerable lengths of time. Other babies are more soothable, settling down promptly when fondled after a distressing incident.

5. *Habituation rate* – Some babies habituate more rapidly than others. A new stimulus holds their attention for a while but quickly loses interest value. Others stay with a novel stimulus for a long period of time and go back to it time and again.

6. *Cuddliness* – Some babies respond positively to being held, fondled, and comforted. Others are less positive in their reactions and are less effectively soothed by being held or cuddled. Some infants will struggle to escape the clutches of the adult (especially when it is not the mother) and seem more content on their own than in the arms of an adult.

A significant dimension related to temperament is *soothability*. Various stimuli soothe a distressed child, including gentle rocking, soft, melodic sounds, a sweetened pacifier, and even placing of a foot in warm water. Each child develops a preference for his own particular soothing. Happily, infants easily soothed by one technique tend to be easily soothed by another; unhappily, infants not easily soothed by one technique tend to resist others as well. Without doubt some infants are more easily soothed than others, some infants transfer from a distressed state to a calm state more rapidly than others, and some infants react to stimulation far more happily than others.

R. Q. Bell (1968) believes that the child, primarily by merit of temperament, is a reinforcer of adult behavior. He hypothesizes that temperamental differences among children are a determining factor in the behavior of the adults who care for them. Irritable children elicit irritability (and the tense behavior associated with it) from their parents more than passive or playful children. In other words, how parents treat their children is greatly influenced by the children themselves. This hypothesis claims that the child actively influences his human environment, that he is considerably more than merely a shaped product of the environment. Significantly, Bell's hypothesis finds widespread agreement among mothers, pediatricians, and other adults who spend considerable time with young children.

Difficult Babies and Easy Babies

One of the most basic temperament categorizations is description of children as "easy" or "difficult." This sounds more simplistic than it is. Thomas, Chess, and Birch (1970), using parents as a source of information obtained data on characteristics such as fussiness, playfulness, and baby responsiveness to mother and father. The general findings support the notion that some children are more difficult than others on a wide variety of behavioral criteria. Not all children fit into the "easy" or "difficult" category; some are more accurately described as "slow to warm up." Of great import to developmental psychologists was the finding that children tend to retain their general temperament throughout infancy and into toddlerhood, even into the preschool years.

For example, research disclosed that at two months of age some babies do not squirm when being dressed or having their diapers changed, have regular eating and eliminating schedules, smile and gurgle a great deal, and cry very little. These are (for those of you who have not raised children) "easy" babies. Other babies at two months sleep restlessly, wriggle when being changed, awake at different times each morning, cry when being fed, have irregular, stressful, bowel movements, are easily startled, and do not soothe easily. These are "difficult" babies.

The same babies, at two years of age, manifest a rather similar profile. *Easy babies at two months have the following characteristics at 24 months:* They enjoy quiet play, they are soothed by music, they eat well and have few digestive problems, they sleep well on their first trip to grandmother's house, (an indicator that they handle unknown situations well), they obey quickly, and they smile and giggle a great deal.

Difficult babies at two months have the following characteristics at 24 months: They get in and out of bed while being put to sleep, their nap times changes from day to day, they avoid strange children on the playground, they whimper in new situations and cry and scream during haircuts, they yell when excited, and cry when mother leaves. They tend to have trouble with toilet training because their bowels are unpredictable.

These general behavioral trends are just that – general trends. Few children are uniformly perfect as here depicted in the easy child, and few are uniformly difficult. However, consistencies occur with such regularity that the classification system has become part of pediatric parlance.

General Infant Temperaments	
Difficult Child	Easy Child
Irregular body functions (sleeping, eating, etc.)	Regular body functions (sleeping, eating, etc.)
Intense reactions	Low to mild intensity of reactions
Withdraws from unfamiliar situations	Approaches new situations positively
Adapts slowly to new routines	Adapts easily to new routines
Mood generally negative	Mood generally positive
Cries frequently	Cries infrequently
Distressed easily Resists soothing	Easily soothed Easily reassured

(Based upon the research of Thomas & Chess, 1977)

Birth Order and Family Size

The order in which children are born and the size of the family into which they are born exerts some influence on their childhood traits. One general trend is for first-born children to score higher on intelligence tests than their younger brothers and sisters. They also tend to be less aggressive than younger siblings.

Some psychologists argue that first-born children receive more attention and greater amounts of affection than later children and therefore are more secure and confident. Others note that first-born children are given more responsibility (looking after the younger children) and thus acquire greater competence.

Family size is also related to certain traits and characteristics. Research indicates that the more brothers and sisters the lower are one's scores for verbal and number abilities on IQ tests. Another study reported that as family size increases children's intellectual ability decreases. Additional studies indicate that children from smaller families tend to be "taller, stronger, and more energetic than those from larger families" (McCandless, 1977, p. 129).

Zajonc's Hypothesis on Family-Size and Birth Order

A slightly different twist in the explanation of this phenomenon has been formulated by Zajonc and his associates (1975). According to Zajonc's hypothesis, a child's intellectual development is influenced by *The average intellectual level of all family members,* including the child. Thus first-borns are at a "mathematical" advantage because their home is composed of two adults (usually) and only one child. First-borns are exposed only to adults; therefore they experience a higher level of intellectual exchange. A fourth-born child would have his intellectual environment "watered-down" by the presence of three older siblings. The substance of this controversial hypothesis is best explained by Zajonc himself:

> Children who grow up surrounded by people with higher intellectual levels (that is, first-borns and children from small families) have a better chance to achieve their maximum intellectual powers than . . . children from large families who spend more time in a world of child-sized minds . . . (p. 39).

In essence, with each additional child, the family's intellectual environment lessens.

Sex Differences

Boys and girls show measurably different traits from the earliest days of life. Current research indicates that differences between the sexes exist during the first year in the following general areas: (1) size and body composition, (2) vulnerability, and (3) sensory ability.

By most measures, female infants are more physically mature at birth. Their skeletal maturity is slightly ahead of males', and their neurological maturation tends to be slightly more advanced. Although girls are marginally smaller than boys, their overall body development is from one month to six weeks ahead of boys'. Boys have a greater percentage of their body mass taken up by muscle, and girls have a greater percentage of body mass taken up by fat. In terms of activity level, no noticeable differences are apparent between boys and girls. However, some differences between the sexes obtain in the maturation rate of specific bones.

In terms of vulnerability to deficiencies and deficits, females have a noticeable advantage over males. Premature males are significantly inferior to premature females of the same age and are more likely to manifest a wide variety of perceptual and/or learning disabilities. Males are more susceptible to birth injury and prenatal damage; they have a higher mortality rate during the first moments, weeks, and months of life, regardless of race or socioeconomic status. More boys have lower Apgar scores at birth, by definition this means poorer general health and less responsiveness.

Differences in sensory ability are the least noticeable of the three types. The research data are not nearly so consistent in this matter. Some research indicates that females demonstrate greater sensory keenness, but other research does not support this generalization. In short, we see little certainty in this area.

Wearing Your Baby

William Sears, Professor of Pediatrics at the University of Southern California, believes that a newborn should not spend hours each day alone in the crib. Rather, she should be "worn" by the mother (or father) in a sling, similar to the way of certain tribes in Africa and South America. The following are Sears' own words:

> My experience suggests that baby-wearing enhances not only the baby's development but also the parents' overall enjoyment of the baby. I noticed that the more babies were carried, the less they cried. Mothers with fussy babies would calmly say, "As long as I carry him, he's content!" Based upon these observations, I developed a sling carrier and advised parents to begin carrying their babies as much as possible right after birth. I then noticed that exciting things were happening to carried babies and their parents.

> Over a period of three years I studied mothers who wore their babies at least several hours a day. I observed that carrying greatly improved the behavior of their babies. Carried infants cried much less, showed fewer colicky episodes, and in general, seemed more content. As the babies became more content, their parents became more content. Parents who carried their babies also seemed able to read their babies' cues. In essence, parent and baby appeared to be more in harmony with one another.

Benefits: What are the benefits to "wearing your baby"? Sears claims that:

1. wearing your baby soothes the baby and encourages better sleep patterns,
2. wearing your baby helps babies thrive
3. wearing your baby helps babies learn better because they remain in a state of quiet alertness more than do non-carried babies,
4. wearing you baby fits in well with a busy lifestyle because you take your baby with you, eliminating trips to baby-sitters, etc.

As Sears points out, "Baby-wearing is a style of parenting that requires us to change our mindset about what babies are really like." Despite Sears' enthusiasm for baby-wearing few developmental psychologists are convinced that the benefits are as impressive as claimed. On the other hand, for parents who want to wear their baby, no evidence (at this time) suggests it is harmful. As with breast-feeding, perhaps the most significant effects of "wearing" your baby lie within the parent rather than the child.

During the past decade an increasingly popular trend has been to describe the sexes as "equal" with regard to important hereditary factors, and to claim that the differences between them derive primarily from differential environmental treatment. Very young humans seem to defy such an equalitarian outlook. The evidence indicates that females hold a superiority over males in numerous critical areas, the most important of which is the ability to stay alive. As Gordon points out, "It is interesting to note that the male is born inherently weaker, in terms of disease susceptibility, than the female. Color blindness and hemophilia are essentially male disabilities. . . . On the whole, perhaps because of the mechanism that determines sex, the female of the species is stronger and healthier" (1969, p. 27). As pointed out elsewhere in this chapter, males have a considerably higher mortality rate than females throughout the childhood years and are plagued by a greater incidence of virtually every major illness and defect.

The Formation of Basic Trust

The child loves and trusts before he thinks and acts.
Johann Pestalozz

During the first year of life the infant develops patterns of trust that significantly influence the remainder of childhood and perhaps even reach into the adolescent and adult years. Infants who experience basic trust have a positive attitude toward themselves and their social environment and have garnered a sense of self-confidence that enables them to better cope with life difficulties, with other kids, and with themselves.

Infants' sense of trust is most influenced by the treatment they receive from their parents. Parents who are warm and comforting, who nurture with consistency and who attend promptly to distress contribute a very important role in the formation of basic trust. On the other hand, parents who resent their child, who treat the child with aloofness or coldness, who share little time, and who make the child the target of their hostilities help to instill in the child a fearful belief that the world is cold, unpredictable, and unstable. The extent to which the child develops trust or mistrust greatly influences the outlook she takes into toddlerhood, and perhaps even into adulthood.

The Absence of Trust

One is tempted to ask why parents would behave in such a manner that their child would develop mistrust. Erik Erikson (1950), who developed the concept of basic trust, suggests several factors, focusing on the role of the mother: (1) Motherhood is not always a welcome status. Many mothers resent the restrictions imposed on them by child care and release their frustration on the child. (2) Occasionally the experiences of pregnancy and delivery are sufficiently unpleasant (physically and/or psychologically) to predispose the mother negatively toward her child. (3) Finally comes the role the baby himself plays. Many infants are difficult and unpleasant. A distressed child may cry for long periods, constantly demand attention, have irregular feeding and sleeping schedules, and give little affection to the parents. Each of these factors contributes to child-mother interaction that fosters mistrust rather than trust.

The absence of basic trust has several effects on infant development. First, and perhaps most important, mistrust inhibits normal curiousity. Further, mistrust makes it difficult to relate spontaneously and openly with others, drastically reducing opportunities for gaining praise, recognition, and achievement – all essential to the one-year-old. Surprisingly, some parents prefer mistrust in their children, because preventing the growth of self-reliance keeps the child closer to them. For parents whose own psychological development is incomplete, the child's dependence is rewarding.

Basic trust does not guarantee the child will learn to speak more clearly or to walk more swiftly; *it simply means that the child feels safe enough to explore the world within the limits nature imposes.* (As you will observe in the next chapter, exploration during toddlerhood is based in great measure on the willingness to "gamble".)

Whether children grow through toddlerhood or merely survive it is in large measure determined by their trust in the adults who share their lives. In the larger discourse of human events, these bonds of trust welded in the formative first months may chart more paths than any of us presently recognize.

Love Your Baby: 1920s Style

In the 80s and 90s we have grown accustomed to experts who shower advice on every topic to anyone who will listen. Among the most "radical" of the original advice givers was John Watson, the famous American psychologist. He believed that children are easily spoiled, and that the more they are loved the more spoiled they are likely to become:

> Loves are home made, built in. The child sees the mother's face when she pets it. Soon, the mere sight of the mother's face calls out the love response . . . So with her footsteps, the sight of the mother's clothes, of her photograph. All too soon the child gets shot through with too many of these love reactions (Watson, 1928, p. 75).

And even though in the 90s we consider love and tenderness vital to child-rearing, Watson held no such sentimental attitude:

> Remember when you are tempted to pet your child that mother love is a dangerous instrument. An instrument which may inflict a never healing wound, a wound which may make infancy unhappy, adolescence a nightmare, an instrument which may wreck you adult son or daughter's vocational future and their chances for marital happiness (p. 87).

How Effectively Can We Engineer Children?

Among the most practical, yet theoretically complex questions that psychologists ask is, "To what extent is our behavior learned?" Do children act as they do because of learning, or because of the way they are genetically programmed?

Behaviorism is a school of psychology which claims that most human behavior results from environmental rewards and punishments. Rewarded actions tend to be repeated, punished actions tend to disappear.

John B. Watson (1924), the prominent American behaviorist was largely responsible for behaviorism's entry into the mainstream of American psychology. He believed that psychology is the study of stimuli and the responses that follow them. Human behavior to Watson was a series of responses evoked by a series of stimuli. The science of human behavior, therefore, was the science of the the relationship between stimulus and response.

In 1924, Watson issued a statement that has become one of the most famous in American psychology: "Give me a dozen healthy infants, well-formed, and my own specified world to bring them up in and I'll guarantee to take any one at random and train him to become any type of specialist I might select – doctor, lawyer, artist, merchant, chief, and yes, beggar-man and thief, regardless of his talents, penchants, tendencies, abilities, vocations, and race of his ancestors." Thus, Watson claimed to be able to engineer children to become whatever he chose. He did not consider their individual talents (or temperaments) to be important in this engineering process.

Watson's challenge provides us with an opportunity to examine the relative importance of several factors in child behavior. He believed that behavior is elicited, rewarded, and punished, and gradually shaped as a result of this interaction. An objection to this theory is that it does not sufficiently consider temperament differences between children. Some children, for example, are passive in the face of both reward and punishment, whereas others respond vigorously to reward but much less to punishment. A second criticism is that he did not sufficiently credit the role of maturation. Children can perform feats and respond to stimuli only to the extent that they are developmentally ready to do so. Therefore, certain stimuli have little effect at certain ages but are highly influential at others. (Peer pressure exerts almost no influence on the one-year-old but has great impact on the middle-years child.) Another criticism directed at Watson's behaviorism is that it does not fully consider the importance of natural abilities. Since some children are more gifted at physical skills than mental skills, it is easier to teach these kids sporting activities than, for example, algebra. Psychologists who believe in the importance of natural ability think Watson's claim to mould the child "regardless of his talents, penchants, tendencies, abilities" is not only boastful but naive.

The Impact of Heredity on Human Development

Identical Twins during the First Year of Life

In this book I have created a set of identical twins for the sole purpose of making it easier to explain fundamental concepts of human growth and development. These hypothetical children, whose age changes at the end of each chapter, will prove extremely helpful in demonstrating some of the subtle (and not so subtle) facets of human growth and development.

As long as I am inventing these twins I may as well do it right: here are their background specs. These identical twins are born full-term with no adverse effects and with no known hereditary defects; they are both of average intelligence, height, weight, and personality. They are being raised by two parents without noticeable defects in a "typically" North American way. These children are the prototypes of scientific "averageness" and will grow through the life cycle as scientific averages predict they would. They represent the norm in all important childhood traits and juvenile growth patterns; thus, they will serve as examples of the human growth process as it is most frequently manifested in North America.

Because these identical twins are invented, I shall periodically have them do miraculous things, purely for your education. Their primary purpose, however, is to serve as theoretical examples of trends in child growth and development. Because the twins derive from identical heredity, the genetic considerations discussed throughout this text are constant; for purposes of elucidation I shall speculate on how these girls would differ if their environments differed, and how they would remain the same even if their environments differed – the net effect being a speculative assessment of how children are influenced by heredity, environment, interpersonal relationships, and chance factors.

Twins tend to have a more difficult prenatal period than singleton children because they require more space and their placental systems are more likely to be faulty. Twins are also more likely than singletons to be born prematurely. Our twins, special creatures that they are, were born full-term without unusual difficulty, and without inborn errors of metabolism. Birth shock may have been more taxing for one child because identical twins are not identical in their responses to stress.

The early weeks of life are dominated by reflexes, although one twin may have a stronger sucking or grasping reflex while the other possesses a more consistent rooting reflex or a more streamlined tonic neck reflex. The girls will gradually outgrow their reflexes at about the same pace. The twins may show inconsistency in temperament, one being irritable and the other calm, one quick to respond to new stimuli and the other less so. On the other hand, these girls may be quite similar in temperament: the important point is that little reason exists to assume that the girls will be identical in their temperaments, even though they are identical in heredity.

A hypothetical question: "What if one twin were delivered by the Leboyer technique and the second twin delivered by traditional methods?" What differences might appear several months later because of the different delivery techniques? At the time of this writing (1990), no studies have provided a conclusive answer to this question. We do not know if babies delivered by one technique fare better, say at 18 months or at 36 months, than babies delivered by another technique. A good case can be made that the baby undergoes less shock in a method such as that devised by Leboyer, but we are uncertain whether this reduced shock positively influences the growth of the child.

As noted in the previous chapter, teratogens can destroy hereditary ground plans during prenatal development; therefore, even though twins inherit the potential for normal vision, their sight could have been destroyed if their mother had contracted rubella during the early stages of pregnancy. Teratogens can alter (or even destroy) the genetic potential inherent in the growing child, providing us with our first example of the power of environment to alter the forces of heredity.

Because our twins are healthy at birth they achieve similar Apgar scores. By the fourth month their scores on measures of intelligence will be similar; if they are not, this fact is as likely due to invalid measuring instruments as to actual differences in intellectual abilities.

Our twins will show similar increases in the effectiveness of their sensory equipment. During the early weeks neither will manifest much sensory precision, but by the eighth or tenth month they will taste, hear, touch, smell, and see with considerable clarity. Special training would result in little significant improvement in sensory efficiency. This holds true for other maturation-regulated behavior, such as walking and talking, where the law of readiness, more than the quality of the environment, determines the child's ability to benefit from practice.

In the first weeks of post-uterine life both children demonstrate generalized states of excitement, especially irritation; however, their emotional range is initially extremely limited. By their first birthday, however, the girls possess diversified emotion and clearly demonstrate happiness, playfulness, fear, anger, jealousy, and competition. Even though our twins are mature enough to enjoy a range of emotion, one girl possibly will experience one emotion more consistently than the other; thus, one twin may show few flashes of jealousy, whereas the other seems obsessed by it. Thus differences sprout, blossom and evolve their own patterns.

In intellectual abilities we note parallel growth. During the first month behavior is dominated by inborn reflexes; during the third and fourth months the girls will commence repetitive practice of simple manoeuvres; in the seventh through tenth months both girls will solve simple problems and acquire some capacity for object permanence; and in the vicinity of the first birthday active experimentation begins.

As with most developments during the first 12 months, coaching helps, but not much. As long as the child is well cared for and provided ample stimulation, growth proceeds in an orderly sequence that can be accelerated very little by further enrichment.

Neither twin will be able to pronounce many words by the end of the first year, although both will skyrocket in their speech abilities during toddlerhood. Their developmental progression in preparation for speech, however, is synchronized. The girls begin babbling and manufacturing nonsense chatter at about the same age; they will produce recognizable syllables at about the same age.

One twin may be a better walker than the other at 12 months and a better runner at 36 months simply because of normal differences in motor skills. However, while learning to walk the girls will show much similarity (see Table 6-2 for twin resemblances in other motor skills). Even in this generalization caution is necessary because children are unique even in maturation-based skills such as crawling and walking. Most kids quit crawling after they have learned to walk, but not all do so. (I once observed for several weeks a youngster who moved herself from place to place by "rolling" in a sitting position, using her extended arms as stilts. Emily Ruth began upright locomotion before she learned to crawl, and in this unique approach to walking gave early warning that she would be a unique and feisty individual.)

Twins show some personality similarities but not with the regularity of more biologically determined traits such as walking or talking. Even when twins are given equal treatment they likely will assume different profiles on important personality dimensions such as introversion or extroversion. In growth and development the dimension least influenced by genetics is personality; at least, that is the way psychologists perceive the situation as the 20th century lumbers to its conclusion.

We will keep close track of our twins as they inch through childhood. These girls will continue to demonstrate considerable similarity in their growth, although while doing so they will also evidence great individuality in social outlook and personality composition.

The Major Concepts of this Chapter

1. Piaget's stages of infant intellectual development recount the progression from simple reflexes to purposive behavior; from being able to solve simple problems and recognizing object permanence to using trial-and-error experimentation.

2. Memory in infancy advances rapidly. Newborns can't remember for even a few hours, while at 4 to 6 weeks they can, and by 5 months they may retain memories for up to two weeks. During the second half of the first year a rudimentary ability to store information in categories and to process numerical information develops.

3. Speech in the first year of life follows a progression from the vocalization of single syllables, to cooing, to babbling, to repeating syllables, and finally culminates in the first words being spoken near the first birthday.

4. Near four months the infant brings her hands together; near six months she transfers objects from hand to hand; at eight months finger-thumb opposition occurs, and at 12 months the infant is able to throw and drop objects.

5. Locomotion is regulated by maturation and usually progresses from sitting up, to crawling, to creeping, to standing, and to taking first steps. Some children skip milestones in this progression, but most do not.

6. As the child learns to differentiate self from environment, and to monitor her own behavior, self-awareness emerges. Self-awareness is the building block of human personality which results in self-direction and self-control.

7. Individual differences are revealed in infant temperament, which remains somewhat consistent throughout childhood. Some babies are "difficult" while others are "easy," or "slow to warm up."

8. Patterns of basic trust developed in the first year influence future development. Basic trust engenders assertive confidence while mistrust instills the feeling that the world is unstable and unpredictable.

9. The study of identical twins provides insight into the relative influence of maturational and environmental forces in human growth and development.

5

The Origins of Human Genius: Thought and Speech During Toddlerhood

The very genius of childhood lies not in analysis, but in response.

Joan Selby

Children between the ages of one and three years have been called many things, some of them not the least bit flattering. I refer to these children as "toddlers" because they really do toddle (especially between 12 and 24 months) with short, tottering steps – a gait characteristic of no other developmental age. "Toddler" is expressive and familiar and helps convey the innocent charm of children between 12 and 36 months.

Toddlers are not an easy subject for study, although they are more suited than our two previous subjects - the fetus and the the one-year-old. The major problems associated with the psychological investigation of fetuses and one-year-olds are their inaccessibility and their inability to speak. Toddlers speak and are accessible and on these counts make psychological research much easier; however, they also are far more complex and possess greater freedom than pre-toddlers, and this makes them more difficult research subjects.

During toddlerhood (especially the latter half), children act with intention, purpose, forethought and strategy. Toddlers "soak up" the environment, but not passively. They discard certain rules and retain others; they like certain foods and dislike others; and they flourish with some kinds of learning and flounder with others. A toddler's speaking skills may be advanced beyond his chronological age while his bladder control is less developed than typical of other children his age. This unevenness, is in accord with the principle of asynchronous development. Toddlers are no mere blank slates on which experience writes. Neither are they helpless, fragile, or weak. Toddlers are feisty, resilient and exploratory creatures who constantly act upon their world and in turn are acted upon. They actively participate in their own programming but certainly are not responsible for all of it. They are usually sturdy and durable and, if unpampered, are frequently the most physically healthy members of their household.

Toddlers experience a great deal of frustration in day to day living because their ambitions always seem slightly ahead of their capacities. In response to this disparity they cultivate an essential skill: getting assistance from others. If toddlers are gifted at getting into things, they are geniuses at getting others to bail them out.

Throughout this chapter the reader will observe references to the *early* toddler and to the *late* toddler. This distinction is made because fundamental differences exist between the skills of the 12- to 24-month child (early toddler) and those of the 24 to 36-month child (late toddler). Intellectual and physical skills of late toddlerhood are not only more numerous, they are qualitatively superior to those of early toddlerhood. Thus, it is often inaccurate to sweepingly say that the toddler can do this or can't do that, because what he can't do in early toddlerhood he may master during late toddlerhood.

Curiosity, Exploration and Competence

Most developmentalists believe that children possess an inherent, genetically programmed drive to explore their environment. This concept has been most forcefully (and persuasively) presented by Robert White (1959). The substance of the idea is this: evolution has equipped humans with the drive to attain competence with their environment. Children, in response to this drive, disassemble objects, turn dials, flip containers upside down, and otherwise engage in an endless range of actions designed to enhance their mastery and maximize their understanding of the world in which they live. This inherent impulse to competence generates its own pleasure, excitement and mental stimulation, which are powerful enough to motivate continuous exploratory behavior. Adherents to this concept believe that children possess natural curiosity and that all learning, in its foundation, is based upon the drive for competence and mastery.

In this text it is accepted as a tenet of development that every child possesses a basic, unlearned drive to acquire competence, to solve problems, to learn new skills, and to master their own developing body. Curiosity encourages competence, but they are not the same because as the toddler becomes increasingly competent in mastering specific skills his curiosity toward them lessens. Curiosity and exploration are sometimes ends in themselves, but their main evolutional purpose is to enhance competence (mastery).

Most exploration during the first half of toddlerhood is trial-and-error: observe what happens when this is stacked on that; taste this when mixed with that. Toddlers learn an incredible amount from their trial-and-error approach. But they are susceptible to bumps and accidents during their initial experimentation.

Overprotective parents inadvertently hinder their child's growth by discouraging natural curiousity or by destroying self-confidence. During these years exploration provides valuable knowledge about physical objects, geometric relationships, and causality. Childhood simply could not unfold as it does without the impulse to explore and the inherent drive to attain competence.

Egocentrism

Fraiberg gracefully describes one variation of toddler egocentrism:

The magician is seated in his high chair and looks upon the world with favor. He is at the height of his powers. If he closes his eyes, he causes the world to disappear. If he opens his eyes, he causes it to come back. If there is harmony within him, the world is harmonious. If rage shatters his inner harmony, the unity of the world is shattered. If desire arises within him, he utters the magic syllables which cause the desired object to appear. His wishes, his thoughts, his gestures, his noises, command the universe. (1959, p. 107)

Egocentrism influences every phase of toddler existence and, more than any other mental trait, contributes to their sublime imperviousness to the outside world. It is the core of their self-engrossed charm, and adds immeasureably to their innocent loveability. It also, however, adds to their daily frustration because toddlers constantly encounter realities that their singular frame of reference hasn't prepared them for. Toddlers eventually overcome some of the limitations imposed by egocentrism, but it is a lengthy and troublesome process.

Most forms of egocentrism weaken with age: *perceptual egocentrism* (the assumption that there exists only one perception of a physical object) diminishes with the onset of perceptual constancy; *emotional egocentrism* diminishes when the child learns that everyone does not have the same emotional reaction to the same experience; and *intellectual egocentrism* loosens as the child realizes that every issue has two sides. For the most part, however, egocentrism dominates toddler thought.

Self-centredness demands expression and toddlers quickly learn cute and charming behavior designed to focus attention upon themselves. The toddler will dance for applause, role somersaults for praise, or laugh boisterously in order to direct the attention of parents to their splendid child. Showing-off rarely occurs before toddlerhood because younger children have a limited ability to engage in activities designed to elicit specific reactions from adults.

By the end of the second year the child's vocabulary is sprinkled with self-reference. Toddlers know their name and respond to it (unless they sense that trouble beckons). They talk about themselves in the third person: "Timmy is hungry." They also punish themselves verbally: "Timmy is a bad boy"; praise themselves: "Timmy is a good helper."

Toddlers are possessive and they demonstrate emotional attachment to their possessions. They cry when forced to share something they want for themselves; they sometimes hit or bite another child who plays with their favorite toy – which in the world of toddlerhood is quite different from a mere toy. Egocentrism generates possessiveness, and possessiveness evolves into ownership. Both of these features become embedded within the toddler's personality and they are virtually immune to extinction. There is no social-ism in the egocentric world of toddlerhood!

Self-Awareness in the Egocentric Toddler

Jerome Kagan has generated some of the most innovative ideas in con-temporary child psychology. Pertaining to the emergence of self-awareness, he suggests that three interrelated events guide the child toward a more com-plete and mature sense of self: (1) awareness of adult standards, (2) a desire for mastery, and (3) self-as-me (Kagan, 1981).

Awareness of Adult Standards

Schematizing and organizing the world is a full-time job for the toddler. Among the first tasks is to differentiate actions which bring praise from those which bring punishment. This distinction becomes refined when the child recognizes adult standards and expectations. Even in the early phase of self-awareness children know the difference between events which are simply unusual (Dad wearing his hat inside the house) and unusual events which bring adult disapproval (crayon marks on the wall). In other words, the child begins to perceive the relevance of events in terms of *adult standards,* not merely her own. Meeting adults standards brings feelings of right-doing and self-satisfaction. Failing adult standards brings wrong-ness and disapproval. Once this level of development has been attained self-awareness is never completely independent of adult standards.

Mastery

From adult standards evolve self-standards. These are goals the child sets for herself; mini-accomplishments actualized by mini-skills. Children experience self-satisfaction when they master these tasks, and frustration when they fall short. Mastery at this age is influenced by the child's increas-ing awareness of completion and finality, and by her recognition of the differ-ence between a task completed to specifications and one that isn't.

Self-as-me

Near the second birthday youngsters realize that the person in the mirror is "me," and that the baby in mother's arms in a photograph is also me. Pictures of me are "me." Things that belong to me are "mine." With these realizations self-awareness blossoms and the toddler attains the self-consciousness reserved for those few creatures in nature who think about themselves.

Self-Awareness and Emotions

Pride manifests itself as a sense of worth, specialness or self-respect. It does not develop until the child attains a rather well defined sense of self awareness. Shame, an emotion of guilt or incompetence likewise cannot exist without a measure of self-awareness. Even the famous toddler temper owes its existence to the sense of self, most particularly the frustration and anger the self experiences when thwarted or denied.

Self-awareness is riddled with alternating pleasures and disappointments. Toddlers not only experience their selves, they assert their selves, sometimes merely to elicit confrontation – to exercise the muscular portion of their personality.

Research indicates that at 24 months toddlers laugh more and get angry more than they did at 18 months, and that at 18 months they demonstrate more of these emotions than they did at 12 months. Thus a progressive self-expression tags along after the galloping self-awareness which highlights this period of human growth.

Mental Growth During Toddlerhood

Few periods in the life cycle equal toddlerhood in quantity or quality of intellectual growth. The one-year-old and the three-year-old possess such vastly different modes of intellectual functioning that it is difficult to think of them as being in the same developmental stage. The one-year-old has primitive learning skills while the three-year-old has sophisticated capacities. One-year-olds are narrow; behavior and thought is severely constrained by as yet undeveloped potential. Compared to these infants three-year-olds are intellectual expansionists and social entrepreneurs of the grandest order. Understanding these transformations of human intelligence is one of the greatest challenges facing the developmental psychologist.

The Emergence of Human Thought:

Mental Development during Early Toddlerhood (12-24 months)

Before 12 months the child possesses an extremely limited range of intellectual skills. Memory is exclusively short-term, and the ability to benefit from experience is minimal. Infants less than a year old possess such a primitive notion of causality that they do not recognize themselves as an instrument of causality (the baby will strain to lift a blanket that she is standing on). During the second year these deficiencies are partly outgrown, as the child discovers a new and bewildering world of cause and effect.

Toddlers naturally experiment with and explore the unknown. However, they *learn to modify* their behavior when it proves unsuccessful because they eventually recognize themselves as active agents possessing the ability to act upon and modify their environment.

Some scholars are actually very impressed with the thinking abilities of toddlers:

> It turns out that not only do infants notice many more details of their environment than adults ever suspected but they actively invent rules or theories to explain what they perceive . . . . By the age of 2, the normal child has learned to speak, built himself a large framework of theories about the world, and taught himself various intricate skills which he can use in new combinations whenever the need arises – an extraordinary achievement. (Pines, 1970, pp. 72-73)

Despite these commendable features, young toddlers posess only minimal capacity for abstract thought. Learning is primarily trial-and-error, mostly error; fortunately, growth in memory helps eliminate endless repetitions of experiments that were conducted the day before. Before 24 months children learn that they can draw an out-of-reach object that rests on a support, such as a blanket, toward themselves by pulling on the blanket. They also learn that an object can be retrieved with a tug on a string attached to it. At this developmental level the child learns to tilt wide objects in order to draw them through the narrow bars of the playpen; they come to realize that objects will not pass through an opening smaller than the object itself.

Early toddlers solve problems through the process of *active experimentation*. They must actually try to squeeze a four-inch ball through a two-inch opening before they realize it will not fit. They have a very limited ability to process new information without some form of active experimentation. In other words, they must actually *do* it, or *see* it, before much learning takes place.

Near 24 months toddlers advance to a new stage of mental development: they think by mental combinations and devise solutions without the physical process of active experimentation in a process known as *mental experimentation*. Flavell (1963) describes this breakthrough:

> This important new pattern can be summarized as follows. The child wishes to achieve some end and finds no habitual schema which can serve as means . . . However, instead of fumbling for a solution by an extended series of overt and visible sensory-motor explorations . . . the child "invents" one through a covert process which amounts to internal experimentation, an inner exploration of ways and means. Unlike any previous stage, the

acquisition of something can now take place covertly – prior to action, instead of through, and only through, accommodations. (p. 119)

Some examples will clarify. A child attempts to rest up against a stool, but the stool scoots backward. After several unsuccessful attempts to lean against the sliding stool, the toddler gets up, places the stool against a sofa, and then leans against the stool with assurance that it will not slide backward. This response demonstrates the capacity to invent a solution without active experimentation. (It is assumed that the child has had no previous occasion to prop the stool against the sofa.)

During the second year several geometric relationships are mastered; thus, the child does not expect square blocks to roll or pyramids to remain upright when placed on their apex. At 24 months the child gives every indication of being a thinking creature, and sometimes his moments of reflection are as painfully obvious as those of the preoccupied professor.

The toddler learns to deal with plural and develops an interest in "many" and "more," which represents an advancement over his previous preoccupation with singular items and events.

He likes to assemble the many cubes into a pile or to disperse the pile into the many cubes. He likes to store and to hold four, six, or more cubes which are handed to him individually. In comparison, the 1-year-old is single and serial-minded. The 1-year-old infant has a typical one-by-one pattern; he takes one cube after another and places it on the table or platform in a repetitive manner. This is a genetic anticipation of counting. The 18-month-old infant cannot count, but he has a vigorous interest in aggregates, and that also is a developmental prerequisite for a higher mathematics. (Gessell, 1940, p. 31)

The Emergence of Constancy

Object constancy is the recognition that the physical properties of objects do not change, even though they appear to change. *Size constancy* is the ability to see size as constant even though the retinal image actually is smaller or larger. For example, when a person is walking away from you, the image on your retina actually becomes smaller. You do not perceive the person as becoming smaller, you perceive him as the same size but moving away. Size constancy involves placing a constant object into a changing perceptual field without losing awareness of its original size. *Shape constancy* is the ability to recognize that shapes remain the same even though they look different from different angles. *Color constancy* permits the child to recognize that colors remain the same even when they are seen in varying degrees of light or alongside various shades of the same color.

When the child has acquired size constancy, color constancy, and shape constancy, the world acquires greater overall object constancy, thus becoming more understandable, manipulable, and predictable. Without the achievements of constancy the world is an irregular collage of misrepresentations, an unworkable conglomeration of inconsistency.

A New Quality of Mind:
Mental development during Late Toddlerhood (24-36 months)

The second half of toddlerhood is characterized by growth of all previously acquired skills, as well as spontaneous development of several additional capacities. Manual, perceptual, and verbal discriminations become considerably more precise. Exploration and investigation are greatly enhanced by refined prehensile skills. Random and disorderly activities are partially outgrown, and there is an almost universal tendency to arrange and organize environmental objects. Play blocks often are grouped into geometric or color classifications. The child easily solves three-hole board tasks, invariably placing triangles, squares, and circles in the slots that correspond to their shape. At about two-and-a-half the sense of completion is so well developed that some toddlers experience emotional distress upon observing a torn picture or a statue with a missing limb.

Although not talented at bartering, toddlers assimilate the notion that one object can be traded for another; however, their impulsivity inclines them to change their mind a moment after the transaction has occurred. Late toddlerhood witnesses the primitive beginnings of cooperative work. The child now recognizes that two people can work together to accomplish a desired goal, although it takes a somewhat skilled adult to get much cooperation from the toddler. Toddlers are rewarded for their attempts at cooperative labor (cooperation is one of our society's most highly prized behaviors); it is not unusual for parents to invent activities that require cooperation in order to further entrench the importance of it in the toddler's growing social awareness. Cooperation works most effectively when there is something tangible in it for the toddler because they are, by nature, self-centred and minimally sensitive to the needs and feelings of others. Altruism comes ever so slowly to the egocentric toddler.

Representational Thought

By the second half of toddlerhood *representational thought* becomes a central part of mental activity. Representational thought is the ability to represent in one's mind the possible (or probable) consequences of a given action. It permits the thinker to anticipate the influence of A on B. In representational thought one is able to grasp the relatedness of an entire sequence of events. For example, if suddenly it strikes the toddler's fancy to sneak a cookie from the kitchen, the child will recognize that a chair is needed in order to reach it. Discovering that the cookie is still out of reach, the child might employ a spoon to scoot it forward. While engaging in these activities the child is aware that if mother catches him, he is in trouble;

therefore, upon her unexpected entrance, he may "freeze" in anticipation of a reprimand. The cookie theft demonstrates the following representations:

1. the chair and spoon can be used to reach the cookie,
2. eating the cookie may bring mother's disapproval,
3. mother's disapproval will occur only if she discovers what has transpired (this point is critical, because it distinguishes general knowledge from private knowledge; stated differently, the toddler knows that everyone does not know what he knows), and
4. mother's disapproval, like the cookie, must be approached with strategy.

It is no wonder that mothers describe daytime routine as a war of wits.

Toddlers possess only a vague understanding of *causality;* their thought is more correlational than causal. Event A is thought to be caused by event B because they occur together. The child believes that blowing branches cause wind because they occur simultaneously; or she may think that inflating the wading pool brings warm weather. Flavell (1963) provides us with further examples of the toddler's capacity to understand what causes what:

> If one asks the reason for A, the child will supply a B as cause, B being simply some element which co-occurred with A in perception and had hence co-fused with A in a global, syncretic schema. Since cause-and-effect requirements are so lax for the young child, anything and everything must have an identifiable cause. One interesting consequence of this orientation is that he is unable to form a genuine concept of chance or probability. (p. 161)

Object Awareness during Toddlerhood

As we discussed in greater detail in Chapter three, during the first year of life children come to remember where objects have been placed even when these objects cannot be seen. This perceptual breakthrough advances the child beyond the confines of immediate sensation and, as well, increases problem-solving abilities. As one might expect, however, the capacity for object permanence is not fully developed during the first year. When searching for a hidden object the one-year-old reflexively searches in locations where it has previously been hidden. When the object is not found, alternative searches are limited. Thus, if not successful on the first try, the child may never locate a hidden object, even if it is only a few centimetres from where she is searching.

During the toddler years great advances take place in the child's understanding of the physical world. For example, when searching for a hidden object that fails to turn up where it was previously hidden, the late toddler simply begins to search elsewhere because he is no longer confined to one exploratory option. Also, the late toddler is able to deal with transparent obstacles. When an object is placed inside a glass jar with a closed lid, the early toddler is powerless to devise a manoeuvre that will retrieve the object and soon forgets about it and moves elsewhere. The late toddler, however, will rattle the container, tip it, and glance at the adult in a quest for assistance, thus applying at least a social strategy to the solution of the problem. Finally, the late toddler's capacity for object permanence becomes so advanced that even when an object has been moved behind three barriers in succession, he will search behind each barrier until the object has been located.

Older toddlers develop such a sophisticated understanding of permanence that they can see through deception or trickery. For example, when an adult shows a three-year-old a coin, then "hides" it first behind screen one, then screen two, then screen three, and asks the child to locate it while secretly palming the coin, the child will follow directions and search behind the barriers (where a sporting experimenter would have left it); however, when the coin does not show up, the child may look in the experimenter's hands or pockets, indicating not only an awareness of object permanence, and possession of a disciplined memory but also an intuition about the psychologist's penchant for deception.

Logic

During the third year logic makes its presence felt in the child's mental processes. The earliest form of logic is referred to by Piaget as *transductive* because it is neither purely inductive nor purely deductive in form. Transductive reasoning proceeds from particular to particular and is not based on a concept of causality. Thus, if the cat is furry, all furry creatures are thought to be cats. If dogs have four legs, all four-legged creatures are thought to be dogs.

In the following passage Lefrancois (1974) effectively summarizes the important differences between mature forms of logic (inductive and deductive) and the simplistic form employed by toddlers (transductive):

> The child reasons from particular to particular, following the same general form of thought as he would were he reasoning inductively or deductively. Transductive reasoning, however, frequently leads to incorrect conclusions. Consider, for example, the observation that a sparrow flies. A sparrow is a small bird that comes in a variety of species: tree sparrows, house sparrows, and song sparrows, to name but a few. To say that birds fly, sparrows are birds, therefore sparrows fly, is a correct illustration of deductive reasoning. To observe that all sparrows fly, that all robins fly, and that a variety of other birds fly, and to then conclude that birds fly is correct inductive reasoning. To say, on the other hand, that a specific house sparrow flies, that another specific bird flies, and then to conclude that the second bird is a sparrow is an example of transductive reasoning – reasoning that could well be a sparrow, but it might just as well be a robin, since robins fly also. (p. 147)

Inductive reasoning and deductive reasoning are disciplined attempts to extract truth from established points of information. Transductive reasoning, which is the most primitive and least accurate form of reasoning, simply joins things that are close in time, or somehow correlated with one another. If father comes home from work each day at six o'clock, moving the hands of the clock to that time should cause him to return home. A thought process governed by such logic generates preposterous conclusions. Indeed, a great deal of toddlerhood folly is anchored in this mental process.

Transductive reasoning is an intellectual process which, in its foundations, is faulty. Toddlers think poorly not only because they possess incorrect information. They think incorrectly because their *mechanism of thought* consistently draws false conclusions.

Ultimately transductive reasoning is outgrown, but its importance as a stage of intellectual development should not be underestimated. Nor should its outcomes because from them equations unique to toddlerhood are repeatedly brought into existence: blanket is equated with security and the absence of blanket with insecurity; departure through a door equals "gone" rather than gone for a moment; and Johnny may equal brother and no one else, and brother may equal Johnny and no one else. Transductive reasoning, fortunately for the human species, is outgrown in the preschool years and replaced by more advanced reasoning.

Because of the abundance of transductive errors in the thinking process, the young child's deployment of reason is a constant source of amazement to adults.

> Parents who try to reason with young children often find themselves sinking in a guagmire of rapidly changing premises, logical inconsistencies, unforeseen implications, word magic and dissolving obviousness. Told that toy he wants is too expensive, it follows for the child that his parents must be willing to buy him another, less expensive one. . . . The young child has no doubt that a single object can simultaneously be in two widely separated locations. A new adult encountered in the home of other children is almost certain to be classed as a parent of those children, even though this may provide them with two or more mothers or fathers. (Church, 1966, pp. 77-78)

Stimulation versus Understimulation

Maturational unfolding follows its genetic blueprint only when the environment provides basic necessities. If the environment is impoverished, children simply do not mature to their hereditary potential.

The Institutional Studies

Rene Spitz (1965) conducted pioneer research on a group of children reared in a home for abandoned children. Their physical environment was barren, devoid of playthings, and visually restricted by bed sheets draped over the crib sides so that they could not look around and see other children. These children lay on their backs all day, and at 12 months many of them could not even roll over. Their social environment was as understimulating as their physical environment. They were not held or cuddled during the day, their contact-comfort needs were not met, and they did not experience playful, physical affection of any kind. The combined effects of physical-sensory understimulation and the absence of personal contact inflicted severe damage on the growth patterns of these children. Virtually all of them were retarded in their physical development: they could not crawl, walk, or engage in eye-hand skills with nearly the competence of children their age reared in normal environments. Their intellectual and speech development was severely curtailed. In essence, their development was retarded in virtually every significant phase of social, physical, and intellectual functioning.

Another group of children observed by Spitz were raised in a prison nursery that was not geared for young children. However, these children were played with and handled each day by their mothers (who were delinquent girls). These children did not display the listless passiveness of the first group; nor were they globally retarded. When these two groups were tested, at two years of age, the prison-nursery infants were about normal on most measures, whereas the abandoned children gave every indication of mental retardation. The hypothesis put forward by Spitz, and subsequently adopted by most experts in developmental psychology, is that contact, unto itself, is necessary for normal development.

Allied research indicates that children who spend the first year of life in an orphanage and who are then placed in a foster home tend to score better on developmental measures than children who spend the first three years of life in an orphanage. On many personality measures, including impulsiveness, ability to concentrate, and general interpersonal skills, long-term orphanage children consistently achieve lower scores.

One of the most widely reported studies in the field of stimulus deprivation was carried out several decades ago by H.M. Skeels (1939). While working at an orphanage characterized by the bleak environment typical of institutions of the time, Skeels observed two young girls who were extremely retarded in their behavior. They were physically underdeveloped, passive, and disinterested and spent most of their time rocking back and forth in a manner typical of severely disturbed children. They were transferred to a mental institution because it was unlikely they would erlyer be adopted. Skeels observed the children at a later date and was startled at what he saw. The girls were active, alert, inquisitive, and, in general, normal. He administered and intelligence test to the girls and was surprised that they scored in the normal range. A scientific investigator, Skeels began to isolate the factors that could possibly have brought about such dramatic changes in the personalities and abilities of these children. He discovered that each child had been "adopted" by one of the retarded women at the mental institution. The women played with the girls, fondled them, made them the focus of attention, and talked with them. Social interaction, and physical contact, provided the stimulation the girls required, and their natural abilities blossomed.

In an attempt to verify that the "treatment" received from the mentally retarded women was the key to the girls' improvement, Skeels set up an experiment. Over the course of several years, 13 infants were removed from the orphanage and placed in the mental institution. All showed signs of improvement, and all increased their scores on tests of development. Follow-up research on these youngsters showed that by adulthood all were living on their own and none of them was mentally retarded. Another group, who remained in the orphanage and were not adopted, did not fare nearly so well. Of this group of 12 children, 10 spent most of their lives in an institution for the mentally retarded.

Provence and Lipton (1962) observed children reared in an institutional environment in the United States several decades after the studies conducted by Skeels. In the institution, nutrition was adequate and the physical facilities, in general, good. However, the amount of child-adult interaction was minimal, and the children suffered as a result. Here is how the authors describe living conditions in the institution:

> The infants were fed in their cribs with bottles propped. When cereals, fruits and vegetables were added to the diet they were also given in a propped bottle with a large holed nipple rather than given by spoon. . . . Each infant in this group shared the time and attention of the attendant with 7 to 9 other infants in the same age range for the 8 hour period of the day when she was present. For the remaining 16 hours of the day, there was no person in the nursery except at feeding time when an attendant who also had similar duties in other nurseries heated formulas, propped bottles, and changed diapers. (p.47)

Children reared in these conditions were retarded in both speech and vocalization. They did not coo much; neither did they cry as much as normal infants. They did not respond to being picked up and in general demonstrated little of the responsiveness typical of children raised with normal contact and stimulation.

The Meaning of the Institutional Studies

These studies demonstrate that potential awaits stimulation before it manifests itself. These studies also indicate that normal abilities wither when the environment is bleak and barren. The research conducted by Spitz and Skeels greatly illuminated the issue of early-childhood stimulation and also legislated improvement in orphanages, foundling homes and other institutions that care for the young.

Stimulation in the Household

The institutional studies documented adverse effects which accrue when children are neglected and do not receive satisfaction of their basic needs. In North America, however, these are rare circumstances. What do we know about stimulation and understimulation as it relates to the typical home environment? Numerous researchers have tackled this problem focusing on the behavior of the mother. Among the most significant findings were those compiled by Clarke-Stewart (1973) who observed that verbal stimulation from mothers enhanced the verbal competence of the child and that the amount of time the mother spent in play with the child influenced the child's ability to handle cognitive complexity. It was also noted that mothers who scored high on traits such as affection and responsiveness had children who scored higher than average on measures of social development. Of special interest to many researchers (and to the government agencies that fund early-childhood programs) was the finding that the physical environment was not correlated with child competence as strongly as were mother-child interaction patterns.

The amount of time spent with the child is not so important as the kind of behavior shared. Clarke-Stewart's research indicates that mothers who allow their children to initiate an activity, and then respond verbally to what the child has done or offer suggestions on how it could be done more efficiently, tend to have more competent children than mothers who spend an equal amount of time with their children but who are more preoccupied with control and physical care than with stimulating interaction. Children who receive the kind of optimal stimulation described by Clarke-Stewart tend to acquire greater competence in dealing with their physical environment and to possess greater interpersonal skills than children raised by mothers who do not employ stimulating interaction strategies. From these findings emerged what is popularly described as "quality time." Implicit to the concept is that time itself is not of primary concern, rather the quality of interaction is of greatest consequence. As we shall note in a later chapter, quality time is also an important factor in the emotional and social growth of the child.

A further finding of this research was that the child greatly influences the response patterns of the mother. Children who respond with interest and zest encourage a similar response from the adults in their environment, whereas an apathetic child tends to make adults lose interest. (See Bell's hypothesis in Chapter three.)

Language Retardation and Understimulation

Of all human skills, language is perhaps the most seriously affected by an impoverished environment during the first years of life. Provence and Lipton's research with institutionalized youngsters gives evidence that the language retardation of these children began early in life: they failed to speak words by their first birthday, and their expressive language was considerably behind that of children reared in normal environments. Most research indicates that early understimulation in language has long-lasting effects. Goldfarb, in a series of now classic observations, (1947) found that children who had minimal language stimulation when they were very young remained weak in language skills even at age 12, with about 80 percent of them being below average in speech fluency.

The upshot of this line of research is a universal recognition by early-childhood specialists that the child learns more when exposed to a rich verbal world during the first years of life and that such exposure, unto itself, reduces language retardation.

Speech During Toddlerhood

How can I know what I think till I see what I say?

G. Wallas

Between the twelfth and thirty-sixth months normal children learn to speak the language of their household and also learn a great deal about the grammatical and syntactical structures of their native language. Before the third birthday toddlers acquire spoken mastery of about a thousand words and an understanding of thousands more. English-speaking children learn that nouns usually are placed at the beginning of sentences, that objects of action follow verbs, and that adjectives come before nouns. They also learn that words communicate intents, that words used incorrectly may lose their communicative power, and that words are integrally related to affection and love.

How the child acquires language and grammar is not precisely understood. There is little controversy, however, about the general requirements of language acquisition, most notably, that it depends on (1) maturation of brain functions, (2) exposure to the language, (3) reinforcement for using language, and (4) a genetically based capacity for symbolization. *The relative importance of each of these factors is controversial,* however, and different theories explain the acquisition of speech with differing emphases. In this abbreviated section I shall concentrate primarily on *describing* speech habits rather than analyzing various theories associated with speech acquisition, even though the theoretical issues are exciting and thought provoking.

Individual Differences in the Attainment of Speech

Children do not possess equal language abilities, for several important reasons. First, all children do not possess equal hereditary capacity for speech. Second, children are not equally exposed to rich verbal environments, therefore, they do not benefit equally from experience. Third, as with all abilities, a normal range of individual differences occurs within a given population; each child's position within this range derives from a mixture of hereditary and environmental factors.

Girls as a group tend to be slightly more advanced in language abilities than boys. They tend to develop their language skills slightly earlier, and they have larger vocabularies, more complex sentence structure, better articulation, and a lower probability of speech defects during the early years of life.

Thus, even at the basic level of gender difference we observe variation in speech ability.

Only children tend to possess greater language abilities than children with siblings, the most widely accepted explanation being that only children experience more one-to-one contact with adults (see Zajonc's hypothesis, Chapter four). Children with brothers and sisters must share adult time and, as well, are exposed more to child talk. Twins tend to have less developed language skills than single-birth children; however, as noted elsewhere, twins have a greater probability of incurring a wide range of deficits than the single-birth populations, and their vulnerability to language problems may derive from this fact.

Despite the wide range of individual differences in the rate of children attaining speech, a considerable degree of predictability characterizes the entire process. In the following pages we shall overview some of these general trends, reminding the reader that they represent norms (averages), and apply to large segments of the child population, but not to every child.

How Children Acquire Language

Toddlers not only learn words, they construct grammatically sound sentences. In English most sentences begin with a subject which is followed by a verb and sometimes and indirect object. Adjectives tend to come before the nouns they are describing. English-speaking toddlers learn these general rules of grammar (just as Russian-speaking children acquire the grammatical rules that govern the Russian language) without specific instruction and follow them in their speaking habits without awareness that their speech is regulated by grammatical machinery. The speech of the two-year-old, immature though it may be in vocabulary, is grammatically sound. The moppet who claims "Johnny want Breakfast" not only is expressing an idea; he is adhering to general English grammar prescriptions. The speech is telegraphic and egocentric and makes no use of the first person pronoun, but note how different the sentence becomes if the words are re-arranged: "Breakfast Johnny want" or "Johnny breakfast want." Interestingly, a youngster who displays faulty general grammatical construction is more likely to have serious speech problems than a child who uses particular words incorrectly or who has a minimal vocabulary.

Language acquisition begins at birth when the newborn is greeted as a member of the community of language users. Most authorities now believe that language acquisition occurs naturally given even a minimal language environment. However, enhancement of the language environment does have significant long-term benefits for the child. Thus, most educators advocate such practices as reading and singing to babies from an early age. Such parental practices may relate to the quality and speed with which the baby acquires language.

During the first year of life the baby grows from the reflexive communication of cries and general mouth movement, that are the same in all languages, to the consonant vowel sounds and intonation patterns of the native language. At three months the reflexive noises become babbling which includes many of the consonant and vowel sounds of the native language. During the remainder of the first year of life this babbling increases on many levels of language development. The baby's delight in babbling becomes a self-reinforcing style of acquiring language. Deaf babies, for example, babble the same sounds up to six months as other babies, but since they can't receive self-reinforcement they discontinue babbling and begin to communicate with movement instead.

Even before the baby utters an understandable word in the native language, she has already demonstrated other aspects of language such as intonation patterns, turn taking, and response to other language users. From an early age babies understand and respond to language at a level beyond their ability to express themselves. At one month some babies distinguish the sound of mother's voice, even to the point of being soothed by it. Later, pleasure is derived from language and action games such as "pat-a-cake" and "touch your nose, touch your toes." The baby is an acute listener who can distinguish the native language in surprising and parent-pleasing ways. The ways in which the community uses language with babies builds upon the baby's skills and reinforces language with pleasurable activities.

Around 12 months the baby has in her repertoire the first spoken words that can be deciphered as part of the child's native language. Babbling continues and the baby begins the addition of words, but not at the accelerated rate that one might suppose. Language acquisition remains influenced more by its own natural momentum than the household environment.

Around 21 months (later for some children) the first two-word sentences are created. At this stage the rate of language development increases dramatically. By two years many babies have acquired grammar in the sense of word order, tense, pronouns, and use of suffixes and prefixes. It is also in this stage of development that significant differences between children's language development are noticeable. A significant number of children at two years still have a very limited vocabulary and use the point and grunt system for communication. However, some children are prolific talkers. Even so, these differences do not yet indicate a malfunction in the system. Given time, the majority of children acquire their native language with the same ease with which they learned to sit and walk.

The Humble Beginnings:

Language at Twelve Months

The child's first word, which usually is spoken within a month of the first birthday, is little more than a conditioned response to an object or person. First words are difficult to distinguish from the random, playful vocalizations that the child has been making during the past few months. A few additional words usually are acquired before the fifteenth month, but it is within the normal range for a child not to have uttered a recognizable word by this time. Between 15 and 18 months children jabber and chatter, and assault their world with a barrage of syllables, but they do not use very many "real" words. Communication at this age is carried out primarily by gesture and mannerism (as it has been since the first months of life). At about 15 months the toddler begins to experience frustration at being misunderstood because not until then do words communicate intent or desire.

The quality of vocalization at this age is influenced by several general factors, most notably: (1) parental encouragement or suppression, (2) the opportunity to hear the conversation of adults or other children, and (3) the presence of inhibiting emotional experiences such as neglect or abuse.

A universal principle of speech is manifesting itself by 12 months: language comprehension precedes language production, usually by several months. In other words, the child understands much more than she is able to speak.

Between 12 and 18 months a period of *speech readiness* occurs, when the child is maximally sensitive to learning words and, by the same token, is particularly susceptible to impairment of normal speech by conditions such as severe illness and acute emotional trauma. For most toddlers a dramatic upswing in the production of words, the use of words for specific purposes, and singing with words takes place during this critical 6-month period. (Note vocabulary growth as it is described in Table 5-1.)

The Marriage of Words and Thought:

Language at Eighteen Months

Word production increases spectacularly between 18 and 24 months. An increase of 250 words between 18 and 24 months is not unusual. (At about 18 months the Broca region of the brain, which is integrally related to speech development, undergoes rapid development.) At this age language assumes a communicative function of greater importance than ever before. Spontaneous word combinations are emerging; by 24 months the toddler *creates original phrases* that express desires or describe objects. (This ability poses special problems for those psychologists who claim that speech results primarily from imitation.)

Despite the increased number of words 18-month-olds use, they still have only a minimal capacity for two-word combinations, and only among verbally advanced toddlers are three-word, grammatically sound phrases used. At this age the child relies on one-word sentences (called *holophrasiastic speech*), which express a complete idea. "Eat" means "I want something to eat." "Bath" means "I want to take a bath now."

Word comprehension is increasing rapidly, as is the ability to interpret the meaning of a sentence. Between 18 and 24 months adjectives work their way into the vocabulary, the most common being good, bad, hot, cold, and others that have direct bearing on the toddler's personal world.

The Tumble into Phrases:

Language at Twenty-Four Months

First phases are an early warning of better things. They do not possess the streamlined fluidity or the factual precision of the sentences issued by the 36-month-old. Parents are pleasantly surprised to hear their toddler's first phrases even though they may disagree as to what the child is trying to say. The progression from words to phrases seems almost accidental because of its clumsiness, but it is far from an accident of nature since it is one of the most important transitions in the acquisition of speech.

Two-word phrases are spontaneously formed by most children somewhere near 24 months. These phrases usually relate to immediate needs ("Go potty") or to environmental objects ("Dog big"). Children may spontaneously invent new words when the words in their vocabulary are insufficient to express an idea. These inventions are known as *neologisms*. Examples of toddler neologisms are "fator" (food is in the refrigerator) and "uvkiss" (give me love and a kiss).

Between 24 and 30 months toddlers experience considerable frustration in their attempts to communicate, because words now have purpose and are intended to elicit specific responses. The two-year-old is deluged by words, only some of which are understandable. Because the verbal world sometimes overwhelms the toddler, the role of the parent is crucial in language development.

Parents influence speech in innumerable ways. They expand vocabulary and syntax. The toddler exclaims, "Man come tomorrow," and the parent responds, "Yes, the man will come tomorrow." The toddler claims, "Mailman here ago," and the parent responds, "Do you mean 'The mailman was here a few minutes ago'?" The toddler counts, "Two cookies," and the parent responds, "There are three cookies." The interaction produces a continuous dance of language with the child following the parental lead into the world of words, grammar, and syntax. It is not surprising that youngsters who share rich verbal interchange with helpful adults acquire skills beyond those of children who experience no such joy.

For most two-year-olds usable vocabulary is approaching 200 words. Pronouns are used for the first time, indicating the movement away from exclusive preoccupation with nouns, verbs, and adjectives. "I," "me," and "you" become differentiated, although "I" and "me" remain interchangeable for some time. "My" and "mine" come before other possessives in the toddler's vocabulary (in accord with their egocentric nature). Many two-year-olds still use their proper name, rather than the correct pronoun, when referring to themselves. Investigators who have tabulated the vocabulary of two-year-olds report a range of from 5 to 1212 words; at 30 months the range extends from 30 to 1509 words. These data serve to remind us that individual variation is normal in speech acquisition. Occasionally a child considerably below the norm in speaking skills at 24 months will make an impressive breakthrough and by 30 months be an average, or perhaps even advanced, speaker.

It is important to keep in mind that even trained specialists have difficulty calculating the exact number of words in a child's vocabulary at any given age. When a word is added to the vocabulary, it may not become part of everyday (working) usage; rather, it may remain dormant for several weeks, pop into usage for a few days, and then disappear again. Because the child understands such words when they are used by others, the words become part of the *receptive* vocabulary. On the other hand, some words are used with considerable frequency, even when another word would be more suitable. For these reasons, when a specialist claims that a child has 1150 words in her vocabulary, a certain amount of scientific guesswork is involved. The discrepancy between receptive vocabulary and working vocabulary must be taken into account when assessing children's verbal abilities.

Table 5-1   Vocabulary Growth in Children

Age (years and months)	Average Number of words
0-8	0
0-10	1
1-0	3
1-3	19
1-6	22
1-9	118
2-0	272
2-6	446
3-0	896
3-6	1222
4-0	1540
4-6	1870
5-0	2072
5-6	2290
6-0	2562

From "An investigation of the Development of the Sentence and the Extent of Vocabulary in Young Children." by M.E. Smith, *University of Iowa Studies in Child Welfare,* 1926, 3(5). Reprinted by permission of University of Iowa Press.

Infant Communication

Arnold Gesell's pioneering research provided us with perhaps the richest body of information ever assembled by a single developmental psychologist. The following information highlights some Gesell's findings concerning communication trends during the first half of toddlerhood.

Gesell's Developmental Sequences for Infant Communication (15-24 months)

15 months

1. Uses total-response gestures.
2. Indicates refusal by bodily protest.
3. Responds to key words, repeatedly used by mother or father.

18 months

1. Communicates both by gestures and words, but words are beginning to replace gestures.
2. Responds to simple commands.
3. Verbalizes ends of actions such as "bye-bye," "thank you," "all gone."
4. Refusals may be expressed by "no" but more usually by bodily response.

21 months

1. Asks for food, toilet, drink.
2. Repeats single words said to him, or last word or two of a phrase.

24 months

1. Speech accompaniment of activity.
2. Asks questions such as "What's that?"
3. Verbalizes immediate experiences.
4. Much vocalization in a group, but little conversation.
5. Refers to himself by name.
6. Refusals expressed by "no."

(adapted from Gesell, 1940)

The trends observed by Gesell in the late 40s parallel the speech development of most toddlers in the 80s and 90s. However, they are not *completely* appropriate for all toddlers. With increased parental encouragement, with greater verbal enrichment, some babies today are ahead of the developmental milestones put forth by Gesell. Speech, as we have already noted, is more susceptible to environmental enrichment than walking or crawling. An enriched environment *tends* to improve children's communication abilities.

The Leap into Sentences:

Language at Thirty Months

Prior to this age most children speak as though they were sending a telegram, eliminating all unnecessary words. Messages are direct, to the point and possess little literary merit; allusion and metaphor are nonexistent. At two and a half children mature beyond purely descriptive speech, but it will be another year before they can speak with sufficient skill to hold the attention of adults. At 30 months new words are added every day, and children go out of their way to learn the proper label for an object or person. They enjoy rehearsing and flit about a room naming object after object. Toddlers engage in this behavior even without praise; it is part of their built-in programming for mastery and competence. As with so many toddler developments, the practice of words is its own reward.

At 30 months few toddlers still babble; phrases usually have communicative intent, and sentences may be five words or longer. Children understand rather well what is said to them, which is just as well, because parents expect their verbal commands, even complex ones, to be acted on. Words have praise value, and toddlers go to painstaking lengths to receive a "What a good boy" or "You are my most wonderful helper." Toddlers especially enjoy the gestures of affection that accompany verbal praise, but they willingly accept spoken praise alone – a landmark in the socialization process.

As one would expect, the slight maturational superiority of females during the early childhood years is manifested in their greater facility with words. At three years girls surpass boys in many areas of speech development, including vocabulary size, length and complexity of sentences, and general communicative ability. The developmental difference between normal girls and boys at this age is from three to six calendar months. Even among girls, however, words are not used to precisely differentiate reality from fantasy, and sometimes the only way to determine whether the 30-month-old child is talking about a dream or an actual event is to ask her outright.

A Renaissance of Words:

Language at Thirty-Six Months

Toddlers now have about 1000 words in their working vocabulary and comprehension of thousands more. Speech is intelligible even to strangers, and grammatical complexity is roughly that of colloquial adult language. At 36 months the child may introduce the main points of a message with appropriate comments rather than stating only the exact message. By the third birthday toddlers spontaneously initiate conversations that have no purpose other than social pleasure.

Despite impressive achievements in the acquisition of language, the toddler has trouble with many particulars of speech, especially prepositions. A command in which a preposition plays a central role ("Get the paper under the table") usually meets with failure unless the child knows that the paper is somewhere in the vicinity of the table.

If mother says, "Go in the bedroom and bring me the . . ." she is surprised when her toddler goes searching into the bedroom. The child does this because mother's tone indicates command, and from the particular words the child knows that she is expected to retrieve something. Lack of cortical maturity prevents her from realizing that the first part of a command is meaningless (or at least ambiguous) without its conclusion. (Adults learning a second language encounter similar difficulties when dealing with someone who speaks too rapidly.)

Perhaps the most significant breakthrough at this age is the ability to talk about nonpresent events. The three-year-old talks about past events, although future happenings are discussed in more restricted terms. Compound and complex sentences emerge, and usually plurality and past tense are mastered. The toddler is creative at inventing past-tense words that are grammatically sound but technically incorrect, such as "runned," "sitted," "taked," "eated," and "wented." Interestingly, the toddler has probably passed through a phase in which the irregular past tense, such as went and sat, were used properly. The seeming regression to incorrect usage occurs because the child first learns correct irregular forms from imitation and "then discovers the 'ed' rule for past tenses and generalizes the rule to all possible verbs. Only very slowly does she rediscover that not all words work that way, and the irregular past tenses have to be learned all over again as exceptions to the rule" (Bee, 1989, p. 148).

Language in Deaf Children

Children born deaf do not learn speech unless they are given special instruction, and even then speech usually is weak and underdeveloped. If a child is born with normal hearing and becomes deaf before the age of four, he will not speak as an adult without special instruction. The native abilities that regulate the acquisition of speech do not unfold if words are not heard. If the child becomes deaf between the ages of four and six, learning of grammatical rules is especially difficult. Children who have heard speech even for a short period of time are more proficient at acquiring language than children born deaf, because even minimal exposure to sounds facilitates the acquisition of speech. Interestingly, children who are born deaf pass through the same stages of *very early* language as normal infants. They coo at about three months and babble at about six months; however, advanced vocalizations and speech are severely curtailed. Because of the normality of sound making in the very young deaf infant, deafness may go undiagnosed for several weeks or months if routine medical examinations are not conducted.

Summary: Linguistic Genius or Super Computer?

Just as psychologists in the early decades of this century were fascinated with the child-as-machine metaphor, psychologists in the latter decades are fascinated with the child-as-computer metaphor. The fields of cybernetics and computer technology have inspired the mind-as-computer metaphor, and has also encouraged the image of the growing child as an increasingly complex symbol-manipulating system. Many of these comparisons are in order since children are information processing "systems" who handle a complex flow of data and information and who solve difficult tasks and problems. Differences do exist, however, and even in the 90s the science of computer technology lags far behind the linguistic capacities of the five-year-old, if not in power certainly in complexity.

In order to equal the speaking capacities of a five-year-old child, a computer would have to be capable of (1) inferring the intent of ambiguous messages, (2) putting into context words or phrases that do not make sense, (3) omitting words not central to the verbal message being received, (4) reconstructing the meaning of words when they are used humorously (when adults use words playfully the intended meaning is often the opposite of the spoken meaning), (5) spontaneously inventing new words, and (6) distinguishing pretend words from real words. Most assuredly, the state of computer technology is far from attaining these language comprehension abilities.

In the span between the eighteenth and thirty-sixth months the child completes the transition from a pre-verbal to a word dominated organism. Thus, in 540 days the human toddler accomplishes what other primates have been unable to accomplish in a million generations.

The Pursuit of Toddler Excellence: The Superbaby Syndrome

The 80s witnessed a phenomenon for which there was no equivalent in the 40s, 50s or 60s: the commercialization of educational programs designed to teach two-three-and four-year-olds to read, write, calculate numbers and even operate computers. "Maximize your baby's potential" is the message, and super babies are the promised product. Perhaps the single most prominent person in this recent phenomenon is Glen Doman, author of *How to Teach Your Child to Read,* (translated into 16 languages), and founder of the Better Baby Institute, where parents learn to educate their infants.

Toddlers, being the remarkable creatures they are, have responded with impressive accomplishments in these enriched and accelerated programs. Many have learned addition and subtraction with a facility unthinkable only 30 years ago.

The parents of these children tend to possess distinctive features in their own right: reading to their babies before they are born, taking them to the gym at 6-months, violin lessons at two-years, competitive gymnastics at four. One commentator known for an objective eye had this to say about parents of "super babies:"

> Most consumers of superbaby programs are successful couples who postponed parenthood until their 30's. Older and wealthier than most new parents, they are convinced that there are lessons for everything. Their own identities are founded in their achievements, and they want their baby – often their only baby – to be a high achiever, too. They approach parenthood in much the same way they approach their careers: planning ahead and working overtime. Their child must be prepared, they feel, for the quality preschool program that leads to the right nursery school that feeds into the prestigious kindergarten. (Scarr, 1983, p. 163)

Fascination with superbabies runs higher among parents than among professional educators. As of this writing (1990) the general consensus among preschool educators and developmental psychologists is that accelerated programs run the risk of negative side effects on the child's social and emotional development. Some kids suffer from achievement anxiety, and others from reduced interpersonal skills. Very few developmental psychologists believe that the benefits which derive from massive intervention at this age have long-term value. The mood among contemporary experts (which does fluctuate from decade to decade) is that it just isn't worth the strain, the cost, or the loss of play time to accelerate children this rapidly.

Parents do well to remember that toddlers and preschool age children require:

1. A secure, predictable environment so that they can learn to anticipate events and to make choices,
2. A stable relationship with a responsive care-giver who is sensitive to the child's interests and needs,
3. Respect for the child as an active participant in the family and not merely a passive recipient of training,
4. Ample space in which to play, and other kids to play with, and
5. Achievements and accomplishments relevant to the social world in which they live.

The Major Concepts of this Chapter

1. Developmentalists suggest that children possess an inherent drive toward competency which results in curiousity and the desire to explore.
2. Egocentrism influences every phase of the child's existence. Perceptual egocentrism, emotional egocentrism and intellectual egocentrism are dominant features of thought during toddlerhood.
3. The development of self awareness is guided by an awareness of adult standards, the desire to master tasks, and an unfolding understanding of "me." As self awareness develops so does the range of emotions experienced by the toddler.
4. In early toddlerhood the need to attain competence is manifested by trial-and-error experimentation followed by mental experimentation. Expansion of memory capacity and the emergence of object constancy are further manifestations of intellectual development. Transductive reasoning is the precursor to further logical reasoning and is the primary logical mechanism of toddlerhood.
5. Language development requires brain maturation, exposure to language, reinforcement for the use of language and a genetically based capacity for symbolization. Language development in toddlerhood is characterized by a progression from first words near the first birthday, to a few additional words near the fifteenth month. Rapid development of the area of the brain responsible for speech (Broca's area) is accompanied

by vast increase in word production between 18 and 24 months. By 30 months speech has communicative intent and sentences may be as long as five words. At 36 months speech is intelligible, socially appropriate and can refer to nonpresent events.

6. The "superbaby" syndrome of the 1980s refers to the proliferation of educational programs designed to accelerate the development of the infant and toddler. Some psychologists doubt the benefits of these programs and suggest there are detrimental effects (e.g., achievement anxiety, negative effects on social and emotional development).

7. Toddlers and preschoolers require a secure and predictable environment which allows for ample play and achievement opportunities in the context of respect for the child as an active, valued family member.

6

The Origins of Selfhood:
The Dynamics of Toddlerhood Growth

Children do need to be guided and reminded and
corrected – no matter how well disposed the are –
and that's the truth.
Benjamin Spock

The phenomenal transformations brought into existence by the staggering intellectual and speech abilities of the toddler are not the only achievements of this developmental period. An additional spectrum of developments are simultaneously asserting themselves which solidify the toddler's position in the world of childhood. These developments are usually referred to as "personality and social," but the more general term "dynamics" seems equally appropriate.

In this chapter we will overview the inner dimensions of toddler development, focusing on the subjective dynamics which mould the developing child.

Affection and Attachment

During toddlerhood affection and attachment are intermingling forces. They are among the most powerful and compelling features of childhood, even though we understand them in only a limited scientific way. Fortunately, we possess a wealth of knowledge at the human level from which our investigations of affection and attachment may begin.

Affection

At one year of age the child is affectionate, sensitive and has formed the solid beginnings of emotional attachments. The one-year-old feels anxious when separated from loved ones and gains reassurance upon their return. During the next two years, he learns to give love in addition to merely receiving it, and to contribute more tangibly and substantively to the love relationship.

All toddlers possess a fundamental need for affection and they are genetically programmed so that this need is *gratified by embrace and caress.* All primates (including humans) have a genetically based predisposition toward receiving contact comfort. Harlow's research with monkeys confirmed their need for contact, and the observational studies of human infants conducted by Bowlby (1952), Spitz (1965), and Goldfarb (1947) confirmed its importance to humans. The need for touch and caress is so powerfully ingrained in our nature that Spitz reported that a severe lack of contact comfort from the sixth through the fourteenth month may cause irreparable damage, possibly even death to the human infant.

Specialists in child behavior know that normal children enjoy *giving* as well as *receiving* affection and that contact comfort has the power to restore confidence and security. They also agree that healthy interaction between parent and child involves considerable contact beyond that which is required to satisfy all other physical or psychological needs.

Toddlers learn that a smiling embrace or an acknowledgment of care is a powerful adult reinforcer. The parent, upon whom nature imposes a special susceptibility to toddler affection, is emotionally vulnerable to these gestures. The toddler extracts love from adults. Thus, part of toddlers' lovability lives in their capacity to make adults want to love them.

Attachment

What is attachment? According to Mary Ainsworth, who has made enduring contributions to our understanding of this process, attachment may be defined as "an affectional tie that one person or animal forms between himself and another specific one – a tie that binds them together in space and endures over time" (1973, p. 42).

Psychologists view attachment as among the most important forces in the formation of personality. Erik Erikson, perhaps the most prominent personality theorist since Freud, believed that attachment is the foundation upon which child personality is established. Erikson claimed that the first major crisis in childhood is the formation of trust, which is based upon the child's effective attachment to mother. If a secure and loving attachment is not formed, the child responds with a sense of mistrust, which adversely affects further personality growth and development.

The Origins of Attachment during the First Two Years of Life

The most widely accepted explanation of human attachment is found in *ethological theory*. This theory understands human behavior in terms of its survival value and its evolutionary function. A significant contributor to ethological theory, John Bowlby, observed and described infant attachment with considerable precision. Bowlby emphasized that a baby comes into the world equipped to interact (in a primitive way) with a caregiver, and the baby's role in this interaction actually triggers the mother to respond even more – this interaction contributes greatly to the infant's chances of survival. The attachment bond, for all intents and purposes, is anchored in our biological nature.

Humans are more complex than lower animals, and the attachment process for us does not remain stable or unchanging. It modifies with time, especially with the increase in baby's abilities. The end-product of attachment during the first two years is for the child to attain enough self-reliance to become at least somewhat independent of mother.

The Developmental Sequence of Human Attachment (Bowlby's theory).

1. *The preattachment phase (birth to 6 weeks).* – At this age the infant exhibits a series of genetically programmed reflexes such as smiling, tracking, and crying which have some survival value. Infants seem (there is not unanimous agreement on this) to be soothed more effectively by their own mother, and to respond to soothing and holding. This stage represents the primitive beginnings of human attachment, bonding and love.

2. *The increasing attachment phase (6 weeks to 8 months)* – At this stage baby orients toward, responds to, and has a strong preference for mother. The attachment is not "solid," however, and the infant usually does not protest when separated from mother. At this stage of attachment the infant may protest when isolated for too long, but usually is not overly distraught by brief separation from mother.

3. *The phase of solid attachment (8 months to about 2 years)* – Attachment to the mother is now solid and unmistakable. When mother departs unexpectedly baby experiences anxiety. Attachment is physical in that baby follows mother wherever she goes in the house. At 18 months some toddlers become fearful or weepy when they sense that mother is getting ready to leave the house. Attachment in this phase is rendered more powerful by the fact that *object permanence* is now part of the child's cognitive repertoire. Therefore, "out of sight" is not "out of mind." Baby howls and complains when mother is gone because she knows that she is somewhere. Interestingly, infants who attain object permanence early tend to manifest separation anxiety early.

4. *The formation of a reciprocal relationship (begins about 2 years)* – In this phase of attachment the child has outgrown the genetic programs of

Phase 1, the generalized attachments of Phase 2, and the fearful anxiety of Phase 3. Now, in the final phase of toddlerhood attachment, the child manifests more systematically the benefits of representational thought, and increased skills of social engineering. The child now better understands (and accepts) that mother will come and go in the course of a day, but that she will return. Toddlers learn about schedules and routines, therefore, separation anxiety lessens. Toddlers also learn how to do things with mother, and thereby share her presence more completely than merely being near her. Toddlers who are provided with interesting play alternatives tend to get over mother absence rather quickly. Some youngsters at age three anticipate mother's departure in a matter-of-fact way, bringing her purse, or saying "See you later, Mommy."

Thus, in the two-year period since birth the attachment process undergoes considerable change. Once attachment has been formed, however, it retains a powerful force throughout the childhood years.

Attachment to the Working Mother

In most North American families it is mother to whom the child forms the strongest attachment during the first years of life, because it is the mother who most frequently spends the day at home with baby. However, with a growing number of mothers working outside the home, a question of particular relevance is, "To what extent does the daily separation of mother and child influence the child's attachment to the mother?" The following response to this question was based upon research conducted in the 70s, and it seems as appropriate now as then:

> First, it seems very clear from the available research that it is not whether or not the mother works that is important for the child's well-being but what kind of alternative care is provided. In particular, it seems to matter whether or not the alternative care is stable over a period of time. The child seems quite able to form attachments both to her natural family and to alternative caretakers, but her emotional and mental health seem better when there aren't a lot of shifts from one caretaker to another. (Bee, 1989, P. 247)

This remains a widely accepted viewpoint on the matter of mother-child separation. Most experts also agree that the most important variable in mother-child interaction is not the amount of time spent with the child but rather the quality of the interaction between the two and the extent to which affection and warmth permeate the relationship. In other words, it is the quality rather than the quantity of the relationship that most matters.

Research indicates that children who spend the day with caregivers other than the mother do not have less mother attachment than children who spend each day at home with their mother. Bee concludes that "we can say with reasonable confidence that alternate care . . . does not interfere with the child's attachment to her own mother if the separation occurs at 1 year or later.

Before that we cannot be as confident" (1989, p. 248).

The Prototype Hypothesis

It is not known how attachments formed during childhood influence our later attachments. This topic has been of both popular and scientific interest for the past several decades. Some of the most influential thinkers in modern psychology believed that early childhood attachments exert significant influence on all future attachments and, perhaps, all love relationships. Sigmund Freud and John Bowlby, though for quite different reasons, claimed that the child's first attachment becomes a foundation for future bondings. This is sometimes known as the *prototype hypothesis* because first attachments become a prototype for attachments throughout life.

Believers in the prototype hypothesis argue that one's sense of trust toward the world and the willingness to share one's self with another person are greatly influenced by early attachments. Therefore, first attachments in which parents provide little love, or parents who give love then hostility, produce a child who feels unwanted or unworthy. On the other hand, first attachments of unconditional love produce a child who feels wanted, worthy, and willing to give love.

The prototype hypothesis holds an intuitive appeal even though, like most hypotheses which link the events of childhood with adulthood, it has little convincing evidence to persuade the doubting disbeliever. Perhaps the most convincing "evidence" stems from our recognition that youngsters who undergo *extremely negative experiences* in their early years are susceptible to emotional disturbances in later life. This link appears time and again in our study of emotionally disturbed adolescents and adults. The link is not without weaknesses, however, because we simply do not know how many youngers have terrible relationships early in life and nevertheless develop into healthy and loving adults. (Healthy adults rarely seek psychotherapy, therefore, we know little about their childhood relationships.)

We do not understand in any precise sense how loving attachments in childhood affect later attachments. Very few adults are able to accurately recollect the quality of their attachments in infancy and toddlerhood, and very few parents write verifiable reports on this topic. The net effect of all this is that the prototype hypothesis is a hypothesis which is difficult to confirm or deny. Therefore, generalizations about it are extremely tenuous.

Fears, Anxieties and Apprehensions

No passion so effectively robs the mind
of all its powers of acting and reasoning as fear
Edmund Burke

Despite abundant talents for exploration, adventure, and, occasional destruction, toddlers are not the swashbuckling daredevils one might think after observing them in the protective confines of their household. Actually, a streak of cowardice marks toddlers, and, like the antiheroes of contemporary cinema, they make no attempt to hide their lack of courage. When frightened, they run away, cry, whimper, and shun conversation.

Unfamiliar environments and unknown adults cause apprehension, uncertainty, and downright fear in most toddlers. For the most part, these fears are not overcome until the child is assured that the unknown person (or environment) is not dangerous or threatening.

Fear is first experienced during the first year of life, when the infant reacts to strangers, as well as to separation from mother, with fear. During toddlerhood a sharp increase in fears occurs, and by the third birthday children have more fears than at any other time during the first ten years of life.

For our purposes toddlerhood fears are divided into three general categories: (1) fear of strangers; (2) fear of separation; and (3) general fears and anxiety. Other categories could work almost as well, but here we have the opportunity to observe the relationship between toddler fears and normal developmental progressions.

Fear of Strangers

Fear of strangers appears during the first year of life, most typically between the seventh and tenth months. At first infants react to strangers with a blank, empty expression more suggestive of uncertainty than fear. In time this reaction changes to apprehension, and eventually into outright fear. Some psychologists believe that stranger anxiety comes into existence when the child learns that the presence of a stranger signals the departure of the parents – as the case with a babysitter. From this perspective, fear of strangers really is distress over losing one's parent. Other psychologists claim that fear of strangers is exhibited *before* the infant has unpleasant experiences with strangers, and this viewpoint has the most adherents. Many mothers have found themselves explaining to a doting grandparent: "She's never acted like this before. I can't imagine what's wrong with her today!"

Some babies do not exhibit stranger anxiety at all, whereas others are frozen with fear. Adults, far more than children, elicit stranger anxiety. When another child unexpectedly appears in the room toddlers rarely respond with fear – although they initially show cautious reserve.

Some researchers claim that fear of strangers derives from the discrepancy between what the child sees and what he expects to see. Thus, when the child is accustomed to seeing mother, the appearance of another person evokes fear. This viewpoint has credence among some psychologists, but others find it lacking, because youngsters sometimes respond to perceptual inconqruity with smiles or even laughter. Thus, when mother makes unfamiliar sounds with a protruding tongue and extended lip, baby may find this funny and laugh out loud. So difference, unto itself, does not create fear.

Human infants are not the only primates to fear strangers. Newborn chimps, like humans, show no fear of strangers at a very early age but soon acquire it. Whether they are taught this by older chimps, or whether it emerges as part of their instinctual repertoire is not known – just as it is not known in humans.

To further compound the issue, fear of strangers is influenced by the child's base of security – that is, by the presence of someone or something that reassures the child. Some toddlers, when safely held in the protective arms of mother, are not the least bit frightened by strangers; however, they may experience sheer panic if they have to confront the stranger on their own. Stranger anxiety can thus be understood in two distinct contexts: (1) coping with strangers when mother is present and (2) coping with strangers when mother is absent. (Mother refers to the adult who cares for the child; obviously, this could be the father or a guardian. In our culture, however, it most frequently is the mother.)

When an unfamiliar person enters the room toddlers scurry directly to mother, whereupon they latch onto a leg or somehow indicate that they want to be held. If the stranger proceeds directly to the child, she will offer a hesitant greeting at best and tears of fright at worst. Within moments, however, curiousity usually gets the better of the toddler as she slowly disengages from mother and ambulates toward the visitor. Confidence remains tenuous and a sudden burst of laughter or an unexpected facial grimace may send the toddler scrambling back to mother's protection. In most cases the toddler overcomes fear of the stranger within five minutes, especially if mother "protection" is available when needed.

In an attempt to gather data on stranger fear in children one researcher conducted a study in which 36 infants (18 boys and 18 girls) were observed over a period of time (Schaffer, 1966). The infants were observed at home (with their mothers present) every four weeks during the first year. Their reactions to strangers were recorded, and several interesting findings emerged. It was noted that smiling at strangers began to decrease at about three to five months; before this age strangers were met in the same way as familiar individuals. As the child aged, strangers elicited a cautious stare, with very few, if any, friendly overtures from the baby. Finally, at about eight months, the baby developed a "frozen" reaction to strangers, and some actually showed outright fear that dissipated only after comforting from mother. This sequence of reactions to strangers has been observed by pediatricians for decades (and by mothers for centuries), however, in this study careful documentation has confirmed the systematic emergence of stranger fear in North American infants.

Children's fear of strangers is inversely proportional to the number of adults they interact with each day. That is, the more adults encountered during the course of normal living, the less fear shown to a stranger, and, the fewer adults encountered the greater the fear. It is unclear whether the number of adults encountered creates greater trust or whether the child just quits noticing them so much. Both hypotheses seem reasonable.

Stranger anxiety is not restricted to fear of people. Toddlers frequently display a general restlessness in a strange environment. In general, toddlers have a mild apprehension of anything too different. In most kids, stranger anxiety weakens considerably before their fourth birthday, eventually to become shyness, timidity, or merely reserve. It is, in essence, a form of stage fright in the social theatre.

Fear of Separation

The mother is the child's lifeline to the outside world. The child clings emotionally to this lifeline, and soon the bond between them becomes so powerful that the child fears separation even for short lengths of time. The anxiety that sweeps through the child when separated from mother is known as *separation anxiety.*

Bowlby (1952) initially formulated the hypothesis that separation from mother automatically elicits anxiety in the infant over 28 weeks. Bowlby believed anxiety occurs because the child has a genetic disposition toward clinging and following, and, when these are severed, as in separation, the child experiences anxiety. Separation anxiety is a primary human response which is "instinctual" rather than learned. It is part of our hereditary package.

In his investigations of hospitalized children between the ages of 15 and 30 months, Bowlby observed a consistent pattern triggered by separation from mother. The pattern follows a sequence of (1) protest, (2) despair, and (3) detachment, with each stage having its own unique characteristics. Bowlby comments, "Should his stay in a hospital or residential surgery be prolonged . . . [the child] will in time act as if neither mothering nor contact with humans had much significance for him. After a series of upsets of losing several mother figures to whom in turn he has given much trust and affection, he will gradually commit himself less and less to succeeding figures and in time will stop altogether taking the risk of attaching himself to anyone." These tendencies manifest themselves in disinterest, minimal affective responsiveness, and neutrality toward life in general.

A classic example of the separation syndrome observed by Bowlby is described in the case of Laura, who at age 30 months was brought into hospital for a minor operation. Bowlby describes her changes during an eight-day hospital stay.

1. The first day she was cheerful as she met the admitting nurse. Upon bathing, etc., she began to scream and cry for mommy. She became calm after a few minutes. When alone she appeared calm, but when a friendly person arrived her feelings became known. Throughout the first day she

asked for mommy and showed anxiety and apprehension.

2. During the second day she began to look strained and sad; she gave little response to the nurse. Her parents visited her 30 minutes after her operation. She reached for mother and cried "I want to go home." She was subdued because of her stitches. She waved slightly upon the parents' departure.

3. The third day she was quiet, nondemanding, spent much of her time clutching her teddy bear. She cried for mommy after the nurse played with her for a while. This reaction was very consistent – whenever she was by herself she displayed passivity and detachment, but when a friendly person played with her she would become remorseful and cry for her mother. When mother visited, it took Laura 15 minutes to "warm up to her." When mother left, Laura was remorseful, but did not show it by crying.

4. During the fourth day she played wildly with her doll. Her mother did not visit.

5. On the fifth day the mother visited again and there was a thawing period. When the mother left Laura she cried lightly but soon stopped.

6. The sixth day another child was admitted who cried a great deal. Laura said "You are crying because you want your mommy . . . she'll come tomorrow."

7. On the seventh day both parents visited. Laura showed no excitement when the chairs were being set up, even though she knew what this meant. Laura made no attempt to go to her mother when she entered the room. She remained subdued. When they left the room Laura mumbled quietly, "I want to go with you." She seemed to almost ignore the departure of her mother.

8. Laura cried heavily in the morning. She had been told the night before that she would be leaving in the morning. She remained cautious when her mother arrived. Not until her outdoor shoes were placed in the room did she accept the fact that she was really going home. She demanded that she be able to take all her "possessions." On the way out she was seen walking apart from her mother.

The progressive distancing Laura experienced and her gradual decline of emotional investment are not uncommonly observed in toddlers too long separated from their parents without quality caregivers as replacements.

Separation anxiety and stranger anxiety do not traumatize the normal child and should not be understood as inherently destructive experiences. They are developmental realities made either more difficult or more tolerable by the quality of the toddler's emotional world. The most significant factor in the child's reaction to separation or to strangers, however, is the base of security.

The Base of Security

Harry Harlow's studies with young monkeys are widely known for their contribution to our understanding of contact-comfort during the early years of life. Harlow's experiments also cast light on the importance of mother as a "base of security."

Harlow and his co-workers conducted dozens of investigations during the 50s and 60s into numerous facets of the child-mother relationship in various species of monkeys. In one experiment (Harlow and Zimmerman, 1959) the effects of being "reared" by an inanimate object rather than a real mother were investigated. A terry-cloth mother provided milk through a bottle placed approximately where the mother's breast would be. Being inanimate, it did not move or provide any of the personal comforts of a mother, but, being made of terry cloth, it was soft enough to climb on and snuggle up to. Young monkeys raised under these conditions appear normal in many respects, especially when playing in isolation. Harlow, however, observed some significant changes in these monkeys; most importantly, monkeys living with their natural mothers have more "courage" than their deprived peers and respond less fearfully to frightening objects.

Harlow found that when he placed a fearful object (a large plastic ant) in the play arena, young monkeys immediately flee to mother for protection. The flight to "mother" is intense and uninterrupted – the monkeys were frightened. Upon reaching mother, the monkeys would jump on her, press against her, hold tightly to her arms and shoulders, and slide up and down her front. In time the panic would subside, and, although still not completely at ease, the monkeys would cling less tightly and stop rocking altogether, moving their head away from the breast. Eventually they would climb down from mother, their courage bolstered. Cautiously they would approach the fearful plastic ant, sufficiently cautious that sudden activity from another part of the room would trigger their flight. Within a few minutes the young monkeys would be disassembling the plastic monster, having been transformed from quivering, frightened creatures into normal, curious explorers. Harlow discovered that young monkeys with real mothers recuperated much more quickly and demonstrated greater confidence than monkeys that had a terry cloth "mother."

In another Harlow study, monkeys that did not have a mother to run to remained in a state of fear considerably longer than monkeys for which a mother (real or artificial) was available. Monkeys that had never experienced mother comfort hid face down in a corner, regressing to the fetal position or autistic rocking. The fearful object frightened them beyond their coping resources.

Three conclusions are typically extracted from these famous studies: (1) the mother figure instills courage in the young monkey after it has been frightened; (2) the young monkey instinctively races to mother in an emergency and clings to her until confidence has been restored; and (3) monkeys that have never known mother security (even that provided by an artificial mother) have virtually no capacity to cope with fear, even when it is triggered by motionless plastic ants.

For the toddler, mother is far more than a life preserver in a sea of troubles; she is the builder of confidence and assurance. The mother, unquestionably, is more than a source of love and comfort, more than a need gratifier and caregiver: she is as well the source of emotional rejuvenation the toddler requires to cope with an unpredictable, and sometimes fearful world.

General Toddlerhood Fears

The months near the third birthday show the greatest incidence of fears of the entire childhood period. Girls are most fearful at about 36-six months, boys at about 42 months – the time lag typical of many boy-girl developmental differences.

At age three dogs are feared more commonly than anything else; by age four this distinction has been usurped by the dark. Near the fourth birthday the number of fears begins a decline that will continue until about age nine or ten.

Size is not a major factor in toddler fears. An insect may trigger a fear reaction of greater intensity than a locomotive. Interestingly, mentally advanced children have fears correspondent with their mental age rather than their chronological age.

Because the toddler distinguishes poorly between real and imaginary objects, during the third year a significant increase in fear of imaginary creatures occurs. Many normal three-year-olds spend sleepless bedtime hours watching fearfully the weightless, wavelike "creatures" outlined on their wall, who at any moment may swoop down. Reassurance from Mom and Dad that there is no basis for these fears makes toddlers somewhat less fearful, not because they are convinced there is nothing to fear, but because the brief moment of parent conversation bolsters their courage. As toddlers age they learn about the stigma associated with letting their fears be known and they become more reluctant to talk about them. Toddlers invariably become frightened when they sense their parents are frightened; parental fear is more contagious than parental confidence.

Specific fears (dogs, ladders) do not inhibit the toddler as much as general fears (darkness, strangers). The most destructive fear to the emotional well-being of the toddler is the subterranean (unconscious) fear that the *world in general* is dangerous. Psychologists have not given a name to this pervasive fear, however, it resembles *basic mistrust*. This fear, more than any other, impedes psychological and social growth during the formative years of toddlerhood.

When all is said and done, most toddlerhood fears are caused by one or more of the following circumstances: (1) anticipation of being physically harmed, or of pain in general; (2) sudden unwanted changes in stimulation; (3) lack of congruity between what is expected and what actually happens; and (4) anticipation of loss of people who provide love, comfort, and security.

Helping Children Cope with Fears

Some fears are inevitably interwoven with growing up: fear of the dark, fear of strangers, fear of death or illness. Other fears result from specific events, i.e., being bitten by a dog. However a fear happens to develop, it usually can be lessened with effective adult assistance. A few guidelines for helping children cope with their fears include the following:

1. Help children understand their fears. Factual information often lessens fear, especially when the child does not know much about the feared object. Thunder storms are terrifying to many youngsters because they sound scary and because children usually have no idea what causes them. A brief, low-key explanation of what creates thunder may lessen the fear, especially when reassured that little chance of harm exists.

2. Act calmly. Children become fearful when they see, or sense, fear in adults. Conversely, when a adult is calm and unafraid in a fearful situation this often exerts a calming effect on the youngster.

3. Gradual approximation. An unrealistic fear may be eliminated by approaching the feared object in gradual, brief increments. If the feared object is a tame dog which poses no threat (as contrasted with the dog who bit the child last year) the fear may be lessened by first escorting the child into the backyard (briefly) with the animal, later approaching closer while the dog is leashed, then touching the dog while the dog is being held by a parent, then touching the dog while the child is being held by the parent, then finally, touching the dog while standing alone. This procedure might take an hour or two, even a day or two, depending on the intensity of the fear. Usually, the fear will be overcome by this series of gradual approximations.

4. Base of security. Establish firmly in the youngster's mind the belief that a base of security is always available when he becomes fearful. The base of security being, in most instances, mother or father. It is important that a child know (sense) that no matter what happens, he will be "bailed out" when danger beckons.

The Phenomenology of Impotence:

Frustration and Anger

> *There are times when parenthood seems nothing
> but feeding the mouth that bites you.*
> Peter De Vries

Temper tantrums – Some toddlers, especially between 18 and 30 months, throw temper tantrums everyday, sometimes three or four times per day. Almost all books written for parents of young children deal with temper tantrums because they are especially bewildering and frustrating to parents who cannot make sense out of the "who, what, when or why" of tantrums. Temper tantrums rarely occur during the first year of life, as well, tantrums are not as prevalent during the preschool years (three to six) as during toddlerhood. Toddlerhood is a period for temper tantrums because the child experiences a great deal of frustration and possesses very few resources for dealing with it.

"When a child has a tantrum she simply is going to pieces emotionally for a while . . . all systems are out of control. This is not a time for parents to use restraint; this will only drive her screams higher and her kicking wilder. If the child is not harming herself bodily, the most effective means of control is to let the tantrum spin itself out" (Caplan & Caplan, p. 37). When calm has returned, parents should look into the events that *lead up to the outburst*. Frustration (the toddler's constant companion) is the most common cause of tantrums.

A good deal of frustration for two-year-olds stems from their inability to fend effectively in big-people's world. Most things are just too big, or too unwieldy for the toddler to do with as she wants. The toddler wants to do *everything* despite her comparative ineptitude:

> The toddler seeks to be in the driver's seat of every car, to push every carriage herself, and throw herself into every doll bed. The two-year-old feels she must play the dominant role in every situation, and perhaps that is her temporary right at this stage because ego building is a necessary first step to developing social competence. (Caplan & Caplan, p. 31)

Dealing with Anger

Parents play an important role in all this because they, more than anyone else, help the child cope with the anger that flows from frustration. The following guidelines are worth noting:

1. *Don't reward temper tantrums.* Kids retain with remarkable tenacity those traits which get them what they want, including temper tantrums and dramatic hysterics. When these lead to desired outcomes, the parent is asking for a repeat performance. Try to remain calm until the tantrum has run its course.

2. *Reward children's attempts to solve problems by reasonable means.* Even when results are not perfect, reinforce conflict resolution via discussions, truces, and compromises.

3. *Don't throw tantrums yourself.* Children repeat what they see. If the parent has temper fits, expect the same from the child. Model appropriate behavior. This doesn't guarantee results, but it improves the chances.

4. *Help children understand what caused their frustration.* Anger can be defused simply by understanding why a frustrating event occurred. "The car had a flat tire and that is why Mommy was so late." "Why do you think the usher asked you to leave the theatre?" "What were you doing that would cause that to happen?" This helps kids to look beyond surface behavior, and to search for causes not readily apparent to their egocentric minds.

Play During Toddlerhood

> *You can do anything with children*
> *if only you play with them*
> Otto Bismarck

Play during toddlerhood can be understood as pleasurable work, but just as correctly it may be thought of as the means by which the child learns about the environment and practices newly developing skills.

Developmental factors influence play, determining in part its content as well as its form, but most significantly by establishing upper limits beyond which the child cannot function effectively. Three developmental factors are especially relevant to understanding the form and the function of childhood play.

1. *Mental and physical maturity* – During the second year toddler's construct block towers, string beads, and repeat simple tasks. They do not participate in play that requires extensive memory, manipulation of very small objects, or respect for abstract rules. The play habits of toddlers are so closely related to their cognitive development and general mental maturity that some psychologists actually observe the quality of their play in order to estimate their IQ and their emotional maturity.

2. *Impulsivity* – Toddlers sometimes quit smack in the middle of a project with no regret or remorse. They have only a limited sense of finality, and it usually matters little to them whether or not they complete what they start.

3. *Basic trust* – Toddler play is greatly influenced by whether they are fearful or confident, outgoing or timid, self-reliant or dependent upon their mother. The force which most influences these issues is basic trust: the child's confidence that he can cope with whatever problems arise and that someone will provide assistance or protection when necessary.

Youngsters without basic trust are inhibited, fearful, and apprehensive and it shows in their play.

Types of Play

Toddlerhood play cannot be truly encapsulated into a classification scheme because its range defies imagination much less categorization. However, if one is willing to lose a bit in the translation, the following general categories can be employed to account for a great deal of toddler play: (1) body-contact play, (2) sense-pleasure play, (3) competence play, and (4) role-rehearsal play. Usually these type of play overlap with one another and always they are executed with more zest than grace, and always they leave the environment in a state of disarray that was not present before play began.

Bouncing, jostling, squeezing, hugging, tickling, embracing, and just plain frolicking are forms of *body-contact play*. Body-contact play usually has no other purpose other than the pleasure it brings to both baby and adult. It is the most ancient form of play; all mammals, especially primates, revel in it. During the first 18 months body contact is the chief form of parent-child interplay. Body-contact play contributes in great measure to the child's sense of physical well-being and her sense of emotional security. Toddlers naturally enjoy body-contact play, as long as it is not too strenuous, and will unashamedly beg for it if they have been too long without it.

Sense-pleasure play produces pleasurable experiences in a way that differs from body-contact play because it involves inanimate objects: "Play with raw materials – water, sand, mud, foodstuffs, whatever – can be viewed as sense-pleasure play, as can masturbation, swinging, bouncing, rocking, scribbling, humming, listening to music, and smelling flowers and other aromatic things" (Stone, 1968, p. 271). Toddlers delight in the sensual pleasure of digging in the sandbox, splashing in the bathtub, rolling down grassy slopes, and swinging on swings. Toddler are, first and foremost, creatures of the body.

Competence play is play which exercises abilities which have relevance outside the world or play. Playing with numbers Sesame Street style is competence play. Middle-class North America supports hundreds of corporations that specialize in competence-play equipment, such as pegboards, moulding clay, bouncing balls, tricycles, storybooks, puzzles, toy clocks, chalkboards, miniature athletic kits, water-color paints, kiddy cars, and an infinite array of skill games.

Role-rehearsal play combines fantasy and dramatic play, with the child acting out important roles and activities. (Playing "house," with mother, father, sister, and brother roles.) Pretend activities such as answering the telephone, greeting visitors, combing hair, scolding inappropriate behavior, and commenting on the excellence of food are examples of role-rehearsal play. This play reaches a zenith among preschoolers, who possess more mature imaginations and more impressive vocabularies than toddlers. Role-rehearsal play is a medium by which the child acts out frustrations, insecurities, and guilt feelings; consequently, it has "therapeutic" utility as well as recreational value.

In "make believe" play children pretend to be whatever they prefer, make rules to suit their liking, and conjure up the finale to the whole show. All forms of play eventually get pressed into service in make-believe play: competence play is involved in building block houses; role-rehearsal play allows the toddler to become mother or police officer; and, of course, sense-pleasure play comes in, as sand, mud, and other messy substances get into the act. Toddlers may decide to be flying grasshoppers encircling the city looking for goodies to eat, but then as quickly abandon this imaginary adventure because mother says they can't leave the yard. Play, as with all toddler developments, is filled with paradoxes and illogicalities.

Progression of play

Social play during toddlerhood follows a moderately predictable sequence. First comes *solitary play* which is simply the child's preoccupied involvement with objects, or with himself; it is not social in nature because it does not involve other people. Near the first birthday *parallel play* emerges, in which the child does not play directly with other children but rather independently in their presence. This is an especially fascinating form of play because in it children really do not take notice of other children playing nearby. Sometimes they bump into one another, or accidentally tip the other off balance, and neither child responds differently than if they bumped into a chair. By late toddlerhood *mixed play* begins in which play is influenced by the presence of others, and toddlers actually modify their behavior to comply with the expectations or demands of other children. Not until after toddlerhood, however, does genuine *cooperative play* take place with any degree of proficiency. Simple games requiring only a minimum of cooperation (such as London Bridge) usually are doomed to failure during toddlerhood (most assuredly during the first half of toddlerhood), but they prosper at age four or five.

The functions of play are diverse, but most psychologists conclude that play creates opportunities for children to explore, to assume new roles, to practice sex roles, and to rehearse important activities they cannot do in real life such as driving a car or shopping for groceries.

Toddlers require a great deal of assistance and supervision in their play. For one thing, they need help getting play started because they do not focus well, and they resist starting something new or unknown. More importantly, their lack of foresight prevents them from predicting which kinds of play may be dangerous, and their lack of self-constraint results in unsupervised play (especially when more than two children are involved) deteriorating into pushing, shouting or biting.

Games and play – Games and play are not the same even though some games are playful and some play naturally evolves into games. Generally speaking, play refers to the child's activities "characterized by freedom from all but personally imposed rules (which are changed at will) by free-wheeling fantasy involvement, and by the absence of any goals outside the activity itself." Games, in more complex vein, "are usually competitive and are characterized by agreed-upon, often externally imposed, rules, by a requirement to use the implements of the activity in the manner for which they are intended and not as fancy suggests, and frequently by a goal or purpose outside the activity, such as winning the game" (Bettleheim, 1987).

Play is an in-and-of-itself phenomenon, it is narcissistic and egocentric, a self-indulgent pleasure with a modicum of purpose. The by-products of play, however, are extremely relevant to the developing child since play is the primary learning mode in the daily routine. Play releases selfish and aggressive tendencies as well as loving and sharing tendencies, it expands the range of parent-child interaction, it cultivates spoken language and body language, it elicits laughter and love from mother and father. Play is the essence of toddler existence.

Games are, so to speak, a different ball game. They attract only after the child has attained the mental and emotional maturity to handle rules and structure. Games subordinate the participant to rules. If you do not (or cannot) adhere to the rules you are expelled from the game or fail in its execution. The egocentrism of toddlerhood opposes games because toddlers will not deny their impulses simply to comply with abstract rules. Preschoolers, and most assuredly, 9- and 10-year-olds are a different matter. They enjoy structure, rules, and competition. They evaluate themselves in terms of game competence, and they take pride in winning games such as checkers. When all is said and done, games have rules and they usually have winners and losers determined by a pre-established set of rules. Play, on the other hand, is its own sport. Toddlers are geared emotionally and intellectually for play; it is their medium for experiencing and actualizing themselves. Games attain their grandeur in a future universe.

The Developmental Tasks of Toddlerhood

During toddlerhood four centrally important developments take place that mark the child's transition from a comparatively helpless creature to one who looks after a considerable number of her own needs, desires, and ambitions. Successful progress through these developmental tasks prepares the child for the biological and social demands of the preschool years. (See Chapter one for a more thorough description of developmental tasks).

Learning to walk – Walking is the most important of all motor achievements because it converts the environment from a narrow, confined area to an open, expansive laboratory for investigation. Toddlers are dominated by the urge to explore – an urge that cannot be fulfilled in the absence of ambulatory skills. Learning to walk heralds the onset of many social behaviors from which the pre-walker is excluded. The impact children make on their household is directly related to their ability to walk; likewise, the impact of the environment on the child depends on the ability to move through the environment and learn from it. The advent of walking greatly expands the role of the environment because the child in now more fully exposed to it.

Learning to talk – Speech is one of the crowning achievements of childhood. As far as is currently known, no other creature shares our advanced capacity for speech. With words come symbols, and with symbols comes an entire new realm of vicarious existence. With words comes the ability to express thoughts and feelings as well as the ability to learn from the thoughts and feelings of others. The toddler works hard at acquiring speech and is not reluctant to interrogate anyone who might provide a morsel of information. The onset of speech affects all other toddler developments – even walking. With speech, the toddler will walk or stop on command and can be guided from one place to another with the spoken word. And the ability to walk allows the child to move to that particular spot in the environment most advantageous for asking questions or presenting arguments.

Learning to control elimination – Humans, no matter what their age, prefer social gatherings where the participants do not spontaneously eliminate waste material. In our society it is expected that by a certain age children will look after their elimination requirements with minimal inconvenience to others. During the first year of life no demands are made in this regard. However, by their third birthday children are expected to have acquired toilet habits fairly similar to those of adults.

Sphincter control depends on maturation as well as learning. The child can't be toilet trained until he is maturationally ready, however, the learning he receives may either facilitate or hinder this biologically based phenomenon. If the child learns to feel guilty or dirty about the natural activity of elimination, these learned responses may actually interfere with effective toilet training. In any event, the preschool child is expected to have control over bowel and bladder, and for the vast majority of children this capacity is acquired during the toddler years.

Learning to be independent – Toddlers work very hard at establishing themselves as independent individuals even though they are extremely dependent in every social and biological regard. The task of toddlerhood is not to attain genuine independence, but to learn elementary gestures of independence. For the most part these are awkward, sometimes stubborn, attempts at self-reliance, but they occur with such persistence that they become part of the toddler's insignia.

Toddlers insist on making their own decisions even when they produce an outcome they don't want; they want to do things for themselves even with only half the proficiency of mother or father.

Sometimes it is easy to confuse unpredictability with independence. The distinction is relevant because a great deal of seemingly "independent" toddler behavior derives from their inability to predict the outcome of their actions. Wearing one's trousers backward stems not from a desire to originate independent clothing trends but from not paying attention to antecedents and outcomes.

When two alternatives present themselves, one sensible and the other not, the toddler usually will choose the former. If, however, an adult makes the more reasonable choice for the toddler, the child may insist on the less desirable alternative simply to exercise choice. No hero, our toddler will change her mind when unwanted consequences accrue from a poor decision. Then again, she may stubbornly suffer through the entire event, deriving a faint sense of triumph from the indirect control over the parents that her suffering brings.

These embryonic flickers of self-conscious independence are the stuff from which childhood self-reliance and rugged individualism originate.

Other Significant Breakthroughs of Toddlerhood

Toilet Training

The ability to control elimination is a complex achievement that depends primarily on maturational readiness and partially on training and practice. Urination (also called *micturition*) is controlled by both voluntary and involuntary muscles: the detrusor muscle is involuntary and is stimulated to contract by impulses from the spinal cord, but the external sphincter is voluntary, and its control becomes possible when the child has achieved maturational readiness, which for most children is between 18 and 30 months. (After all, it takes children more than a year to learn to open and close their hands voluntarily.)

Stories of children toilet trained by their first birthday invariably prove false. What usually is meant is that the child defecates or urinates when placed on the pot; but this occurs because the mother has been alerted by some cue from the child and hurriedly places the baby at the proper location. The ability to defecate or urinate upon locating the correct place is only one aspect of toilet training; the most significant part is voluntary control of the anal and urethral sphincters so that elimination can be temporarily postponed.

Despite individual differences as to when bladder or bowel control is achieved, there is a sequence to which elimination almost universally adheres: (1) walking occurs before bowel control; (2) bowel control occurs before bladder control; and (3) daytime control of bowel and bladder takes place before nighttime control. This sequence unfolds between 18 and 30 months for the majority of children throughout the world.

Developmental psychologists generally agree that toilet training is most efficiently learned within six months of the second birthday. "There seems to be a critical period roughly between the ages one-and-a-half and two years or so in which toilet training happens quite easily (provided the baby's life is going well in general), and outside which [toilet training] can be very strenuous" (Stone & Church, 1968, p. 135).

By middle toddlerhood bowel control is achieved, and when accidents occur they really are accidents. Daytime bladder control is fairly well mastered before the end of the third year, but the child still occasionally fails to make it to the bathroom, often stopping just a few feet short after a desperate sprint from the playground. Despite the high esteem in which bathroom urination is held by parents, for some toddlers the bathroom is little more than an inconvenience. Many toddlers prefer to wet their pants rather than leave the social hub of the sandbox, even though they are perfectly capable of making it home. For the most part, defecation is a different matter, and, whether because of parental censure or merely personal inconvenience, most toddlers show considerable self-displeasure after soiling their pants.

Nighttime bed wetting (*enuresis*) occurs for many children well into the preschool and even early school years. Bed wetting among children five years and older may signal emotional distress, although many bed wetters show no noticeable emotional problems. Some children go to startling lengths, such as changing sheets in the middle of the night, to prevent parents from learning about their bed wetting.

As urine accumulates, the bladder wall stretches, stimulating nerve fibres to transmit impulses to the spinal cord that are then relayed to the brain and interpreted as the desire to urinate. At least three factors contribute to bed-wetting: (1) the child may be a deep sleeper, and the brain may thus not respond to bladder impulses; (2) the bladder may accommodate less than normal volume and therefore require more frequent drainage; and (3) the child may go to sleep with a comparatively full bladder, thus ensuring need for relief before morning. This last factor is widely blamed by parents of children for whom enuresis chiefly occurs when the child is not taken to the toilet in the middle of the night, or when the child consumes a good deal of liquid before bedtime.

The basic premise of maturational readiness, as espoused by Arnold Gesell and other developmentalists, is that children will toilet train *when they are ready* and not before. In the extremely influential *The Second Twelve Months of Life,* the authors make the case that for parents, waiting is better than hurrying when it comes to toilet training their toddler:

Thus parents who are content to wait for toilet learning until their child essentially is ready to "train" herself generally will have no problem with this developmental step. The child needs a model of what to do, the physiological capacity to control the muscles responsible for holding in or letting go purposefully, the cognitive capacity to recognize when she has to go, and the motivation to assume control of her own body functions. (p. 135)

Caplan and Caplan then claim:

When all these elements are present, children will learn fairly quickly to assume control of their own body functions. Until such a time, the parents are merely *training themselves* to catch their child at the right time. At the same time, they might be creating emotional roadblocks to their child's learning on his own when he is ready. (p.136)

The role of maturation in toilet training was ingeniously investigated by McGraw (1940). She experimented with a set of identical twins, starting early after birth with one child in an attempt to establish consistent toilet training. The second twin received no toilet training until he evidenced considerable bladder control. At this point the second twin received the training the first had been receiving for several months. Differences between the twins with regard to toilet training were almost nonexistent. Thus, the months of practice and coaching received by the first twin did not accelerate the onset of sphincter control. The twin who received no practice acquired mature toilet habits very quickly once training commenced, because he was maturationally ready.

A consistent finding is that parents who wait are able to toilet train their youngsters more quickly than parents who begin too soon. This finding reflects an elementary fact of developmental readiness: bladder control does not occur until the regulation of this function has shifted from subcortical to cortical centres; practice before biological maturity is essentially useless.

The following guidelines concerning toilet training are generally accepted by developmental psychologists and pediatricians:

1. Haste, shame, pressure, and anxiety should be avoided during toilet training.

2. The matter should be left largely to the maturational readiness of the baby.

3. The child should be kept clean, dry, and comfortable so he is able to notice the difference when wet or soiled.

4. A comfortable toilet that adjusts to the measurements of the child should be employed.

5. Interest and approval should be shown at the child's successes, but he should not be given the impression that it is the most   important event in the world.

6. Enemas or suppositories should not be used except on a doctor's advice.

7. The total family atmosphere is an important factor in achieving the developmental task of controlling elimination.

Learning to Feed Oneself

The maturational ground plan that regulates human growth during toddlerhood exerts significant influence on the eating habits. Like all toddlerhood skills, feeding oneself undergoes a stunning increase in efficiency and precision. At 18 months toddlers lift a cup to their mouth and drink rather well; grasp a spoon and insert it into a dish; place the spoon in their mouth, usually twisting it slightly before or immediately after putting it into the mouth. By 24 months most toddlers can hold a small glass in one hand and have mastered the art of inserting a spoon without twisting it. They refuse certain foods but they devour others. They will, if allowed, turn their tray into an arena for sense-pleasure play, stirring pudding, grinding potatoes, and stuffing everything squishable into their glass. By 36 months (the end of toddlerhood), they pour liquid from a pitcher, although they have poor judgment about the size of the pitcher they can comfortably handle; they take in food without much messiness on floor or table; and they consume most foods without parental assistance. Three-year-olds will chatter and socialize at the dinner table but must be reminded repeatedly to sit still and remain in the chair. Occasionally at this age the toddler reinforces parental suspicion that civilization is having some effects by offering to assist in setting the table or picking up dishes after the meal.

Eating time abounds with social learning for toddlers. They learn about sharing, etiquette, and conversation. Equally important, they learn how mother and father treat each other and how brother and sister interact with each other at the dinner table. They learn to associate mealtime with anxiety and bickering or with pleasant social intercourse, and in the ultimate scheme of things, this may be the most significant outcome of mealtime gatherings.

Handedness

The fact that most children are right-handed has received considerable attention during the past several decades. The topic is of special interest because we really can't figure out why only about 10 percent of the world's people are left-handed while about 90 percent are right-handed.

Hand preference usually manifests itself during the last part of toddlerhood (in the vicinity of the third birthday), at which time over 80 percent of all children show a preference for using their right hand in situations where either hand would serve as well (such as reaching for an object directly in front of one's face).

T. H. Blau (1974) evaluated thousands of disturbed children and found that a greater proportion of them are left-handed than is true for the population in general. He concludes that left-handed and mixed-handed children are more likely to have behavioral and physical problems during the first five years of life; to have school problems; to have reading, arithmetic, and speech problems; to be enuretic; and to suffer headaches and dizziness. These negative symptoms do not, of course, typify all lefties; they simply occur more frequently among the among the left-handed population.

Of the explanations for handedness, the *cerebral-dominance theory* has received widest acceptance. The left side of the brain controls the voluntary muscles on the right side of the body and the right side of the brain controls the voluntary muscles on the left side of the body. In most instances the left hemisphere is dominant; therefore, most people are right-handed. Since hemisphere dominance does not become established until after age two, consistent hand preference rarely occurs before the third birthday, and for some children it does not occur until age five or six. Research also indicates that eye and ear dominance relates to cerebral dominance, with right-ear-dominant and right-eye-dominant patterns associated with left-hemisphere activity.

The relationship between brain organization and handedness was cleverly demonstrated in a study where it was found that when right-handers tap with their right hand it interferes with their speech, but when they tap with their left hand it does not. Left-handers are more likely to incur speech interference when they tap with either their left hand or their right hand (Schell and Hall, 1979).

Gesell, whose research during the 40s greatly influenced handedness theory, observed that at age 18 months toddlers are clearly bilateral and equally competent with either hand. At about 24 months hand preference appears, followed once again by a period of bilaterality. However, in the vicinity of the fourth birthday a consistent preference emerges that lasts throughout life unless the individual is required to change. The dominant hand can be changed, but not easily, and months or years may pass before a complete handedness transfer occurs. It used to be thought that changing a child's handedness could result in emotional damage or stuttering, but few empirical data support this belief.

Although theoretical explanations are diverse, the following facts seem clear. The vast majority of humans are right-handed, and this has probably been true for thousands of years. Cerebral dominance is related to body-side preference, and for most humans the left hemisphere is dominant. When children are allowed to choose handedness they consistently prefer right-handedness. After hand preference has been established it can be reversed, but this process is both slow and difficult. Finally, left-handers (as a group) have a greater incidence of developmental problems than right-handers.

The Impact of Heredity on Human Development:

The Growth of Identical Twins during Toddlerhood

Heredity exerts such a powerful force during toddlerhood that most abilities are directly influenced by it. Greater variation is observed in speech development and personality formation because these are more influenced by social and environmental factors.

Of the five major growth advances during toddlerhood, four of them: learning to walk, talk, think, and control elimination are regulated primarily by maturation. The fifth, learning independence, is influenced more by parent-child interaction and the range of experiences to which the child is exposed. Thus, identical twins tend to be very much alike on the first four factors, even when their upbringing differs. As long as their environment provided minimal necessities their abilities are, in all probability, very similar.

Toddler phenomenology is influenced by maturation factors. Identical toddlers are both highly egocentric because they have not as yet undergone sufficient growth to transcend this state. They both possess a strong sense of curiosity and exploration and a drive to acquire competence, although we can rightfully expect individual differences, not only because of differences in temperament, but also because children react differently to the same treatment.

Toddler growth very much depends on the richness of the environment. Thus, even though identical twins grow through the progressive phases of active and mental experimentation at about the same time, one will learn considerably more than the other if she receives quality feedback from an adult. The onset of logic will most likely appear in similar sequence, with both twins acquiring transductive reasoning at about the same age. If one identical twin were sent away to a bleak and desolate institution of the type described by Spitz, or Skeels, dramatic deterioration would most likely take place in her mental abilities. Mental skills simply do not proliferate without interpersonal communication; her curiosity would wither, perhaps even disappear; and the surplus vitality that characterizes children reared in normal conditions would degenerate into apathetic lethargy. If one twin remained in this understimulating environment, she might, with time, become functionally retarded, falling further behind in her abilities each successive year.

If one twin, on the other hand, were sent away to a "super" environment where she received rich mental and verbal stimulation, she would probably undergo more development than would have occurred in a normal environment. However, improvement from extra stimulation would not be as great as deterioration from understimulation. (A generalization that applies to virtually all toddler development.)

Table 6-1   Intelligence, Weight and Height Correlations
for Identical Twins Reared Together and Apart

	Intelligence (group test)	Height	Mass
Identical twins reared together	.92	.98	.97
Identical twins reared apart	.73	.97	.89

Based on data from Newman, Freeman and Holzinger, 1937.

Table 6-2   Resemblances in Motor Skills of Young Twins

Motor skill	Correlation within Fraternal pairs	Correlation within Identical Pairs
Accuracy of eye-hand coordination	.51	.95
Steadiness of arm control	.43	.83
Speed of rotary arm, wrist and finger movement	.56	.82
Speed and accuracy in coordinated movements of both hands	.44	.71
Speed of card sorting	.39	.73

Adapted from "Twin Resemblances in Motor Skills and the Effects of Practice Thereon," by Quinn McNemar, *Journal of Genetic Psychology,* 1933, 42, 70-90. Reprinted by permission.

Speech, like mental abilities, is blueprinted in a general fashion, with room left for both acceleration and deceleration. Identical twins utter their first word, form their first two-word sentence, and begin using the past tense at approximately the same age. If either twin were struck with deafness, however, or placed in a nonverbal environment, her acquisition of speech would be diminished, perhaps irreversibly. If Mommy and Daddy took a shine to one twin and spent countless hours in cheerful word play with her and gave her sister no such enrichment, the first twin would, in all probability, be more gifted with words, have a larger working vocabulary, and use more complex sentences than her sister.

Separation and stranger anxiety, although demonstrating considerable developmental lawfulness, are tinged by individual differences. The tendency to fear strangers, and to be anxious when separated from mother, occurs in almost all children, but the extent to which these fears take hold or significantly influence day-to-day behavior is a highly individual matter. It is easy to heighten childhood fears, difficult to lessen them, and still more difficult to avoid them altogether. A cantankerous adult could easily turn normal stranger anxiety into downright panic simply by confirming that strangers actually do nasty things, thereby reinforcing a natural apprehension.

Affection and attachment are rooted in human genetics, but the focus, strength, and durability of these tendencies depend on the child's personal experiences. One twin might be more affectionate or better able to elicit affection than the other, even though the *predisposition to enjoy affection* exists in both children.

In all likelihood our identical twins will undergo the same sequence in toilet training and will become toilet trained within a month or two of each other. They will also begin to show hand preference at about the same age and settle into either right- or left-handedness at about the same age. They could be *taught* to be either right- or left-handed, regardless of their natural preference, but learning to use the non-preferred hand would be difficult and frustrating.

What picture do we now portray of our hypothetical identical twins? First, if their upbringing is approximately equivalent, they will possess remarkably similar skills and abilities. Second, if their upbringing is dissimilar but not negligent, they will mature in a parallel sequence, achieving breakthroughs at similar ages with similar outcomes. Ample room exists for individuality because no two children react to the environment or to their own growth in exactly the same way. Further, all areas of child growth that depend on interpersonal cooperation for their actualization become individualized in accord with the interaction of particular child and adult personalities.

Summary

In this chapter many of the key developments between the ages of 12 and 36 months have been presented. We have observed that growing is not a one-way street, with children passively acquiring cultural habits or mental processes identical to the people who raise them. Rather, growth is a perpetual give and take, with the environment making fundamental adjustments in favor of the child on certain occasions and holding its ground on other occasions. Toddlers are bound to the dynamics of toddlerhood, which, not infrequently, conflict with the dynamics of society. Confrontation is an inevitable but necessary requirement of growth.

Without doubt the toddler is something of a housewrecker because she is learning to walk when psychological life is dominated by the impulse to explore. Curiosity is at an all-time high but intellectual judgment is not. The inability to anticipate the consequences of behavior gets the toddler into predicaments she will rarely encounter during the preschool years. This also is the age for learning about physical, social, and personal limits, but, of course, this learning takes place at an age when the child is quite limited in what she is able to understand.

The toddler is not only a cause of, but the epitome of, environmental pollution. Toilet habits are a major contributor, but rambunctious play habits and messy eating habits add the finishing touches. By late toddlerhood daytime sphincter control is usually achieved with modest consistency, but enuresis occurs well into the preschool years for many children. Sense-pleasure play accounts for most toddler messiness, but other forms of play, especially body-contact play and competence play, produce their share.

Toddlers are lovable because of their need for contact comfort, their need for trust and acceptance, and their unique ability to elicit love responses from adults. Even though the nature of love during the early years is difficult to study scientifically, evidence gathered from direct observation points clearly to the conclusion that children function better at all levels of development under conditions of trust and affection than under conditions of mistrust and lack of affection.

By the end of toddlerhood the child has been assimilated into the culture of the family and, via the family, into the culture of the society. Thus, toddlers learn the language of their culture, but traces of pronunciation, intonation, and word usage unique to the family will influence speaking habits for years to come. Similarly, toddlers acquire knowledge of the sex-role differentiations enforced by society but are most impressed by the assignment of roles in their own home.

Thus, toddlers undergo Herculean growth, acquiring skills and developing competencies on a weekly, sometimes daily, basis. The metamorphosis is remarkable though certainly not complete. As you shall shortly observe, the staggering pace of toddler growth is equalled during the preschool years and, in a few instances, exceeded.

Major Concepts of this Chapter

1. Toddlers need affection and contact comfort. Attachment is recognized as an important determinant in the formation of personality. The toddler's understanding of object permanence is a cognitive precursor to separation anxiety. Some psychologists suggest that the earliest attachments (mother attachment) act as a prototype for further attachments, so that if the toddler has formed strong and secure attachments she will continue to form similar attachments over the life span.

2. Play is the mechanism through which toddlers learn about the world and manifest their developing skills. Play habits are closely related to physical and cognitive development and are characterized by impulsivity. Body-contact play, sense-pleasure play, competence play and role-

rehearsal play are each manifested during these years and each promotes development.

3. Play progress from "the one" to "the many" both in terms of the participants and the physical and cognitive skills involved at any one time. Initially play is solitary involving only the child and the object of play. Parallel play emerges near the first birthday and is characterized by independent play in the presence of another child. By late toddlerhood mixed play begins when the presence of others influences the nature of play. Truly cooperative play does not emerge until after the toddler years. It is not until this later stage that games requiring the observance of rules become part of the child's play.

4. The developmental tasks of toddlerhood include learning to walk, talk, feed oneself, be independent, and control elimination.

5. Toddlerhood is marked by the emergence of fears, anxieties and apprehensions. Stranger anxiety and separation anxiety are virtually universal toddler phenomena.

6. As cognitive capacities expand so do fears and apprehensions. The origins of these fears include, anticipation of physical harm, changes in stimulation, lack of congruity between expectation and experience, and anticipation of loss. Pervasive fear that the world in general is dangerous may relate to basic mistrust. More than specific fears, pervasive fears impede social and emotional development.

7. Children can be helped to cope with fears if adults understand the fears, act calmly, help the child to gradually overcome the fear, and provide a base of security to which the child may return.

8. Temper tantrums are a response to the frustrations involved attempting to fend effectively in an environment controlled by others. Parents may look into the events which lead to the tantrum in an effort to help alleviate these frustrations. Modelling appropriate behavior and helping the child to understand frustrations reduces the incidence of tantrums.

9. Most abilities during toddlerhood are influenced by heredity. Learning to walk, talk, think and control elimination are profoundly influenced by genetic programs. In all realms of development the richness of the human environment has important effects on the fulfillment of the child's potential. Identical twins with similar environments will progress at approximately the same rate, but differences in the quality of environment can result in radical differences in development.

7

Intellectual Development:
Years Three, Four and Five

*Genius learns from nature,
from its own nature*
Arnold Schoenberg

The years between the end of toddlerhood and the beginning of the first grade are called the preschool years. Traditionally children begin school when they are six years old, thus three-, four- and five-year-olds are thought of as "pre" schoolers. During the past few decades, however, so many youngsters attend a variety of different kind of "schools" before they enter Grade One that the appropriateness of this term has been questioned. Nevertheless, the term "preschooler" is so soundly embedded in everyday usage and so uniformly refers to three-, four- and five-year-olds that it is our choice in this chapter.

Psychologists are fond of preschool children because they are easy to study, naive about psychological tests, and innocent enough to declare freely their opinions, interests, and conclusions. Also the psychologist is fascinated by children of this age because the influence of the environment is becoming more discernible and that of heredity less discernible. Individual differences are more pronounced among preschoolers than among toddlers. Environmental effects are everywhere visible; dress, social skills, mannerisms, speech habits, and intellectual versatility are drastically influenced by the preschooler's environment.

The daily life of the three-, four-, and five-year-old is active and expansive. Growth is relentless, almost frighteningly persistent. During these years the child blossoms physically, socially, psychologically, morally, and intellectually. The biological innocence of the toddler is outgrown and replaced with the social innocence of the preschooler.

During the preschool years the psychological foundations of trust and confidence are significantly structured; the social foundations of extroversion and self-expansion are solidified; the intellectual foundations of investigation are blueprinted; the moral foundation of conscience is laid; and the physical foundation of the childhood body is developed.

Mental Abilities of the Preschooler

Some Preliminary Observations: Strengths and Weakness of Preschool Thought

The child grows in all cognitive realms during the preschool years and is vastly more adept at concept formation, memory, and quantitative skills at age four than three, five than four.

Recall that between the ages of 12 and 36 months considerable maturing of mental processes occurs: verbal and representational thought come into existence; the environment is mentally schematized and compartmentalized; recognition of number and quantity begin; and language is acquired and developed. Even after these mental advancements have been made toddlers are remarkably restricted in comparison with preschool children. They cannot begin to match their older counterparts in concept-formation skills, duration or depth of memory, intensity or length of concentration, verbal mastery, understanding of the social world, or richness of utilizable experience. Even though preschoolers are remarkably advanced when compared with toddlers, their thought has many limitations compared with older children.

Preschoolers are prerational as well as prelogical in most areas of thought. They have little ability to check the internal consistency of their thought, and they egocentrically assume that their thought mirrors reality. Children of this age resist the notion that their interpretations are the result of their own thought process. To them interpretations simply are.

Preschool children have few means to confirm or authenticate what they assume to be true; for this they rely almost exclusively on authority. When authorities disagree preschoolers simply side with ideas closest to their own. Rarely do they change an idea because it has been shown to be logically inconsistent; however, they will abandon an idea if it proves ineffective or nonfunctional. Preschoolers are not concerned with the origin of their ideas, concentrating instead on how functional or advantageous they are. In this regard they are intellectual pragmatists.

When confronted with a question to be answered, the preschool child does not respond only to the question. When the premise is stated affirmatively, the child tends to agree with it whether it is true or false. When adults attempt to elicit a negative response they usually have success if the question is posed with a negative premise. When presented with two propositions, one positive and one negative, preschoolers tend to choose the negative. Likewise, when an idea coincides with the child's preexisting belief (or prejudice), the child is likely to agree without critical investigation, whereas, if it opposes a personal bias, the child will attempt to detect flaws in it. Because preschoolers are unskilled at differentiating important from trivial details, their thought often misses the larger picture and focuses on the insignificant or the irrelevant.

Thought Rigidity

Children do not live solely in their own little world but most assuredly they live in a more confined mental world than adults. Part of their narrowness is anchored in what developmental psychologists call *rigidity*. That is, "the inability to shift psychological vantage points and take a fresh look at situations" (Stone & Church, 1984). The child simply has too few mental categories with which to process everything he sees, and is unable to construct new, more expansive categories of understanding. Therefore, novel experiences which do not fit are initially ignored or distorted. With increased maturity the child attains greater mental flexibility. Until then, however, all mental operations are restricted by rigidity.

Rigidity can be adaptive to the child, and its adaptive function should not escape our attention. For most preschoolers the world is unpredictable, and, in general, hard to figure out. A certain security derives from routines, habits, and other mannerisms which corridor the world into manageable units. Too much newness can overpower a child, just as it does the adolescent who leaves a small town for the hectic scope of university life.

Thus, two different (but interrelated) types of rigidity constrain the young child's mental apparatus. The first type of rigidity is essentially intellectual and "simply reflects children's limited knowledge and cognitive skills and gives way to more flexible processes as children achieve improved understanding of how things work." (Stone & Church, 1984) The second kind of rigidity is primarily emotional. It strives to keep the world in acceptable balance by not admitting experiences which are excessively disruptive. Both types of rigidity play an important role in the mental world of the preschool child; the first restricts the intellect, the second restricts the emotions.

The Preoperational Stage of Intellectual Development

Piaget, to whom we owe much of our understanding about the preschool child's thought process, believed children of this age are in a stage of "preoperational thought." The remarkable achievements of this stage include the following:

1. The development of symbolic representation – the ability to represent people, places or things with symbols. A broom can become a play horse.

2. The use of mental images to think about people or events that are not present.

3. The use of language as a tool of investigation and exploration.

Quite obviously, since the term "preoperational thought" was coined by Piaget to convey the limits of thought, the child at this stage is not an advanced thinker even though he has gone through many advances in order to reach this stage. Preoperational thought is defined by its limitations as well as its accomplishments. Most relevant to our discussion, it is a mode of thought which deploys only a minimal understanding of causality, and it is characterized by the tendency to see only parts of complicated wholes. By adult standards it is a primitive stage in mental evolution.

Table 7-1   Piaget's Stages of Cognitive Development

Stage	General Description	Age Level
Sensorimotor Period	The child progresses from reflexive action at birth to symbolic activities, to the ability to separate self from objects in the environment. He develops limited capabilities for anticipating the consequences of actions.	0 .5 1 1.5 2
Preoperational Period	The child's ability to think becomes refined during this period. First, he develops what Piaget calls preconceptual thinking, in which he deals with each thing individually but is not able to group objects. The child is able to use symbols, such as words to deal with problems. During the latter half of this period, the child develops better reasoning abilities but is still bound to the here and now	2.5 3 3.5 4 4.5 5 5.5 6 6.5 7
Concrete Operations	At this stage the child develops the ability to perform intellectual operations – such as reversibility, conservation ordering of things by number, size or class etc. His ability to relate time and space also matures during this period.	7.5 8 8.5 9 9.5 10 10.5

Adapted from *Educational Psychology: An Introduction,* by G.S. Belkin and J.L. Gray. Copyright 1977 by Wm. C. Brown Company Publishers. Dubuque, Iowa. Used by permission.

Piaget believed that during every developmental stage thought advances by the interaction of assimilation and accommodation. *Assimilation* is the process of applying previous thoughts to a new object or event. It is the tendency to blend new perceptions into what we already know – to make new experience fit past experience. Assimilation is used by all people (and animals), regardless of their age, and every encounter with new experience involves a certain amount of it. However, sometimes new experiences do not fit. This happens frequently to young children, whose categories of understanding are narrow. Time and again the child is confronted with information that does not process. This is resolved only when the thought process *accommodates* by expanding or changing its boundaries. For example, when a preschooler discovers that other children will take away toys the youngster is perplexed because this does not fit previous experience, thus disequilibrium is created. In time the tot accommodates to this fact and adapts by hiding the toy.

The conflict between past experience and new realities is a fundamental cause of mental expansion because data that do not assimilate into past experience can only be accommodated by an expansion of thought.

Egocentrism

*Egotist, n. A person of low taste more
interested in himself than in me.*

Ambrose Bierce
The Devil's Dictionary

As explained in the preceding chapter, egocentrism derives from a cluster of perceptual and mental tendencies that incline the child to believe that her perception of the world is the only possible one. Egocentrism impedes comprehending the viewpoints of others (especially when they contradict our own).

Egocentrism lessens with age; thus, one can expect a five- year-old to understand ideas different from his own more readily than a three-year-old. And, of course, it follows that a seven-year-old will be able to do the same more effectively than a five-year-old. Egocentrism persists through childhood and well into the adolescent years, and because it influences intellectual, perceptual, and emotional sensations, its impact on the day-to-day functioning is tremendous.

The most completely egocentric humans are newborn infants, whose perceptual and cognitive abilities are so weak that they respond only to stimuli that impinge directly on their sensory apparatus. About a year later, babies recognize that other people exist independently, but little awareness of people as people exists. By late toddlerhood considerable strides are made; the child recognizes that objects and people exist independently of one another, that some things are alive and some are not, and that different people respond differently to the same stimulus.

By the preschool years the child has outgrown many of these primitive variations of egocentrism but nevertheless remains somewhat in its clutch. Preschoolers, for example, believe that adults see things just as they do; they may also believe that parents can actually experience their feelings. Preschoolers consistently begin sentences with a pronoun, assuming that the adult knows the noun to which it refers. Likewise, when returning home after a sandbox quarrel, the four-year-old assumes that mother knows all about it, how it started, and who the primary villain was.

Childhood egocentrism has been researched in a variety of interesting ways, and quite a bit is known about its manifestations. Shatz (1973) has confirmed that five-year-olds are able to differentiate between the abilities of two-year-olds and four-year-olds and to recognize that certain games would be more appropriate than others for children of these ages. Marvin and co-researchers (1976) found that preschoolers know that a secret can be shared by people who have seen a particular event that others have not.

Egocentrism relates all events to one's personal needs and desires. Preschoolers are likely to think that it is raining in the park because it is time to go home, that the sun moves through the sky in order to watch them, or that cartoons come on the television at 9:00 because that is when breakfast is over and they are ready to watch TV.

Four-year-olds have difficulty understanding that dreams take place "inside your mind." They assume that, like television, dreams emanate from an outside source and that, as with television, you must have your eyes open to see a dream. Therefore, they scoff at the explanations of dreaming that adults accept matter-of-factly. Seven-year-olds, however, accept dreams the way adults understand them because they distinguish physical from mental realities; they also recognize that the mind has subjective properties, of which dreaming is one.

Understanding Intentions

In order to understand why people behave as they do we must be able to diagnose their intentions. This is not an easy skill to attain since it requires the evolution of several mental skills as well as the transcendence of egocentrism. It begins with the child's ability to distinguish between actions which are intentional rather than accidental. At an early age children demonstrate some ability to differentiate intention from outcome. Preschoolers, for example, inform mother that sister "is trying" to say something she cannot say, or that she "wants" to go to the bathroom. These demonstrate the elementary beginnings of awareness of intentionality.

By age three most children are fairly quick to comprehend that it is "wronger" to spill milk intentionally than accidentally. "It was an accident, Mom." Or, at a later age: "It was an accident, Mom. Honest.!" The second example indicates that the child knows mother will render a judgment on whether it was an accident borne of negligence or a genuine accident.

Awareness of intentionality signals a breakthrough in intellectual comprehension. Henceforth, the child analyzes personal motivations and becomes more sophisticated at decoding the non-observable aspects of human behavior. "Ms. Smith was in a bad mood today. She wouldn't let us have any fun" is a more advanced line of evaluation than the purely behavioral "Ms. Smith wouldn't let us have any fun today." These breakthroughs in processing the intentions of others lends developmental assistance to the childs gradual exodus from egocentrism. Understanding intentions eventually opens the door to the child's recognition of personality and individual uniqueness, although it will be near the end of childhood before these concepts are deployed with much grace.

General Thinking Abilities of the Preschooler

In this segment we will take a closer look at the following components of the preschooler's thought. (1) concept formation, (2) understanding of causality, (3) knowledge of quantity, (4) memory capacity, (5) Perception of social relationships and, (6) awareness of time concepts.

Concept Formation

The preschool child employs both inductive and deductive thought, although neither very effectively. The inductive method is the more common, because thinking naturally moves from the particular to the general. With age there occurs a gradual shift toward deductive thought (inferring from general to specific).

"Up to the age of six, the child's concepts are determined mainly by his own specific experiences and actions, and are, consequently, naive, inconsistent, diffuse, imprecise, simple, and closely bound up with the immediate perceptual features of the objects. Perhaps as a result of markedly improved verbal skills, a marked shift occurs at about the age of six. Concepts become more logical and differentiated, a trend that continues throughout the school years and into adult life. (Mussen, p. 39, 1963).

Throughout the course of the preschool years concepts becomes more sophisticated, and progress (1) from simple to complex, (2) from diffuse to differentiated, (3) from subjective to more objective, (4) from concrete to abstract, and (5) from variable and scattered to more stable and consistent.

By age five or six most children have not as yet acquired what Piaget calls *class inclusion*, which is the ability to include one class of objects within another class. Piaget conducted an experiment in which children were given a cluster of wooden beads, most of which were brown but some of which were white. When the children were asked whether there were more brown beads or more wooden beads, they claimed there were more brown beads, indicating they did not include the brown beads within the larger class of wooden beads. Children seven or eight years old rarely make this kind of class-inclusion error.

The preschooler's thought is essentially *nonreversible*. That is, the child rarely comes up with a thought and then reverses back to the starting point to double-check the accuracy of the process. When thought is not reversible, the thinker cannot backtrack to locate errors. Thus, when preschoolers make a mental error, they rarely can figure out when or where they made it. (It does not even occur to preschoolers that they can locate errors by reviewing their thoughts.)

The beginnings of reversibility appear near age five or six for most children, although children who have had practice at backtracking, or who are accustomed to being told to think through what they have just said, tend to pick it up more quickly, providing us with one further example of how adults "stretch" and extend the natural abilities of children. (Remember the "rubber band" hypothesis from Chapter one?)

The preoperational child attends to states rather than transformations and responds to outcomes rather than to changes that bring about outcomes. For example, when liquid is poured from a tall, thin container into a short, wide container, preoperational children think there is less liquid because they concentrate on the final product and not the exchange. If the child paid attention to the transformation, he would know that the same volume of water was merely transformed into a different shape. Preoperational children understand stable conditions better than changing conditions because centration impedes grasping an entire chain of events.

Preschoolers also have difficulty with what is known as *transitive inferences*. A four-year old (and many five-year-olds) have trouble with a question like this: If Jimmy is taller than Joe, and Joe is taller than Mary, who is the tallest of the three? Preschoolers think the question is unanswerable because they do not recognize the implicit comparison self-evident to an older child. On the other hand, among a group of seven-year-olds if Johnny is bragging about how far he jumped at the track meet, then finds out that Joe jumped further, and that Fred jumped even further than Joe, he would instantly infer (correctly) that his jump was the least of the three. Piaget claims that children become capable of transitive inferences when they can hold in their minds the logical relationship: A>B>C. In calendar time this ability usually surfaces at about age six or seven.

Understanding of Causality

Among the most significant mental achievements of the entire childhood era is the concept of causality. Causality involves the specification of cause-effect relations; that is, the comprehension of how one event generates another. Children's thinking does not easily bend to the scientific understanding of causality, it is a slow process, and during the preschool years it manifests itself in crude and underdeveloped ways. Like the transductive toddler, a good deal of thinking among preschoolers is correlational rather than causal. When things occur in proximity they are thought to cause one another. Not until middle childhood is causality effectively instilled in the thought process, and not by coincidence, this is the age when the scientific method and other ideas predicated on a systematic understanding of causality work their way into the school curriculum.

Preschool children do not have a firm idea about causality (the origin of tap water is to them as mysterious as the origin of the universe), hence, they readily accept *magical explanations*. Thus, a child is likely to believe that witches cast spells, and elephants can fly, and these beliefs are no more far-fetched to them than distance to the stars being measured in light years.

Magicalism does not dominate preschool thought, but even highly intelligent children are attracted to it. Three-year-olds willingly accept that rain comes from weeping giants in the sky; five-year-olds, as a rule, do not. But Five, while scoffing at a younger sister who believes that Pinocchio is a real person and not a puppet, may believe in Santa Claus or the tooth fairy.

Interestingly, preschoolers are not impressed by the tricks performed by magicians which fascinate older children. Preschoolers are not surprised to witness an apparently inexplicable event, because they do not understand most events in the first place. Nine-year-olds, on the other hand, delight magicians because they are stunned by the magicians' ability to defy chance, permanence, and other principles not yet formed in the preschool mind.

Preschool children are not interested in scientific explanations. They are more concerned with manoeuvring to their advantage the way things are. Rather than understanding the why of reality, preschoolers learn the how of it.

Initial attempts to understand causality include: (1) animism, (2) realism, and, (3) artificialism. When children believe that inanimate things such as clouds and raindrops move because they have purpose, intention, fellings, or other human qualities, *animistic thinking* is at work. Many children attribute physical characteristics to psychological events such as thoughts, dreams, and fantasies. This is called *realism*. A child who refuses to sleep in a room because it is filled with bad dreams is reflecting this kind of thought.

Later the child may assume that all events occur in order to blend with the wants, desires, or orders of some person. It snows so we can make snowballs; the car quits running on the freeway so we can play on the nearby grass. This understanding of causality is called *artificialism*. Children rarely think in terms of randomness, chance, or the impersonal forces of nature.

Understanding What is Alive

Piaget observed that children at different stages of mental development use different criteria in their judgment of whether an object is alive. He observed four variations of the child's understanding. First, children assume an object is alive if it appears to be in good condition – if it is not broken or seriously defaced. Second, children infer life if the object moves; thus are clouds and raindrops judged to be living. Third, objects live if they move of their own volition; thus, the sun is thought to be alive, because it moves through the sky without noticeable assistance, whereas the family automobile is not, because it requires a driver and sometimes remains motionless in the driveway. Fourth, the most mature form of animistic thought occurs when the child comes to recognize that only animals and plants live. Children between the ages of three and six undergo such significant growth in their understanding of the animate world that it is not unusual for them to experience all of the stages of animistic thought observed by Piaget.

Preschoolers attribute life to objects that are inanimate for many reasons, as illustrated by the following explanations of what is and is not alive.

1. Pencil: alive because it writes.
2. Watch: alive if it tells time; not alive if it doesn't.
3. Candle: alive when lit; not alive when unlit.
4. Bicycle: alive because it runs.
5. Clouds: alive because they are moving all the time.
6. Wind: alive because it blows and makes things move.
7. Birds: alive because they fly.
8. Flower: alive because people water it.

Quantity

The preschool child has a long way to go before he grasps the relationships between number and quantity or shape and quantity. It is fairly easy to teach a three-year-old to count to ten or a five-year-old to one hundred. More difficult is that 10 is to 30 what 30 is to 90 or that every number can be doubled. Numbers are memorized by preschoolers but for the most part, they lack functional utility. In the world of mathematics the preschooler lives in stark contrast to the older child, whose understanding of multiples, sums, and percentages affects their day-to-day behavior.

The preschooler demonstrates in other ways a limited acquaintance with numbers and counting. For example, a three-year-old counting her fingers may come up with a different sum each time forgetting to count one finger, or counting it twice.

At this age children have no concept of numbers existing in indefinite quantity. The ability to add, subtract, multiply, and divide does not develop until about six or seven for most children, although exceptions to this generalization are easy to find.

Preschoolers typically confuse cardinal and ordinal numbers. Cardinal numbers refer to quantity (four people, nine eggs, and so on), whereas ordinal numbers refer to order or rank (the fourth person, the ninth egg). Use of numbers does not become efficient until this distinction is learned.

Most preschool children have not learned *conservation of quantity;* that is, that quantity does not change because its shape has been altered or rearranged. Thus, when the contents of a tall, thin pitcher are poured into a short, wide pitcher, preschoolers will insist that there is less water in the wide pitcher. They do not understand that quantity remains the same regardless of the shape it assumes. When the water is poured back into the tall, thin pitcher, the heightened water level is construed by the child as proof that there is now a greater quantity. The child does not see that the same quantity of water has merely been transformed from one shape into another.

When eight coins are placed in a single row very close to one another, three- and four-year-old children believe that the row contains fewer coins than a row of eight coins that are spaced farther apart. Because the second row occupies more space, preschoolers infer that it holds a greater number of coins. Some children persist in this belief even when the middle two coins are taken out, leaving only six coins in the long row and eight in the short row. Children who know how to count solve this problem by simply counting the coins. Children who cannot count but who possess the concept of equivalence are also able to solve this problem. Equivalence is the concept of a one-to-one relationship. Thus, the child compares quantity by matching coin for coin.

Memory

An amazing stockpile of information fills the preschool child's memory. By age six kids have about 25,000 to 45,000 words in their vocabulary. Nursery rhymes, jingles, and idioms by the hundreds are stored neatly away, awaiting only command or an associative cue to be brought into use. Although rich in quantity, the preschool child's memory is poor in quality. For the most part, memory is associative, rote, and clustered – kids who can recall perfectly the words to a jingle often do not have the slightest idea what they mean.

Few children under the age of six can successfully repeat 7-4-9-2-8 or any such five-digit combination. Their memory is hampered by limited attention and a limited capacity for auditory imagery. Despite a restricted ability to recall numbers, the preschooler can repeat sentences or short paragraphs that have a meaningful message. The four-year-old who could recall only three digits usually repeat flawlessly, "The horse ran up the hill." Meaningful clusters are remembered more readily than numbers, as every university student knows.

Much of what the child remembers is merely associative. Upon meeting an adult not encountered for several months, a four-year-old may exclaim "Where is your brown coat?," remembering the coat worn on their first meeting. At the same time, the child may not recall the adult's name or anything else about the earlier visit.

If interrupted in the middle of recital, the preschooler, like the spider interrupted while spinning a web, must return to the beginning and start anew. This is especially true of three- and four-year-olds. Although they remember many things fairly well, preschoolers often do not know in any meaningful sense what it is that they remember.

Short Term and Long Term Memory

Two different types of memory operate within each individual: short-term and long-term. Short-term memory deals with fleeting transitory details that are important at the moment, such as a telephone number for immediate dialing. Information stored in short-term memory does not remain very long, sometimes only a few seconds or moments; it is easily interfered with and, when it has served its purpose, tends to "disappear." Long-term memory, on the other hand, deals with information that needs to be stored for long periods (such as one's home address), that can be recalled on short notice, and that concerns important events in one's life.

Information being processed for long-term memory may be rearranged or even forgotten if a shift of attention occurs. If a preschooler is distracted while memorizing a series of numbers, or is asked to count aloud while listening, the interference will impede both short-term and long-term memory.

The memory power of all preschoolers is limited. Even items of interest are not recounted well. Preschoolers usually cannot recall a TV show without confusing the sequence of events or mixing up the most important facts. Centration causes them to focus on one aspect of the complex event, so that what they perceive, as well as what they remember, is restricted.

Memory improves with practice, sometimes remarkably. Youngsters whose natural memory power permits them to recall only four or five digits may increase to seven or eight with practice.

Social Relationships

Older preschoolers vaguely understand concepts such as division of labor, and organizational hierarchies. However, their understanding is based on the specific workings of their household. A five-year-old takes it as the nature of things that mothers draw bath water, wash dishes, and go shopping, and that fathers shovel snow, and leave early in the morning for work if that is *what they observe in their own home.*

Every preschool child knows about command hierarchies. What they do not understand is that a person at the top of one pecking order can be in the middle, or even at the bottom of another. The concept that mother has a boss or supervisor while on the job is slow to penetrate the inflexible mind of a preschooler, who knows mother only as strength and authority and does not see her as someone's subordinate. Most preschool children assume that all social relationships are like those of the family; thus, the child may infer that all superiors have an emotional attachment to their underlings, just as mother and father have an emotional attachment to their children. This innocent inference is exploded in kindergarten or the first grade, but through the process of *accommodation* the child reconciles the complexity of reality with the simplicity of the thought process.

Time Concepts

Children have considerable difficulty understanding how past, present, and future time are schematized in our culture. Three-year-olds have little knowledge of time as it is understood by adults. Time is present time, with an occasional exception made for important events about to occur or recently completed. Five-year-olds know how old they are, how old they will be on their next birthday, and how old they were before their fifth birthday. Children know that some people are older than others, but they may assume they will catch up in age with older persons, especially their parents. Few five-year-olds distinguish past time with accurate labels. When asked how long it has been since he returned from an out-of-town trip, the preschooler may reply, "two weeks," "20 hours," "a year," or "50 months," when in fact he returned three days ago.

Fibbing, falsifying and pretending

> *Do you think my mind is maturing late,*
> *Or simply rotted early?*
> Ogden Nash

The phenomena of rearranging reality to suit personal desires is of special interest to developmental psychologists because the ability to execute it is based upon advancing mental abilities. Youngsters fib in proportion to their mental skills. Thus, preschoolers rarely establish a false premise in order to cause the listener to draw a wrong conclusion from it. Eight-year-olds, however, are pretty good at it. To wit: "I left my boots on the back porch" says the eight-year-old upon mother's return from work. Mother may thus infer he was not the one who tracked mud into the kitchen. This deception does not occur among preschoolers because it requires knowing that mother will draw a false conclusion if given a false premise.

Preschool lying begins with the most elementary (and least demanding) form: denial. "Did you walk through the kitchen with dirty boots?" "No." A slightly more advanced effort occurs when the child announces falsely "I've washed my hands for dinner." "Are you sure?" "Yes."

During the preschool years kids play with far-fetched ideas knowing they will eventually be rejected but nevertheless enjoying the ploy. It is, more than anything, idea play. "Me and Stella swam across the river." "Don't be silly, the river is too cold and too wide. Besides you can't swim." "Oh yes we can. We did it yesterday." "You were at Grandmother's yesterday." "She went, too. She loves to swim in the river." The exchange continues with the child knowing the whole story is made-up but half-heartedly trying to convince her audience of its truth. The contrivance usually ends with "I'm just pretending." Extending reality, re-arranging it, and playing with it are all part of the preschooler's mental package. Otherwise, they would be mere empiricists – describers of reality.

Preschoolers lapse in and out of reality with such fluidity that their stream of consciousness is a heady mixture of fact and fantasy. Accepting as true everything a preschooler reports is naive. Most parents, and all preschool teachers, of necessity become mini-detectives in their daily interchange with children of this age.

Near age five the child's migrations in and out of reality are a source of great pleasure in many households. "Don't look in the closet." "Why?" "My hippopotamus is in there." Great laughter. "Can I keep it?" "No." "OK, I'll give it to mommy." Great laughter.

Playful pretend, of course, is not the same as intentional lying. However, the mental processes which allow their cultivation are the same. In sum, the capacity to understand reality makes possible the falsification, re-alignment, and playful manipulation of it.

Preschool Witnesses in Legal Trials

Do preschoolers qualify as good witnesses in a legal trial? Are their statements clear, consistent, and, most importantly, accurate? The general answer to these questions is "No" because preschoolers tend to alter their statements under the pressure of cross-examination. However, when required merely to report what they have seen, they sometimes prove to be reliable witnesses. For example, consider the following:

> One summer day a man in an orange Datsun pulled up in front of the neighbor's yard where Lori was playing and told her to get in. She did. Three days later the police found Lori, crying and bruised, in the pit of a deserted outhouse. Lori told the police that the "bad man" had hit her and left her there. The next day, when the police showed her a set of twelve photographs, she gasped and identified one man as her abductor. The man Lori identified was arrested, and a week before the case was scheduled to come to trial, he confessed. (Goleman, 1984, p. 19)

In rare circumstances children make even better witnesses than adults because they notice details adults sometimes ignore. For example, Neisser (1979) reports a study where adults and children watched a basketball game on videotape; 75 percent of the first graders, 22 percent of the fourth graders, and no adults recalled seeing a woman with an umbrella walk through the gym.

In general, however, young children do not make good witnesses in a legal trial. The limitations of their thought process impose too many restrictions on their recall. They are inclined to mix reality with imagination and, as well, reality with desire. Several other reasons also stand out.

1. Preschoolers are prone to give answers they think the questioner wants to hear.
2. Preschoolers are prone to give affirmative answers to affirmative questions: "It was a blue car wasn't it?" "Yes."
3. Preschoolers are prone to give negative answers to negative questions: "He was not the man was he?" "No."
4. Preschoolers are prone to dwell upon specific detail at the expense of the overall picture.
5. Preschoolers are prone to confuse the sequence in which events occur.

Preschoolers are accustomed to their memories being inaccurate, and they are also accustomed to looking to an adult to validate or invalidate the accuracy of their statements. For all these reasons believing a preschooler's statement is tenuous. This is not too imply that preschoolers do not recall events accurately. Rather, it means that many factors incline preschoolers to alter the truth; therefore it is difficult to know *with certainty* when they are reporting accurately.

Summary Comments on the Preschooler's Thinking Abilities

Since the pioneer research conducted by Jean Piaget near the beginning of this century developmental psychology has found itself in the awkward position of describing preschool intellectual abilities in terms of limitations rather than strengths. This chapter has adhered somewhat to this trend, but not completely. The child is growing toward a more sophisticated intellectual level, thus his limitations are far more obvious than if he were lodged on a three- or four-year plateau. Preschool thought truly is rigid when compared with the eight-year-old, and it cannot grasp concepts of causality that nine-year-olds take for granted.

When we compare the preschooler with the toddler, however, we paint a far brighter picture of mental development because preschoolers are more advanced in every thought category than toddlers. Logic is better, language is richer, memory is more fully developed, and concentration span nearly doubles. So the investigator has choices as to whether preschool thought should be evaluated in terms of limitations or strengths. For our purposes, the emphasis has been on the mental skills beyond the preschooler, thereby setting the stage for the renaissance of middle childhood.

In terms of the limited intellectual abilities which preschoolers bring to their daily lives it is worth our while to remember the following. First, preschoolers are essentially prerational and prelogical, therefore, what they are able to intellectually comprehend is intrinsically limited. Second, the mechanisms which regulate thought and process information are rigid rather than flexible. Third, the preschooler does not double check his own thought or even fully comprehend that thoughts are subject to re-analysis. Fourth, memory is not very systematic nor very reliable. Finally, egocentrism, our child's constant companion, twists and bends information in order to make it more suitable to the youngster. All in all, the preschooler has a great intellectual future, but a limited present.

Schooling the Preschooler

Education must have an end in view,
for it is not an end in itself.

Sybil Marshall

The Controversy over Preschool Education

Preschool education in North America has a limited history. It really did not take hold with any vitality until the middle 60s, and then it did so because of a massive campaign in the United States to enhance the educational skills of minority children from low income households. The most significant program was called "Head Start," and it has been the most widely researched, criticized and praised of all North American preschool programs.

Head Start began as an eight week intervention program for children getting ready for Grade One, but it has since matured into a year-round program with about 500,000 students. The educational activities of children enrolled in Head Start are similar to those of traditional nursery schools: coloring, learning rhymes and songs, art work, numbers and letters, learning about animals,trips to the zoo and other activities within the preschoolers range.

Initial investigations of the effectiveness of Head Start were encouraging, especially the research conducted during the late 60s and early 70s. Head Start children, on average, demonstrated sightly higher IQ scores, slightly better school achievement, and slightly better social adjustment to elementary school than similar kids with no preschool experience. At this juncture the optimistic (and practical) ambitions of early intervention seemed justified. Follow-up studies, however, were not as encouraging. Several studies indicated that the positive effects of Head Start were short-lived and difficult to spot at Grade Three. The sheer bulk of the research investigating this topic is difficult to report succinctly, however, the following themes pervade virtually all of the commentary on this topic: (1) changes in Head Start children were positive but short-lived; (2) most educators report gains in self-confidence but these cannot be measured by IQ or achievement tests; (3) public school is sufficiently different from Head Start programs that the transfer between the two is not significant; and (4) the Head Start programs are sufficiently different from one another that lumping them together generates misleading averages.

Nursery school attendance escalated dramatically in the 70s and 80s. In 1970 15 percent of the three- and four-year-old population were attending nursery school while in 1983 about 34 percent were in some kind of nursery school program. About 93 percent of five-year-olds were enrolled in kindergarten in 1983 (Galinsky, 1986).

For developmental psychologists the controversy is not primarily with the numbers of children in preschool (although this unto itself becomes a social and psychological fact of childhood existence) rather, it concerns the child's readiness for schooling, and the impact it exerts on the intellectual, social and emotional well-being of the child.

The Nature of Preschool Education in Canada and the United States

Preschools that are educational rather than merely custodial can be classified into three categories: (1) compensatory-education programs; (2) academic-preparation programs; and (3) personal/social enrichment programs.

Compensatory Education

All children do not enter the first grade equally prepared. A wide range of individual differences exists in emotional stability, intelligence, manual dexterity, and other traits related to schoolwork. Differences also exist among children from various socio-economic groups; as a limited generalization, children from low socio-economic families are less prepared to cope with the demands of the first grade than are children of middle socio-economic families. Two factors seem to best account for this difference: (1) middle-income families find their value structure fairly harmonious with the school's value system; and (2) children from middle-income families, in the course of their daily living, acquire more of the verbal, auditory, and concentration skills required in the first years of school than do children of lower-income families. The attempt to compensate for the disadvantage that lower-income children face upon entering the first grade is referred to as compensatory education.

Children from lower-income families tend to be weaker in the kinds of auditory and visual discrimination crucial to the acquisition of reading skills. Vocabulary differences between socio-economic classes are also noticeable; lower-income children are not as adept with words for categories, classes, and nonconcrete ideas. At least not the categories, classes and ideas most commonly dealt with in school. Middle-income parents tend to place greater emphasis on precision and clarity of verbal messages. As a result, their children enter school rehearsed in these skills. In addition, they possess listening skills that allow them to understand the language of the typical school teacher.

Negative self-concept leads the child to expect failure, and this expectation, in turn, contributes to the likelihood of failure, a phenomenon referred to as the *self-fulfilling prophecy.* "The available evidence, seems to indicate that the ego development of the deprived child is more likely to be characterized by lack of self-confidence and negative self-image than that of the middle-class child" (Bloom, 1965, p. 72).

Another factor that favors middle-income children is that they have been reared with an orientation toward the future and are prepared for delayed or symbolic gratification. This preparation proves advantageous for academic achievement and psychological survival in school.

Children with minimal preparation in auditory discrimination, visual discrimination, verbal clarity, abstract vocabulary, delayed gratification, and group participation soon fall behind in classroom work. Not only do they fall behind, many of them fall further behind each year. Thus, a child who performs near the average in the first grade may fall slightly below the average in the second year and, by the third grade, may be among the lowest achievers in the classroom. This tendency to drop further behind one's age group is called the *cumulative deficit syndrome,* a term that indicates that the child's deficit increases each year. "On the average, by eighth grade these children are about three years behind grade norms in reading and arithmetic as well as in other subjects. These effects are most marked in deprived children of average and low ability" (Bloom, 1965, p. 73).

The stigma associated with weak school performance is not very noticeable in Grade One, but it is during grades two and three. A coping strategy employed by some children is to act so dull that the teacher and classmates do not expect success from them, a strategy known as *selective stupidity.* Some developmental psychologists believe that it is this tendency to behave as though one were stupid, more than a genuine lack of ability, that impedes classroom learning.

Compensatory education is designed to provide learning the child does not get in the home. Educators assume that this educational experience lessens the chance that the child will fall further behind each year and resort to the defense mechanism of selective stupidity. They also assume that, as a result of the learning acquired in the compensatory-education program, the child is better able to actualize classroom potential and, eventually, social and economic potentials.

Preschool as Academic Preparation

> *I was not a Child Prodigy, because a Child*
> *Prodigy is a child who knows as much when*
> *it is a child as it does when it grows up.*
>
> Will Rogers

Academic Preparation preschools stress skills that directly relate to the schoolwork of the first three grades. In these programs children are taught to count and to add numbers; they learn the alphabet and common phonetic combinations. They learn about the behavior of many species of animals and may even be introduced to plant and animal reproduction. The proper manipulation of a pencil is taught (this is not an easy task for four-year-olds, because of their limited prehensile development). They may even learn to use typewriters and word processors. Large-muscle activity is combined with academic learning. For instance, foot races may be timed, fostering an awareness of time as well as its relationship to distance. Running around the school provides exercise, but subsequent conversation creates an opportunity to discuss the relationship between perimeter and distance. The preschool teacher combines the play of creative art with lessons about texture, color combinations, and even the geometry of space.

Advocates of academic preparation base their reasoning on four arguments (1) The earlier children start on the formal academic path, the earlier they will finish; thus, preschool academic training reduces the total educational cost per child (2) Because learning comes easily to preschool children, their eagerness for academic skill should be maximized (3) Intellectual growth is rapid in the preschool years; education accelerates this growth, whereas the absence of education curtails it (4) Traditional preschool is too concerned with social and personal development and insufficiently concerned with cognitive development.

Not all child psychologists agree with these programs. Some experts contend that the child has physiological limitations that restrict academic preparation at this age. The most common concern is with visual maturity. Opinion is divided as to reading readiness before the fifth birthday. Woodward (1966) is forthright in his opposition:

> Although his binocular vision has improved and he can focus more easily, he is not yet ready for any fine work of any description. In particular he is not yet usually ready to learn to read. The physical effort for a child first learning to read is very great. He has to focus his eyes on the beginning of a line of print, take in a number of symbols, and then stop before going on to the next batch. Then he has to make a new adjustment from the end of the first line of print to the beginning of the second, making a diagonal line. Quite often he will miss the beginning of the second and go on to the third. Even an adult, when tired, will do this, so one can understand how much more difficult for a child, who has only just learnt this difficult skill of focusing, this can be. (p. 50)

Many preschool specialists do not accept this assessment. Kindergarten and nursery-school teachers are as opinionated as developmentalists, with some refusing to begin reading instruction before first grade and others launching apparently successful reading programs for four-year-olds.

Preschools designed to enhance academic achievement do not assume that their students come from an academically impoverished environment. They attract middle class children because of the fascination these programs hold for professional, middle class parents. (See Super-baby syndrome in Chapter five). However, few preschools are exclusively involved with academic preparation; most combine academic preparation with development of personal and social skills.

Preschool as Personal/Social Enrichment

This type of preschool is distinguished from compensatory-education and academic-acceleration preschools by its avoidance of academic skills. An implicit assumption is that when children actualize the potentials of their present developmental level, they will develop the capacity to adjust to school demands when they arise. Personal/social practitioners usually say, in effect: "There is ample time for academic work later. Now we want children to appreciate art, nature, people, and themselves."

Competition is avoided, and sharing, cooperation, and participation are stressed. Excellence is encouraged because of the personal reward it brings but rarely is it emphasized in a hierarchialized sense (highest grade in the class) or in a numerical sense (55 out of 65 correct). Preschools that stress personal/social development are to a great extent modelled after the naturalistic tradition first inspired by Jean Jacques Rousseau, who believed that children inherently possess the "basics" for growth and will grow "naturally" as long as they are allowed to follow the course of their unique development and do not encounter undue stress or hardship in daily living.

Many parents and educators (and an increasing number of developmentalists) find this philosophy to their liking. The belief that four-year-olds can endlessly absorb school learning is falling into disfavor in certain quarters. One of the original Head Start pioneers put it this way:

> Playing is the job of 4-year-olds . . . We shouldn't be trying to raise IQ's. We should be raising socially competent individuals, people who are happy with themselves . . . We are putting so much pressure on these children that we are producing achievement anxiety. You can't hurry human development. It has a pace, and you must respect it...So if you insist that 4-year-olds be 6-year-olds, you are going to be giving many of them a built-in failure experience that can have lasting effects on their attitudes toward school (Trotter, 1987, p. 144).

Montessori Schools

> *And so we discovered that education is not*
> *something which the teacher does, but that it*
> *is a natural process which develops spontaneously*
> *in the human being.*
>
> Marie Montessori

A schooling technique for preschool children devised in the nineteenth century by Maria Montessori has received wide acceptance in North America during the past few decades because it blends academic preparation with personal/social development. Montessori believed that children should proceed at their own pace in an environment filled with games and toys, the proper utilization of which will enhance the child's thought process. The skills children learn in Montessori schools are thought by some psychologists to accelerate development from preoperational to concrete-operational thought. In Montessori schools youngsters learn to classify and order objects, such as beads of various colors. They practice seriating cylinder inserts or steps on a tower, and they play at transforming liquid by pouring it into containers of various sizes and shapes. Performance of these learning tasks requires skills described by Piaget as vital to normal growth.

Montessori based her schooling techniques on the premise that children need to attain mastery and competence within their environment. She believed that learning should be presented in concrete and structured settings and that the child should have a clear idea of what is expected. She also believed that children should learn responsibility for their behavior and that they understand that actions produce consequences. Her techniques are structured but not rigid, challenging but not overpowering.

In order to test whether children educated in Montessori programs possess mental abilities beyond their age level, Yussen and Santrock (1978) conducted an investigation. Children from Montessori programs were matched with children of the same age who had attended traditional programs and were tested on their ability to perform three important concrete-operational tasks: seriation of liquid, classification of liquid, and conservation of liquid. On all of these tasks (which, according to Piaget, are indicators of advancing mental processes) the Montessori students performed better. Whether their superior performance on these tasks reflects genuine mental maturity or merely greater familiarity with these kinds of tasks is open to dispute (Yussen and Santrock, p. 225).

The Assumptions Behind Early Intervention in Schooling

From a philosophical perspective, what assumptions do early-interventionists make about the nature of childhood learning? At least three stand out (1) Proponents of early intervention claim that environmental learning plays a major role in the development of intellectual abilities. In addition, they believe that these influences are advantageously received during the preschool years (2) Proponents of early intervention believe that planned, structured learning environments are superior to the traditional environment of childhood (3) Proponents of early intervention believe that gains made at one developmental stage positively influence future stages. That is, achievements build upon one another in an ever-increasing manner. Thus gains made during childhood serve as the foundation for even greater gains in adolescence.

Do Preschools Work?

Since schools have varied goals and ambitions their success must be viewed in terms of their unique purposes. Supervisors of compensatory-education preschools claim that pupils benefit from them, at least in the short run, and research supports this claim with such consistency that it is impossible to survey the abundant evidence in this brief space. Low-income children who attend compensatory-education programs consistently show improvement on measures of intelligence and academic achievement. They frequently demonstrate increased concentration, and they usually are able to stick with abstract tasks longer than low-income children who do not attend special compensatory programs. Research also suggests that children who have attended compensatory preschools fare better in the first grade.

Long-term studies, however, do not clearly establish that preschool programs have lasting beneficial effects. Nor is there conclusive evidence that the values of lower-income children shift in the direction of the schools.

Thus, many teachers feel that the value conflicts between schools and lower-income students are merely postponed, not eliminated. Research dealing with academic-preparation programs also yield mixed data. Alumni of such programs are, on the whole, more successful in elementary school than children who do not attend, but this is to be expected because children enrolled in academic programs are initially stronger in school-related skills. The least is known about preschools that stress personal/ social development because their goals are difficult to measure.

Compensatory-education programs consistently produce an increase in IQ scores – typically from five to 15 points that, unfortunately, tends to disappear by the time the child reaches the third or fourth grade.

Conclusion

In 1965 Benjamin Bloom (one of North America's leading authorities on preschool education) predicted the dominant future trends in preschool education. Since we are now living in the future he predicted, it is interesting to review his ideas on the topic.

Bloom claimed that early intervention schooling would stress *improvement in the quality of preschool and elementary education.* Specifically, the demands would be for:

1. Increasing emphasis on higher mental processes in problem solving rather than merely the learning of information.
2. Increasing emphasis on "learning to learn" – that is, teaching the child how to approach tasks with workable strategies.
3. Increasing emphasis on cultivating those aspects of interests, attitudes, and personality which will help the individual to further his own growth and development, and also help find meaning and purpose in life. [1965, p. 3]

Now, nearly three decades after this pioneer in early childhood education made his predictions, controversy and difference of opinion remain on the issue of early intervention.

When all is said and done, however, we must look to the scientific evidence. Here most researchers have found some consistency, although the reasons for the consistency are still debated:

1. Children who attend preschools are more advanced and possess a wider range of skills than kids who do not.
2. Children who attend preschools tend to be more socially competent and more outgoing in the elementary school years than kids who do not attend preschool.
3. Children who attend preschools tend to be more goal-directed and more task-oriented than kids who do not attend preschool.

4. In a review of 56 studies on this topic, only 3 studies showed *no differences* between those who attend and do not attend preschools; 53 studies *showed advantages to those who did attend* (Kaplan, 1988, p. 199).

The Major Concepts of this Chapter

1. Compared with toddlers the mental capacities of the preschooler are marked by greater concept formation, greater duration and depth of memory, greater length of concentration, increased language mastery, and superior social understanding. However, compared with school-aged children they are limited by prerational and prelogical thought mechanisms.

2. The preschool years are characterized by pre-operational thinking in Piaget's developmental progression. Thought advances by means of assimilation – fitting new experiences into already existing mental schema, and accommodation – adjusting mental schema in order to allow for new experiences which could not be incorporated into existing schema.

3. Preschoolers come to understand causality more accurately, their memories grow and develop, they gain knowledge of quantity and an awareness of time, their range of concepts expands, and they gain more accurate social perceptions.

4. Education for the preschooler may take one of three general forms, compensatory education, academic preparation, and personal and social enrichment. Compensatory education attempts to offset limited learning opportunities in the home. Academic preparation programs stress skills which relate to school programming, such as number concepts and reading. Social and personal enrichment programs avoid academic skills in favor of sharing, cooperation and participation.

5. Although average I.Q. scores may rise as the result of compensatory education, these gains tend to disappear by the time children reach the third of fourth grade. Many experts agree that parent-child interaction is more important than schooling during the preschool years.

8

Physical Expansion and Social Liberation: Years Three, Four, and Five

Physical Growth During the Preschool Years

> *Throughout life a person's view of himself is*
> *influenced by his perception of his body and its*
> *properties, his strength and skill in physical activities.*
> Arthur M. Jersild

The normal preschool child is a masterpiece of dynamic energy and physical architecture. Although contours and proportions are not in their final state, they are remarkably well suited to the developmental needs of this age. Preschool children move at high speed through their daily routine, with only occasional pit stops for fuel and rest. An ordinary adult would collapse from exhaustion if required to follow the same manoeuvres, contortions, and physical gyrations. Although the preschool span includes the years when the child learns to concentrate energy and focus behavior, a great deal of random, fidgety activity remains. Special attention and care must be given to the developing body because it has special requirements and is undergoing important growth transitions.

Muscles are developing more rapidly than other parts of the body. About 75 percent of the child's mass increase during the fifth year of life is the result of increased muscular development. Muscle development in the legs is especially advanced because the child spends most of the waking hours exercising them. Arm strength is is not nearly as developed, however, a few kids bring barely noticeable biceps to the first grade. Some boys can be distinguished from girls by their expanded shoulders and chest cavity, but not many. Although the difference is not noticeable by visual inspection, boys have longer forearms in relation to their body size than girls and this provides them with an advantage in activities that require arm strength or leverage, but because girls are slightly more mature than boys, it will be a few years before this difference becomes significant.

Physical growth during the preschool years is moderately stable, children who are tall for their age at two years tend to be tall for their age when they are six, and children who are short for their age at two tend to be short at six. Chubbiness is a different matter; it is not uncommon for a chubby toddler to be of normal, even skinny, proportions by the time of entering first grade. The respiratory system becomes more stable than it was during toddlerhood, permitting greater endurance and stamina. Breathing becomes slower and deeper, and heart beat becomes slower and less variable. Blood pressure increases steadily.

The range of normal heart size is considerably greater than previously thought. A child who has been growing fast and who is overweight is likely to have a large heart, whereas a child of average size usually has an average heart size. "When it comes to shape, the hearts of healthy children have differences so great that some of them suggest textbook pictures of congenital heart disease – and yet nothing is wrong. The shape of a child's heart is his own business. After he gets that shape, he is going to keep it, barring affliction with a serious disease" (Gray, 1967, p. 133).

Most parents find it difficult to keep pace with their child in an open park, and nursery-school teachers must impose restrictions on the range and rowdiness of play. Burgeoning muscles demand exercise, but preschoolers' limited experience does not allow them to judge how best to satisfy this need. Boys are especially rowdy and boisterous, but when they inadvertently arouse the anger of a female peer they may find themselves out hustled and out muscled.

Skeletal development is unfolding according to its genetic script with some bones growing rapidly while others barely grow at all (reflecting the principle of asynchronous growth). The skeleton is lengthening. Long bones of the arms and legs are maturing at an accelerated pace creating the lean athletic appearance typical of so many five-year-olds. Muscles grow rapidly to accommodate the expanding skeleton, but the consequences are not nearly as noticeable. Even though preschoolers are growing up, fewer than three percent of them are taller than 120 centimetres (4 feet 2 inches) on their fifth birthday, and fewer than three percent are shorter than 102 (3 feet 6 inches) centimetres at this age. Thus, 94 percent of five-year-olds are between 1.02 and 1.20 metres (3 feet 6 inches to 4 feet 2 inches) tall.

(Table 8-1 shows the growth of boys and girls in the tenth and 90th percentiles for their age group. Note the similarity between the boys and the girls. Note also that height and weight, although they increase continuously, do not increase by the same amount in each six- month period.)

Table 8-1 Height and Weight Increases, Ages Three to Six

Age	Boys 10 Percentile	90 Percentile	Girls 10 Percentile	90 Percentile
	Height in Inches			
3	36.25	39.5	35.5	39.75
3½	37.75	41	37	41.5
4	39	42.75	38.5	43
4½	40.25	44.25	39.75	44.75
5	41.25	45.5	41	45.5
5½	42.5	47.25	42.5	46.75
6	43.75	48.5	43.5	48
	Weight in Pounds			
3	28.75	36.75	27.5	37.5
3½	30.5	39	29.5	40.5
4	32	41.5	31.25	43.5
4½	33.25	44	33	46.75
5	36	48.25	35.5	48.75
5½	38.75	53	38	51.25
6	41	56.5	39.5	54.25

Based on data from Watson and Lowrey, 1962.

Of special interest to psychologists are the bones of the wrist and hand, which show a consistent pattern of development and thus serve as a fairly reliable index to the development of the rest of the skeleton. Children with advanced wrist development tend to have overall skeletal precocity; those with wrist development below the average tend toward skeletal immaturity. At birth, wrist bones are soft cartilage. When wrist bones are present at birth, their owner is much more likely to be a girl than a boy. The cartilage progressively calcifies into eight small bones. The rate of this calcification process indicates the rate of overall bone development.

Preschoolers still have their baby (deciduous) teeth, which they start losing between the sixth and twelfth year. Baby teeth are important because they influence the positioning of permanent teeth.

The tendency to respond to infection with a high fever is not as evident during the preschool years as it was during toddlerhood. Infections generally produce less of a temperature increase than they did during infancy, but the duration of the illness is usually longer. Moreover, the possibility of serious heart symptoms following a disease is smaller than it was during the first two years of life. Some evidence points to a correlation between the levels of the blood proteins (beta and gamma globulin) and the development of lymph

---

Carpal Age as a Measure of Development

Developmental maturity can be estimated from the ossification of a child's bone structure. Here is how this procedure works. X-rays are taken of the wrist bones of numerous children; these X-rays then serve as norms for particular age groups. By analyzing the X-rays it is possible to ascertain an average bone density for each age, against which any individual can be compared. Thus, a six-year-old whose carpal age (wrist age) is equal to that of an average eight-year-old is developmentally advanced for his chronological age. A child of nine years whose carpal age is seven years is behind the average developmentally. Advocates of carpal age as a method of measurement claim that it is a more accurate measure of developmental maturity than chronological age. Skeletal maturity is an important factor to consider in human growth and development because it is positively correlated with other developmental phenomena, including the onset of the first menstrual flow, adult height, and adult weight.

---

tissue in the body. When a child's blood contains high levels of these globulins, she is likely to have larger tonsils and adenoids and more lymph nodes of every kind. Such children are more able to resist colds and other respiratory diseases than are children with smaller quantities of these globulins (Gray, 1967, p. 135).

The growing body has special requirements for exercise, rest, and nutrition. Proper development of the large muscles depends on vigorous exercise. Rest, especially deep sleep, is necessary for cell repair and production. And consumption of foods containing calcium and protein is especially critical if the growing skeleton and muscle fibre are to be adequately nourished.

Global "Athletic" Abilities of the Preschooler

Calendar years are quite reliable predictors of physical skills during the preschool period. For example, as far as running is concerned we note that most three-year-olds run with a lack of control, with flat foot action, and have only a limited ability to turn sharply. Four-year-olds run with good control, stop and start well, deploy a longer stride. They can run 35 metres in about 25 seconds. Five-year-olds are very good runners, they can accelerate while in gallop, and execute some of the open-field skills of a halfback. Very few Threes can equal the average four-year-old in running skill and very few Fours can equal the average five-year-old. This progression is not unfailingly true, but for the vast majority of children is a very safe guideline.

The following chart is designed to provide the reader with a general understanding of preschool athletic abilities.

Physical Abilities during the Preschool Years (by age)

	3-year-old	4-year-old	5-year-old
Galloping	Most children cannot gallop. Early Attempts are some variation of the run pattern.	Most children learn to gallop. The pattern is a run-and-leap pattern.	Most can gallop. Can gallop with a left and right lead foot. Can start and stop at will.
Hopping	Can hop 10 times consecutively on both feet. Can hop 1-3 times on one foot. Great difficulty with hop pattern. Gross movements and a lot of arm movement.	Less than half are proficient at hopping. Can hop 7-9 times on one foot. Hop pattern is stiff and not fluid.	About 80% become proficient. Can hop 10 or more times on one foot. Hop is spring-like – action in ankles, knees and hips.
Climbing	Ascends stairs with alternate foot pattern. Descends stairs mostly with mark-time foot pattern. Climbing onto and off of low items improves with higher heights being conquered.	Ascends stairs using alternate foot pattern. Descends stairs with alternate foot pattern. Can climb a large ladder slowly with alternate foot pattern.	Climbing skill increasing; 70% can climb a rope ladder with bottom free. About 1/3 can climb a pole. Climbing includes more challenging objects such as trees, jungle gyms, large beams.
Balance	Balance-beam walking characterized by mark-time sequences.	Balance-beam walking characterized by alternate shuffle step.	Balance-beam walking characterized by alternate step pattern.
Skipping	Skip is characterized by a shuffle step. Can skip on one foot and walk on the other. Actual true skip pattern seldom performed.	14% can skip. One-foot skip still prevalent. Overall movement stiff and undifferentiated. Excessive arm action frequent. Skip mostly flat-footed.	72% are proficient. Can skip with alternate foot pattern. Overall movements more smooth and fluid. More efficient use of arms. Skip mostly on balls of feet.
Jumping	40% are proficient. Jumping pattern lacks differentiation. Lands without knee bend to absorb force. Minimal crouch for take off. Arms used ineffectively.	70% are proficient. Jumping pattern characterized by more preliminary crouch. Can do standing broad jump 2/3 metre. 90% can hurdle jump 5 inches.	80% are skillful. Overall jumping pattern more smooth and rhythmical. Use of arm thrust at take-off evident. More proficient landing. Can do running broad jump about one metre.

(Based upon information from Corbin, 1980)

Perhaps the most significant research on this topic was conducted by Thomas and French (1985). They gathered data from numerous cross- sectional and longitudinal studies, analyzing over 31,000 subjects between 3 and 20 years of age. Of special interest in this research project were physical tasks including running, jumping, throwing, sit- ups and arm strength. The findings coincided with most previous research in this area, with four tasks (long jump, sit-ups, grip strength, and sprinting) showing predictable trends: slight superiority of boys over girls with differences becoming greater during the elementary school years, and even greater after puberty. Importantly, girls who receive coaching, or who play on athletic teams cut this male-female difference dramatically, causing Thomas and French to conclude that environmental factors were the major cause of male performance in these areas. One exception, however, was throwing ability where boys outperformed girls in both speed and distance from the preschool years onwards. The differences were sufficiently great, and environmental factors sufficiently minor, that the authors conclude that on this measure the differences between the sexes are biologically-based.

Brain Development

At the beginning of the preschool period (three years) the brain has attained about 50 percent of its adult weight; at the end of the preschool years (age six) the brain has attained about 90 percent of its adult weight. In the midst of this impressive growth in size and volume *myelination* within and between several areas of the brain also undergoes impressive advancement. (Myelination is the process by which the sheath of fatty cells that covers the neurons stabilizes them and speeds the transmission of impulses along the neurons.)

Cole and Cole (1989) point out several links in the relationship between brain development and pre-school thought. First, the auditory system develops rapidly "which is consistent with the fact that the preschool period is a time of rapid language growth." Second, more effective connections are established between the temporal, occipital and parietal areas of the brain which are important in the processing of time, space and visual information. "The increased connections among these different centers allow for more efficient synthesis of information about different aspects of a problem." Which, not coincidentally, is one of the major achievements of preschool thought. In addition, these increasingly efficient brain areas become more integrated with the speech areas of the brain which enhances symbolization, communication efficiency and a more proficient linkage of words with ideas.

Other regions of the brain also undergo rapid myelination during the preschool years. The hippocampus, which is vital to short-term memory, matures and refines its functions. The fibers linking the cerebellum to the cerebral cortex also mature, permitting improving control of fine motor coordination such as that required to manipulate a pencil (p. 324).

Nutrition and Malnutrition

Preschoolers are finicky eaters and do not eat something merely because it is on their dinner plate; food that does not meet their fluctuating standards of texture, color or consistency may be rejected. Firm insistence that the child eat a certain food is sometimes successful, but equally often (especially with four-year-olds) the child will refuse to eat or will feign illness upon taking a bite. Sweets are universal favorites and most children will, if allowed, eat them until plagued by upset stomach. When sweets are available upon request, the preschool child will attack them almost as piggishly as when they are available only rarely. Some moderation comes about during the early school years in the matter of sweets, but rarely before then.

Malnutrition – Because the likelihood of malnutrition is greater during the preschool years than in any other period of childhood, the significance of malnutrition should be emphasized. The energy requirement per unit of body weight for the preschooler is high compared with that of the adult. The caloric need increases each year, so that it is unwise to base a judgment about preschool nutritional needs on the needs of the preceding year. Four-year-old boys need, on the average, 100 more calories per day than three-year-old boys. Central to the child's diet is protein. The spectacular rate of muscle growth and the relatively high incidence of febrile (feverish) illness make intake of protein during the preschool years important. Severe protein malnutrition is the most common form of nutritional deficiency among children of the world and is not confined to poor or war torn countries.

Malnutrition is particularly serious during the preschool years because good nutrition is essential to normal brain development, proper skeletal growth, sexual development, resistance to infection, and the ability to tolerate stress. Damage may be subtle or severe, permanent or temporary. Researchers studying children malnourished during wartime have concluded that *chronic malnutrition* results in brain damage as well as permanent height and weight stunting. If the malnutrition is less severe and the child is placed on a sound corrective diet, the effects of childhood malnutrition are overcome, and by adolescence the individual will be about normal in size and physique. Mild malnutrition may cause apathy, fatigue, reduced ability to concentrate, and reduced ability to cope with the environment.

In recent years attention in North America has shifted to what has been called *silent malnutrition,* a nutritional disorder most commonly observed among the poor in technologically advanced countries. It is typified by sufficient caloric intake to prevent the profound symptoms of starvation or protein deficiency, but which nevertheless produces a host of lesser symptoms which are dangerous to the child's health. These children tend to be short for their age (one of the most consistent correlates of malnutrition), and highly susceptible to infections and illness. As a rule, they are victims of a household in which nutritionally sound food is in short supply and nutritionally unsound food (junk food) in greater supply. Preschool kids often don't know the difference between the depleted condition of silent malnutrition and the more exuberant condition which typifies properly nourished children. Frequently a preschool teacher is the first to recognize the problem because under nourished youngsters have great difficulty concentrating, focusing and playing with typical exuberance.

Under ordinary circumstances, if protein, calcium, and iron requirements are met, other mineral requirements will also be satisfied. *If adults eat well-balanced, nutritionally sound meals and share them with their preschooler* the child's growth requirements usually will be adequately met.

Sex Differences: Physical and Behavioral

Research conducted during the past two decades indicates that the physical differences between preschool boys and girls are slight. Girls demonstrate developmental maturity over boys from the earliest days of life and suffer fewer perceptual and mental defects. However, by the preschool years boys have caught up in most developmental areas, and the differences that do exist, although favoring girls, do not seem to give them any conspicuous advantage over boys. Physically, boys and girls are of about the same height and weight during the preschool years, with boys having slightly more weight and being slightly taller. In terms of muscle strength, the sexes are about the same, with boys again holding a very slight advantage. In skills involving balance, agility, speed, and endurance, the sexes are about the some (the species traits that make men stronger, taller, and faster do not surface until early or middle adolescence). Mentally, the sexes are similar. Neither sex scores significantly higher on valid IQ measures; nor does one sex evidence greater capacity for memory, concept formation, or other basic intellectual abilities. Emotionally, the sexes are again about the same, although boys evidence a greater incidence of severe emotional disturbance. Language abilities, which are more advanced among girls during the first three years, tend to balance out by age four or five. Although girls acquire their first 50 words several months sooner than boys and possess better articulation, by age five or six they do not evidence significant superiority over boys in sentence length, sentence complexity, or vocabulary size.

With regard to behavior however, considerable differences between the sexes are evident in North American culture. Boys tend to be more rowdy and more boisterous in group settings; the bully in the day-care centre or kindergarten is almost always a boy. The "bully" issue is important in a theoretical sense, because there is no physical reason why a girl could not be the class bully.

Three-and four-year-olds have a meagre concept of gender. Most of them do not even know what distinguishes a boy from a girl, and few of them know that what you are is how you stay. When children finally learn that your sex does not change over time (boys remain boys even as they get older), that gender does not change by wearing clothes associated with the opposite sex (Stella does not become a boy if she wears cowboy boots), or by playing games associated with the opposite sex (Jimmy won't become a girl if he plays with dolls), they have attained what is known as *gender constancy*. Many four-year-olds believe that if you play girl games you might become a girl, or that if you wear girls clothing you might become a girl. On the other hand, very few six-year-olds hold these beliefs. Three and four-year-olds tend not to pay attention to genital differences when deciding who is a boy or a girl. The classic exemplification of this comes when a four-year-old is asked whether the nude children in a picture are boys or girls and replies "How can I tell? They don't have any clothes on."

In conclusion, the differences among the young in our species in skills or abilities are not based in a significant way on gender; rather, their origin is most consistently found in their differential social treatment. (A brief message to the reader: that the differences between the sexes are minor during childhood does not mean they remain so throughout the life cycle. During adolescence, with the onset of puberty, the differences between the sexes become pronounced, especially with regard to speed, strength, stamina, and general temperment. For a thorough assessment of these differences, consult *The Nature Of Adolescence,* (Mitchell, 1986).

Developmental Tasks of the Preschool Years

Developmental tasks include a broad range of social and biological skills which children must master in order to handle the requirements of the specific developmental stage they are growing through, and as well, the requirements of future developmental stages. During the preschool years many such tasks present themselves, and as educational and social demands are increasingly placed upon three- four- and five-year-olds more tasks will emerge in future years. Three developmental tasks are of special importance during the preschool years because numerous requirements are based upon their mastery by age six or seven. They include: acquiring greater control of biological and social impulses, learning about sex roles, and developing a conscience.

To acquire greater control of biological and social impulses – Preschoolers learn to control their physical energy, to attend to one specific part of the environment, to share and to cooperate and to accept "No." These years are filled with learning self-restraint, self- control, and self-discipline. Most youngsters make remarkable strides in sociability, interpersonal relations, and consistency of action during the preschool years.

Eleanor Maccoby (1980) has outlined four kinds of inhibition that preschoolers attempt to master. Mastering these basic forms of self-control contributes immensely to effective interaction with adults and contributes to the self-regulation required in the forthcoming years of middle childhood.

Inhibition of movement – The ability to regulate one's movement, to sit still when one wants to squirm, or to stand on tip toes even when tired, are skills learned during the preschool years. Learning to stop what one is doing is not easy; even more difficult is to shift quickly from one task to another. Most four-year-olds, for example, have trouble inhibiting their impulses in the game "Simon Says." They fail time and again to restrain themselves because they are impelled to action even when permission is not granted by "Simon Says."

Inhibition of emotions – Children learn not to cry just because their tooth hurts, or not to mope because another kid says something mean. Inhibiting emotions is new to the preschoolers since it is rarely exercised during toddlerhood. By six some kids will not cry during a sad movie even though they want to because they evaluate their own emotional displays. Inhibition of emotions is not the stifling of all emotion, rather it is imposing a certain measure of self-discipline so that emotions are not always worn on one's sleeve.

Inhibition of conclusions – By grade one most children have learned to keep from blurting out their conclusions prematurely. This comes as a relief to teachers bombarded with answers before the question has been asked. Three- and four-year-olds jump to conclusions because they do not grasp that a problem cannot be solved until all information is presented. When asked: "How much do three chocolate bars cost?" a three-year-old may reply "Three dollars... If you answer 'No' the child may then immediately reply "Two dollars." Almost never "How much does one cost?" By age six kids learn to inhibit (somewhat) their impulsiveness, which in turn lessens their habit of jumping to premature conclusions.

Inhibition of Choice – When given the choice between now or later, three- and four-year-olds almost always choose now. Even when later yields more benefits they choose now. "Would you like three chocolate bars tomorrow or one now?" "One now, please." By age six youngsters learn from experience that time passes and future rewards are sometimes worth the wait. Middle class parents are especially prone to teaching the merits of delayed choice and delayed gratification, thus encouraging the child's disposition toward inhibition of impulses.

To learn about gender differences and sex roles – Upon entering the first grade, children have limited understanding of the differences between men and women, and as a result of this meagre understanding they may hold either extremely narrow or remarkably tolerant views on sex roles. Their understanding of sex-role differentiation is acquired at home, from peers, and via the media (especially television). Although over the course of time children change their viewpoints about what is masculine or feminine, young boys generally enjoy doing what they understand as manly and young girls generally enjoy what they understand as womanly. It is comparatively easy to convince a boy that cooking is for men as well as women, but it is virtually impossible to get the same boy to play cooking games if he thinks cooking is for females only.

Boys and girls show different patterns of conflict during the preschool years, especially after age three. Boys become increasingly combative and rowdy in their disagreements, whereas girls tend to quarrel less and less after age three, and the quarrels they have tend to be verbal rather than physical. As with many traits, however, sexual differences of this kind become less distinct when society treats young boys and girls the some. Neither sex displays much poise in disagreements, and both will resort to almost any course of action that will bring about the desired end. One favorite method is to bring in an adult who will rule in one's favor. Because this method commonly backfires, children learn to keep adults out of peer disagreements whenever possible. In fact, one of the essential skills acquired during the preschool years is the ability to terminate a quarrel without hitting, biting, or calling for help from an adult. The preschooler who has not acquired these abilities encounters numerous problems in social living when faced with the complicated social structure of kindergarten or the first grade.

To develop a conscience – The internal set of impulses and guidelines inclining away from what the child considers bad and toward what the child considers good is called the *conscience*. For the most part, conscience is learned, and it is sufficiently powerful that young children may experience shame or guilt when they violate it. The conscience represents an internal reference that permits the child to make decisions on grounds other than the purely pragmatic or egocentric; thus, the preschooler no longer bases decisions totally on impulses. The emergence of conscience adds a new set of complications for the preschooler, who now approaches the world not only in terms of real and unreal but also in terms of good and bad. The preschooler's conscience is narrow because mental abilities are not mature enough to see two sides to an issue, and moral outlook is, essentially a series of learned responses.

Conscience Development in the Young Child

The young child's conscience evolves from two basic sources. The first is the specific teachings (prohibitions mainly) received from parents. The "do's" and "don'ts" of daily behavior. The second source derives from the child's identification with parents, from striving to be like them, and emulating their ideas about right and wrong. Children internalize their identifications, eventually becoming, in effect, junior representatives of family morality. Preschoolers absorb moral rules much as they do rules of games or other structured activities.

Most developmental psychologists underplay moral development among three-four- and five-year-olds because such impressive progress is made in the next developmental stage, middle childhood. Jerome Kagan (1984) is a notable exception to this trend, and some of his ideas concerning preschool moral development are presented here. In essence, Kagan claims that significant strides in moral development occur in the preschool years, and these advances contribute to a more "moral" youngster than heretofore acknowledged by developmental psychologists. Of special significance are the following:

1. Two-year-olds have a limited capacity for empathy, and the beginning indicators of sensitivity to others,

2. Three-year-olds reflect on the appropriateness of their behavior, before, during and after the action. They may be confused or frightened if they sense they have done something wrong, or out of order.

3. By age four children begin to evaluate themselves and their actions as "good" or "bad." Behavior is inhibited by punishment, and by the child's belief (or assessment) that the action is "wrong" or "bad."

4. At age four children think that adults can read their thoughts, and they sometimes scold themselves for their private thoughts.

5. Four-and five-year-olds experience pride and shame as a result of comparing themselves with others.

6. Preschoolers tend to think of adults as "better" than themselves, and do not like to disappoint them.

7. Shame (a painful feeling of blameworthiness) usually appears before guilt (the feeling of having committed an offense) in the preschooler's development.

8. Shame, guilt, and anxiety are feelings which preschoolers experience when they do something wrong – or something they somehow think is wrong.

The net effect of Kagan's evaluation is to help us understand the extent to which children respond to a broad range of right and wrong (thus having a certain morality), and to remind us that the pain of shame, guilt, and fear we associate with older people also exists in the emotional world of three-four- and five-year-olds.

Aggression: Darwin Rules the Sandbox

I understand the fury in your words, but not the words.

Shakespeare

Preschool children around the world show aggression by fighting, kicking, biting, and swearing. Some cultures are effective in curtailing it while other cultures encourage aggression by praising it or by creating environments in which children are continually frustrated and therefore demonstrate more anger and aggression.

Very few youngsters demonstrate aggression before 18 months; by age two, however, many children will slap when angered, or destroy the product of another child's play for the reaction it elicits. By age three or four children are prone toward retaliating against "unfair" treatment, and by age four or five it is not uncommon for two kids to join forces against a third and rough him up soundly. The reasons for aggression are numerous, but usually they are based on anger toward parents, conflict with peers or siblings, and frustration with the world at large.

As children are herded together in group settings such as daycare centres the probability of aggression increases because disagreements over playthings and possessions are typical sources of aggressive behavior. Also, at this age children learn that supervisors do not always take their point of view in a disagreement, as mother usually does; thus kids settle disputes on their own terms, and in the world of preschoolers this usually means some form of aggression.

At age four or five a shift toward verbal aggression takes place in many youngsters. When frustrated a five-year-old may retort, "You jackass" and then walk away; the recipient of the slur may retaliate with "You ugly freak" and move on indifferently to the next event on the agenda. Some children carry a general edginess that easily explodes into aggression at the slightest aggravation. This "free floating" frustration is typical among youngsters whose home life is turbulent or abusive, or whose daily life is riddled with failure and incompetence.

The causes of aggression are not thoroughly understood in either adults or children; however it is generally assumed that frustration greatly increases the probability of aggression; this, in simplified terms, is the famous "frustration/aggression hypothesis." However, many children do not show much aggression even when frustrated.

The family plays an important role in childhood aggression. Rejected or unwanted children tend to be more aggressive than children who receive abundant love and affection. Parents who tolerate aggression from their children tend to get more of it than parents who do not.

A competence factor influences childhood aggression. Kids who are good at aggressing tend to do more of it. Youngsters who lose every shoving match learn not to initiate them, and the same goes for shouting or insult confrontations. "Bullies," for the most part, are better at aggression than their peers.

In our culture a boy is more likely than a girl to receive praise for retaliating against a bully, for settling a disagreement with fists instead of sentences, or for intimidating another with physical threats. Whether this differential reinforcement is sufficient to account for the fact that preschool boys (especially five-year-olds) are physically more aggressive than girls is a matter of theoretical dispute. Interestingly, among virtually all of our evolutional cousins (chimpanzees, gorilas, etc.) males are more aggressive than females throughout childhood and adolescence.

Passive aggression is a type of indirect retaliation. For example, rather than striking out at mother, the child may "accidentally" spill milk at the supper table. Rather than shout at mother, the child may fail to make it to the bathroom and require mother to stop what she is doing and prepare a change of clothing. Passive aggression is a way of venting frustration or anger without being held responsible. Its great allure is that, as a bonus, it sometimes brings attention to a child who feels unnoticed.

It should be noted that assertiveness is not the same as aggression. In the world of childhood survival, one learns to take the initiative, to stand up for one's rights, and to "go for it" when the situation demands. This type of normal assertiveness is sometimes confused with aggression among nervous adults who inadvertently punish children for honest self-assertion. Eventually, every supervisor of children must distinguish legitimate assertion from unjustified aggression. In the sandbox jungle, this is no easy task.

Punishment

Punishment is intended to stifle unacceptable behavior or to promote desired behavior. Because the child is egocentric and has difficulty processing abstract rules, the adult must negotiate punishment (and reconciliation) with fairness and compassion. Kaplan (1988, p. 215) has formulated a series of guidelines of considerable practical value in this matter:

1. Be as consistent as possible about which behaviors are acceptable and which are not.
2. Continually threatening a child without carrying through a reasonable disciplinary action decreases the adult's influence over the child.
3. Never threaten to give a child a punishment that either cannot be carried out ethically or that you would not be willing to administer.
4. Especially when dealing with younger children, punishment should be as immediate as possible. However, do not administer punishments that are too severe for the misbehavior.
5. Moderate punishments are usually more effective than severe ones. After you have used your harshest punishment on a child, you have nowhere to go. In addition, if the punishment is too severe for the "crime," the child tends to reflect on the punishment instead of on what was done to deserve it.
6. Do not use the "wait until father (or mother) comes home approach."
7. Give your child a chance to answer any accusations.
8. Punishment is most effective when it is combined with reinforcement for the correct response. Using positive reinforcement along with

disciplinary action increases the effectiveness of both.

9. Overreliance on punishment decreases communication, as children become afraid to confide in adults. Keep the lines of communication open.

10. Use the minimum amount of punishment that will successfully accomplish your goal.

11. Punish only the child's action. Some parents make statements concerning how bad the child is, which focuses on the child rather than on inappropriate behavior. Punishment should be aimed at reducing troublesome behavior, not at injuring the child's self-concept.

TV and Aggression

Preschoolers watch TV about 120 to 130 hours per month, and much of what they watch contains violence. About two-thirds of children's comedy shows include violent episodes, sometimes four or five per show, and crime and Western TV shows average about eight or nine violent episodes per hour. The net consequence is that preschoolers view several hundred acts of violence per month on the family television screen.

Watching violence and actually engaging in violence are two different things. In order to investigate the relationship between the two, Liebert and Baron (1972) conducted an experiment in which children watched a sequence from a popular television show that included fist fights, shootings, and a knifing. Following the viewing the children were shown a panel in which one button was labelled Help and another Hurt. They were told that another group of children were playing in the other room. The extent to which they pushed Hurt or Help was the indicator in this experiment of aggression. The experiment found that the children who watched the violent TV show pushed the Hurt button for a longer period of time than did children who had watched a TV show of similar length dealing with sports. The experimenters concluded that the willingness to aggress is encouraged by watching violent TV fare. Interestingly, when subjects watched a TV excerpt in which the theme was cooperation rather than aggression they pushed the Help button longer than children who watched nonviolent fare that did not have a cooperation theme. These experiments, in conjunction with dozens of others similar in design, have caused most experts to conclude that children imitate what they see on TV, whether it is violent and aggressive or sharing and cooperative.

TV Viewing For Preschoolers*

1. Don't allow the child to sit too close to the TV set; it places unnecessary strain on the eyes.

2. Don't allow the child to turn up the volume too loud. Kids prefer the sound to be loud, but it is unnecessary and possibly harmful.

3. Don't allow the child to watch TV in the dark, it increases eye strain.

4. Don't allow your child to snack in front of the TV set. Grazing while viewing encourages poor dietary habits and the consumption of empty calories. In addition, TV commercials promote the consumption of junk food, making the habit even easier to acquire.

5. Don't rely on one show or one kind of show; make sure your child watches a variety of shows.

6. Limit preschoolers to a half-hour of TV at a sitting. Longer periods encourage passive blandness and non-responsiveness.

7. Don't rely on TV for family interaction. Watching TV as a family is OK, but it should constitute only a small part of family togetherness and interaction.

8. Don't allow TV information to go unchallenged. Make sure your child questions the claims of advertisers and the heroics or unbelievable achievements of TV stars.

---

* (Based upon materials in *Television and Your Child,* by C. Luke, 1988.)

Yearly Growth Profiles

Growth profiles are attempts to describe and isolate some of the consistently recurring traits typical of children during specific calendar years in the growth cycle. Like most investigations in developmental psychology, they rely heavily upon averages and norms; therefore, they are not prescriptions about how three- or four-year-olds should be, rather they are descriptions of how many three- and four- year-olds really are.

As has been emphasized throughout this book, children grow in moderately predictable directions on moderately predictable time-tables and because of this children of similar ages manifest a wide range of similarities in their physiology, their psychology and their understanding of the world. In the following pages we shall introduce you to some of these commonalities as they manifest themselves in the preschool years.

The Three-Year-Old

Three-year-old children have many things in common, because their physical, mental, and social development has taken them through similar growth experiences and left them with similar capacities, abilities, and inclinations. We cannot say about three-year-olds, any more than about any other age group, that they all possess certain attributes. However, certain traits have been observed so many times and with such consistency that it is safe to say that they characterize *most* three-year-olds.

Perhaps the most significant advancement of the three-year-old is that she has outgrown many of the rigid, narrow, and inflexible traits of the two-year-old. Tension and anxiety are part of every developmental age, but during the year between the third and fourth birthdays children commonly reach the most comfortable balance of social, mental, and physical demands of the entire preschool period.

Three is becoming more streamlined. Although not a creature of graceful mobility, the three-year-old moves with more poise and agility than that shown only a few months before. The average three-year-old weighs about 15 kilograms (33 pounds) but will add two more kilograms (4.4 pounds) by the fourth birthday and another two (4.4 pounds) by the fifth. There is no significant sex difference in size, but boys do weigh slightly more than girls. The average three-year-old is about 92 centimetres (3 feet 2 inches) tall and will grow another 13 centimetres (5.5 inches) during the next two years. Proportions are undergoing change because the body is lengthening. Baby fat disappears, and the torso and long bones of the legs and arms lengthen. The child takes on a lean, sinewy glide that stays until the long bones stop growing more rapidly than the rest of the body.

Threes show a marked increase in body coordination and constantly startle parents with their ability to negotiate tasks that they could not have managed six months earlier without catastrophic results. They run with smoothness, accelerate and decelerate, turn corners with moderate sharpness, and stop suddenly, although not always predictably. High-powered acrobatics, such as standing on one foot for several seconds, hopping, skipping, and smooth backward locomotion, however, are still beyond their ability. Threes make it through the day without wetting or soiling but still have difficulty at night. They bruise easily and have ample occasion for doing so because they run with their head thrown back (in order to maintain balance) and frequently trip over obstructions they fail to see and collide with obstacles that do not bend.

A spirit of cooperation characterizes Three that was almost totally lacking in the two-year-old. There is a strong desire to make social contacts and to have someone with whom to visit, play, and, in general, be with. Nursery-school teachers enjoy three-year-olds because of their desire to tell chatty stories and to visit pleasantly and nonchalantly.

Cooperative play is becoming part of daily routine, as is the tendency to follow suggestions. As Threes enjoy imitation, they may adopt the behavior of the child next to them for no reason other than to do what seems to be working for someone else. Preschoolers are so empathetic they may burst into tears upon observing a friend crying. They can as easily become angry or sorrowful if that is the mood of a comrade. Threes do as they see. The details of daily living, such as eating, sleeping, eliminating, and playing, are coped with far more easily than during toddlerhood when maturational abilities and acquired skills were both less developed. Despite important differences among young children, and within the same child over time, most psychologists conclude that Three is a comparatively delightful age, and most parents agree.

The child has less need for rigidness or stubbornness because alternatives are more easily perceived, and routine can be interrupted without the child's feeling that it has been destroyed. Impulsiveness is reduced, and self-discipline is improved. The three-year-old becomes more aware of the separate existence of mother, father, brother, and sister and learns that they have their own relationships with one another. Threes are still sufficiently egocentric, though, to assume that everyone naturally wants to play or visit with them. This makes them enjoyable when their expectations are correct but a nuisance when they are not.

Three-year-olds love to dart into the TV room for a quick commercial and then as quickly dart back to their previous involvement. Commercials cater to their attention span, their sense of urgency, their enthusiasm for jingle or rhyme, and, frequently, to their intellectual level.

Threes talk when they play. They talk in bed, in the bathtub, in the back yard, at church, in the nursery, and in the movies. Words dominate the three-year-old in a way unfathomable to the two-year-old. Although three-year-olds cannot be dissuaded by reason or logic, they can be sidetracked by the melody of words or by the secure persuasiveness of the person who issues them. Play involves chatter, gossip, and comments that may or may not relate to the goings-on. In language development the three-year-old resembles four vastly more than two. The three-year- old listens to learn and learns to listen.

Three identifies with authority figures and periodically will arrive on the scene prepared to conduct a medical investigation, issue a ticket for speeding, or provide corrective discipline for some misbehavior. Three's readily accept that police officers are friends, that fire fighters are heroic, and that teachers are smart. They also accept that they could grow up to be any, or all, of these professionals. Symbols of authority are also fun. Hats, badges, and other signs of silent power attract.

Tantrums are recuperated from more quickly than before, but this is a short-lived respite because many four-year-olds resume the kind of temper tantrums that typify the two-year-old. A fairly good understanding of "Wait your own turn" is forming at this age. Three can be taught household rules and responsibilities, if they are not complex.

Three-year-olds are not genuinely interested in causality. They learn that events in the external world are regulated by physical causes, but they also accept mythical or magical explanations of natural phenomena. Although they understand that the world has its own permanence, occasionally they will attempt to obliterate it by closing their eyes. In games of hide-and-seek, young preschoolers may cover their eyes in order to become invisible to those who are searching them out. Children of this age believe that everything is potentially alive and that everything that moves is alive.

The Four-Year-Old

By no stretch of the imagination is the year between the third and fourth birthdays a period of serenity. On the whole, however, it is more relaxed and cooperative than the year between the fourth and fifth birthdays. The four-year-old encounters many new realities that take their toll. Parents come to expect more mature conduct; the pressure of growing is felt in increased demands and expectations. Some developmental psychologists and pediatricians believe that life for the four-year-old is marked by a considerable degree of disequilibrium This belief is supported by the fact that anxiety symptoms become more prevalent and temper outbursts increase. Parents report that their four-year-old is more belligerent and aggressive than at any previous age and that temper tantrums sometimes border on the ferocious. In describing the four-year-old, Dodson states:

> Tensional outlets are heightened at this age. The child may blink his eyes, bite his nails, pick his nose, play with his sexual organs, or suck his thumb. He may even develop a facial tic . . . He is given to the same type of emotional extremes: shy one minute, overboisterous the next. Many children are as ritualistic at this age as they were at two-and-a-half. (1970, p. 158)

Fours are prone to dogmatism because they have accumulated enough knowledge to be confident that their interpretations are correct. This confidence was less justified at three, because then information was too limited to be relied on. At four the child believes that the way she understands something is the way it really is.

Mother always came to the rescue of Three; not so for Four. Fours are expected to be more proficient at fending for themselves. They were usually given the benefit of the doubt in social disputes at three; not so at four. Rules at three are made to be broken, or at least to be bent a good deal; not so at four. The baby status of Three is rapidly vanishing. Responsibility and accountability creep painfully into the world of the four-year-old. She hides behind stubbornness and rigidity and actually prefers showdowns and confrontations because they make conflicts more sharply defined.

The workings of the four-year old's social world are not smooth. Although it is common for the four-year-old to play well with one other child, trouble usually occurs when three or more gather. One observer gives this description of social life among four-year-olds:

> Social life among four-year-olds is no tea party; it is stormy and violent. Outsiders tend to be excluded once a clique has been formed. There is a

good deal of commanding, demanding, shoving, and hitting. Bragging is the most common form of language among a group of four-year-olds. Name-calling is also popular. Four is crude and direct. Other people's feelings matter little to him. (Dodson, 1970, p. 158)

Speaking is coming along nicely, with many flashes of genius. In addition to performing Herculean tasks in the acquisition of words, the four-year-old shows admirable creativity in coining words and concepts. Chukovsky (1963) informs us that he is indebted to children of this age for teaching him that a bald man has a barefoot head, that a mint candy makes a draft in the mouth, and that the husband of a grasshopper is a daddy hopper. Chukovsky is of the impression that the preschool child is something of a linguistic genius:

> It seems to me that, beginning with the age of two, every child becomes for a short period of time, a linguistic genius. Later, beginning with the age of five to six, this talent begins to fade. There is no trace left in the eight-year-old of this creativity with words, since the need for it has passed; by this age the child already has fully mastered the basic principles of his native language. (p.7)

Fours enjoy body movement in and of itself, and it is not unusual for them to float through a room, totally engrossed in their own body contortions and the pleasurable experiences that accompany them.

Muscle fibre is considerably more developed than during toddlerhood and largely accounts for the four-year-old's fluidity of motion and adeptness of body control. Because the muscles are not yet firmly attached to the skeleton, muscle fatigue is a central feature of the preschooler's daily experience. Four tires easily and needs rest periods during the day and deep sleep at night.

Fours will defy orders but will also accomplish many tasks correctly. They enjoy friendly attention but also enjoy confrontations and arguments. They like their own special toys but show almost no respect for the toys of others and certainly do not believe in the property rights of others. Fours are prodigious learners, despite the tendency to disbelieve information that contradicts their world view.

At four, children are capable of lengthy and complicated conversation, in which they vacillate between fact and fiction, sometimes sheepishly admitting to fabrication when confronted with an obvious falsity. Questions are increasingly sophisticated and insightful and delivered with straightforward matter-of-factness; Fours expect brief answers that coincide with what they already know. If presented with anything else they may initially reject it, but their sense of investigation is so strong that four-year-olds eventually get around to accommodating new information which contradicts their previous beliefs.

Aided by their advanced verbal skills, Fours can present a credible alibi when they get into mischief. Physical aggression takes on a verbal component that rarely was seen in the three-year-old. Fours accost with threatening and accusing words. Many parents have been pushed to the limits of self-restraint by their four-year-old's announcement that he will kick them the next time they request that he be good. Or by their moppet's reply of "Shut up" to the question, "Why don't you talk nicely?"

Fours like to show off possessions at nursery school and at home. They show discretion in lending, preferring to loan only to trusted friends – a trait almost nonexistent among three-year-olds. When it comes to recreation, Fours enjoy children more than adults and may refuse to play in a park that is devoid of children. Children who have never left their yard without permission may begin to do so at this age.

The Five-Year-Old

> *A child of five would understand this. Send*
> *somebody to fetch a child of five.*
>
> Groucho Marx

The five-year-old is losing a good deal of his young-child identity and is beginning to assume a more mature, school-age demeanor. The child startles parents with dramatic growth spurts, especially in social skills and self-control. Five-year-olds learn to integrate their own needs with those of the family and to discipline appetites and impulses. They come to appreciate (not objectively understand) the sensitivity and subjectivity of others. Five is reaping the benefits of what was learned during the turmoil of the previous year. On the whole, the five-year-old displays the traits essential for participation in school life: he is reliable, stable, and rather well-adjusted. Self-constraint is more evident than at four; many children of five display what adults call good manners. Keeping in mind that behavior has consequences, Five is no longer so dependent on experimentation for information; he thinks things through more completely than ever before.

Body coordination continues to show refinement. Balance, agility, and flexibility improve. Five-year-olds can stand on tiptoe, use the hand rather than the entire arm to catch a small object, and follow the trajectory of a thrown ball with fair precision. Strength, durability, and stamina increase. Fives play on the monkey bars not only to burn off excess energy (of which they have plenty) but also to develop and show off their acrobatic prowess. Fives pride themselves on their physical skills and unashamedly brag, "I'm really good."

Fives brush their teeth, dress and undress themselves (shoe laces are a special problem), set the table, run to the corner store, tidy (in a loose sense) the living room, and, perhaps most important for nervous parents, move through the house without leaving a swath of broken vases, cracked windows, and scarred furniture. Pencils, dishes, brooms, and magazines are handled with passable precision, and the number of out-of-bounds items is reduced monthly.

Words become vehicles for learning how the world works as well as the means by which children inform the outside world how they work. Infantile articulation is, for the most part, outgrown, and the child uses words the way he will later use money: purposefully. Questions conjured up by the five-year-old tend to be to the point and relevant. They are asked for a reason, usually to acquire a piece of information ("Where does Mommy work?") or to weave together a vague relationship ("How come old people are wrinkly?"). Fives express themselves in correct, complex, complete sentences, with hypothetical and conditional clauses.

Fives are conversational and social at mealtime, listening attentively to adult conversation. When their understanding is impeded by just one unknown word, they may ask for a definition of that particular word rather than for a restatement of the entire sentence. And Five can narrate a story with sufficient drama to hold the attention of even an impatient adult.

Fives become self-conscious about nudity and may prefer not to be seen in their natural state by strangers or members of the opposite sex. Toilet activities hold a special fascination. Adult slang for natural functions is readily adopted. Preschoolers, quite aware of the shock value of certain words, experience a sense of power watching adults react to them. Four-letter words such as hell, damn, shit, and other graphic terms usually not found in textbooks punctuate the five-year old's vocabulary.

The five-year-old is curious about deformed or crippled people and wants to know how their conditions came about. The child accepts almost any response, because he is as much concerned about whether there is an explanation as about the explanation itself. Five may become worried about death (although he does not understand the concept very well) or about failure, injury, or illness. The child's emotional range allows for worrying about death and ice cream within the same minute.

Preschool children enjoy poetry because its blend of fact and fancy, description and prescription, metaphor and reality caters nicely to their mixed-up understanding of the world. They like stories about the fantastic and incredible. They identify with these stories and, after a particularly exciting story, may announce that they are going to climb into the clouds or crawl inside the stomach of a whale. At another time they may teasingly claim to have an alligator in a pocket or a hippopotamus in the closet and laugh uproariously when parents feign surprise or shock upon hearing these announcements. Fives are convinced that they possess a masterful wit, and they generally are the first to laugh at their barbs and the last to stop. Fives readily accept that they are lovable – an innocent trait that adds immeasurably to their natural lovableness. Fives joke, ridicule, and make fun of themselves, which they could not have done comfortably at four.

Fives are moralists, but in a crude way. They hate to see anyone get away with anything and consider it their duty to report deeds that get others into trouble. Their sense of right and wrong is based almost exclusively on specific teachings they have received; they have little concept of degrees of wrongness. Five is oriented toward punishment in moral matters, giving little weight to the intent of an action and instead focusing on the consequences of the act. Five follows rules and regulations for three general reasons: (1) to avoid punishment, (2) to get praise, and (3) to take advantage of the personal benefits they bestow. Five is not exactly a theologian's delight, but at least he is acquiring moral properties, and is swayed by his slowly evolving sense of rightness and wrongness in easily observed ways.

Five has only a limited understanding of causality. He may believe that real people are inside the television set or that real musical instruments are inside the radio, yet be confused about how they got inside such a small box. Five has little idea how an automobile works, assuming that key and will power are enough to move an automobile along the highway.

Most Important Age?

When during the childhood years do the most significant growth experiences take place? Is it during the first year of life? Toddlerhood? The preschool years? This question has kindled remarkable controversy in child psychology – controversy that shows no sign of abating.

The importance of the first five years of life in forming our character and personality is an accepted tenet in developmental psychology. No consensus exists, however, as to which is the most important age. Cairns has stated the issue as clearly as anyone:

> Most developmentalists would agree that the early experiences of the child-care critical for his social development. The consensus on this matter has not changed greatly over the past 30 years. The general assumption has changed in one way, however, and this change has had a monumental impact on developmental theory and research. It is simply that nowadays the subsequent experiences of the child (those occurring after the age of 3) are being seen as having as much impact as earlier ones on the organization of social patterns at maturity. In other words, not only are the first 3 years "critical," but so are the next 3, and the following 6, 9, and 12 years, up through adolescence and early maturity. (1979, p. 175)

In this book the relative importance of the different ages is not discussed at length because the vast majority of research indicates that all age levels contribute significantly to the growth of the child and that at every age the child is susceptible to positive as well as negative influences.

The Impact of Heredity on Human Development:

Identical Twins During the Preschool Years

Most children are losing their junior-child profile and rapidly acquiring the lean, sinewy glide that marks the preschool years. Paradoxically, as identical twins grow older they become both more similar and less similar. Skills improve with practice, so that one twin may count numbers and write words if she has attended an academic preschool, whereas the other twin, not having attended preschool may possess no such skills. In physical appearance, however, the girls may actually become more similar than they were during toddlerhood, as baby fat disappears, the skeleton lengthens, and facial features become more sharply defined. It is not unusual for identical twins to appear more similar to outsiders at age five than they did at age two, even though adults who know the children well easily spot differences in personality and temperament.

In measurable attributes twins evidence considerable similarity during the preschool years. They weigh about the same, reach the same height, and have similar body builds, facial features, and body-fat content. They are matched in terms of "raw" physical skills, such as running, but may be quite uneven in skills requiring coaching, such as gymnastics. The girls will encounter fewer illnesses than they did during the first three years of life, but the probability of social disruption escalates.

If one of the twins were to suffer malnutrition certain traits not shared with her sister would emerge, including lethargy, apathy, constant fatigue, inability to concentrate, and reduced capacity to deal with interpersonal problems. If the malnutrition were chronic, deterioration would continue, perhaps until the affected twin became mentally retarded, stunted in physical growth, and constantly ill. Malnutrition is among the most potent saboteurs of childhood growth.

Rarely is one twin obese and the other thin. However, if from the earliest months one child were overfed, encouraged to eat when she was not hungry, and provided low-food-value meals, the chances increase that this child would be obese, or show signs of obesity. Heredity is a powerful determinant of childhood growth, but not powerful enough to overcome a consistently defective environment!

Identical twin girls are not much different from boys their age. Few preschool abilities are distinctly masculine or feminine, and few significant biological differences exist between the sexes. The sexes are not identical but they do hold parity with each other.

Although it has been established for generations that identical twins are extremely similar in height and weight, the discovery that their intelligence quotients are also highly similar is relatively recent and has elicited considerable interest in the academic community. Table 6-1 shows the extent to which our imaginary twins are similar in intelligence, as well as in height and weight, if they are raised in the same household and if they are raised in different households.

Identical twins show great consistency in their mental development. First, virtually all of their mental abilities increase in power and efficiency with each advancing year. Second, preschool twins share thought limitations: neither child understands causality in a scientific way; neither demonstrates much competence with logic; and both are hounded by egocentrism and centration.

You might ask, "How would identical twins differ if they attended different kinds of preschools?" Or, perhaps even more to the point, "How would they differ if one went to preschool and the other did not?" If you addressed these questions to a psychologist, you probably would not get a straightforward answer, partly because psychologists rarely provide straightforward answers and partly because the data, as presently assembled, do not warrant a straightforward answer. A few conclusions with regard to these questions are fairly clear, however. First, youngsters who attend preschool tend to perform better academically and have fewer social problems in the first and second grades than kids who do not attend preschool. Second, preschoolers who attend compensatory-education programs acquire skills they probably would not have learned at home. On the other hand, our knowledge about the long-term effects of preschool is clouded. Thus, if one twin attended preschool for two years before entering first grade, while the other stayed home (and did not receive special coaching from her parents) the first twin probably would be a higher achiever in the first and second grades and have fewer adjustment difficulties. However, little reason exists to assume that this difference would necessarily continue through the fifth or sixth grade.

Our twins are now ready for the years of middle childhood, during which they will continue to run abreast of each other in important developmental areas especially those regulated by maturation. They will, however, continue to grow in their own unique personalities and travel in many separate directions. As you shall observe in the next chapter, nature is far from finished with these girls. The growth of one will to tell us a great deal about the growth of the other, because the girls are, after all, products of identical heredity, albeit products that are processed and packaged with individual styles.

The Major Concepts of this Chapter

1. Physical development during the preschool years is moderately consistent and stable. Important developments include muscle development which allows for greater speed and endurance, development of the respiratory system which increases stamina, and skeletal development (particularly long bones of the legs and arms).

2. Brain development is marked by impressive growth in size, volume, and myelination. The auditory system develops rapidly and more effective neural connections develop. Brain development correlates with rapid language development and the ability to synthesize information.

3. Adequate nutrition is vital to physical and cognitive development. Malnutrition is particularly serious during the preschool years since body systems are developing rapidly. Chronic malnutrition may result in brain damage, although the effects of less severe malnutrition usually are overcome.

4. Sex differences in physical development in the preschool years are slight. Boys tend to have caught up in those areas which were to the advantage of girls before. Differences which remain are negligible. Compared with development, behavior is characterized by greater sex differences, with boys tending toward more boisterous behavior than girls. These differences appear to be learned in a social environment which provides differential treatment for boys and girls.

5. Understanding of sex differences are vague. Often four-year-olds have not obtained a concept of gender constancy.

6. The major developmental tasks of the preschooler include: acquiring greater control of biological and social impulses; learning about gender differences and sex roles; and, developing a conscience.

7. Aggression in preschoolers takes the form of fighting, kicking, biting, and swearing. Boys tend to be more aggressive than girls. Verbal aggression starts to replace physical aggression by four or five years of age. Theories of aggression suggest that children react to frustration with aggression. Passive aggression is an indirect form of retaliation with which the child may vent frustration. Television violence probably encourages preschool aggression.

8. The physical appearance of identical twins tends to become even more similar during the preschool years, while individual character and abilities become less similar. When raised in the same household and given equivalent opportunities identical twins have very similar IQ's.

9

Intellectual and Moral Development During Middle Childhood

*A powerful idea communicates some of its
strength to him who challenges it.*

Marcel Proust

Mental Development During Middle Childhood

The middle child is a considerably better investigator than either the toddler or the preschooler. He has superior intellectual tools that are employed more deftly. Experience is better utilized in tackling and comprehending new problems. Refined social skills result in richer interpersonal relationships and greater exposure to a wide range of people.

The years of middle childhood are the first in which children realize that information that does not fit into their understanding of the world probably fits into a network outside of their limited knowledge. This realization occurs because middle-years children are less egocentric, both emotionally and intellectually, than preschoolers; facts need not directly relate to their personal lives in order to be fascinating. Middle children want to know how grasshoppers eat, how seals go to the bathroom, and whether parents in other countries love their children. The world is a vast question mark that the middle child attempts to convert to an exclamation point.

The world opens up so explosively in middle childhood that most children are in a continual state of discovery. They are amazed daily by new revelations and insights, becoming obsessed with the inner workings of machines and the outer workings of people. History (especially the study of Neanderthal man) holds a special fascination; biology (especially the study

205

of insects) impresses. Children at this age become convinced that all phenomena have some kind of explanation – in contrast with the agnostic preschooler, who often did not know (or care) whether a question was answerable or not.

The Nature of Concrete Thought

The type of thought that characterizes the middle child is called *concrete thought*. This term, coined by Piaget, indicates that thought is dominated by facts of the immediate present and concerned with real objects rather than theoretical ideas. In other words, thought is focused on "concrete" realities. (Table 7-1 provides an overview of Piaget's stages of cognitive development.)

Concrete thought represents a striking advance over the previous stages of mental development. Here children acquire certain logical rules that allow them to cope with the world of objects and facts. Most importantly they learn to deal with (1) *classes,* (2) *relations,* (3) *quantities,* (4) *mental representations,* and, (5) *serialization* in a more sophisticated manner.

With regard to *classes,* children learn to deal with the whole and parts of the whole at the same time. For example, if a child not yet at the stage of concrete thought is asked, "Are there more boys or more children in the classroom?" he may answer that there are more boys, more girls, or more children. His answer is unpredictable because he cannot think about a class and its subclasses (the whole and the parts) at the same time. With the advent of concrete thinking, the child easily recognizes that children must outnumber boys because boys are only one of two subclasses (the other being girls) that compose the class known as "children."

With regard to *relations,* for example, the child comes to understand that brightness is a relative phenomenon. A 60-watt light bulb is "brighter" in relation to a 40 watt bulb but not in relation to a 1000-watt bulb, and the same 60 watt bulb may be the brightest in a group of three bulbs. This advancement of thought makes relative comparisons more effective, and absolutes less necessary; as a result, thought becomes more flexible, versatile, and comprehensive. The concrete thinker becomes aware that the world is filled with phenomena that are related to one another comparatively.

During the stage of concrete thought the child learns that quantity remains the same even though its shape is altered. For example, as you saw in the preceding chapter, the nursery-school child usually believes that if the liquid in a short, wide jug is poured into a tall, thin jug, the latter actually contains more liquid. Because the liquid assumes a different shape, the child infers that the quantity has been changed. During mid-childhood the child learns that quantities remain the same regardless of the shape they assume.

Youngsters who grasp this concept of quantity locate the humor in the following joke: Susy and her friend went into the restaurant and ordered a pizza. The waiter asked "Shall I slice it into four pieces or six pieces?" Susy replied: "Four pieces, please. We're not hungry enough to eat six pieces." Children who have not reached the stage of concrete thought, and thus are less attuned to such subtle refinements of thought, usually think the joke is about pizza, failing altogether to recognize that the topic is mathematics.

Two additional mental traits surface during this stage which are of special importance: the capacity to form *mental representations* and the ability to *serialize* objects. The child is capable of mental representation when he represents physical reality symbolically. (Drawing a map of the route to the neighborhood store is an example of symbolic representation.) To arrange objects according to some measurable dimension (such as height or width) in a progressive sequence is referred to as serializing. Arranging ten pieces of string from shortest to longest is an example. The ability to serialize is essential to understanding the relationship between numbers; without this ability, advanced mathematics is impossible.

In summary, during the stage of concrete thought the emergence of five general (and quite different) abilities improves the child's capacity for thought:

1. the ability to think about a whole entity and parts of the entity simultaneously,
2. the ability to understand that some realities acquire their qualities only in relation to the qualities of another reality (that is, for a light to be "brighter," it must be brighter than another light),
3. the ability to understand that quantity does not change simply because its appearance has been changed,
4. the ability to formulate mental representations of physical facts, and
5. the ability to serialize physical objects according to size or some other measurable dimension.

The Limitations of Concrete Thought

As often as a study is cultivated by narrow minds,
they will draw from it narrow conclusions.
John Stuart Mill

Concrete thought focuses on the real, the physical, and the observable. Its strength resides in the ability to organize facts as they are presented. When thought matures it concerns itself with the origins of facts. A good journalist must explain "who, what, when, where, why and how" to the reader. Concrete thinkers are not ready for this lofty profession since they are primarily concerned with "who, what, where and when" but less concerned with "why and how."

Rarely does the concrete thinker approach a question by analyzing all solutions; rather, he responds to the first or second conclusion derived from piecing together the available clues. Because of this predisposition toward hastily picking one solution, rather than investigating all possibilities before inferring the answer, middle children can easily be lured into viewing only one side of an issue or basing their conclusions on a small particle of the total evidence. Concrete thought lacks comprehensiveness.

General and abstract meanings often escape the concrete thinker. For example, if you ask a six- or seven-year-old to interpret the proverb "You can lead a horse to water, but you can't make him drink," the response might make you cringe. The child may say that you can't force animals to drink, that horses naturally locate water, or some such literal response. Hypothetical problems also confuse our concrete thinker. "If horses had six legs could they run faster?" Many kids draw a blank to this kind of question because it requires them to hypothesize something they know is false. They are likely to reply "Horses don't have six legs." Or, more likely, "What a stupid question. Horses don't have six legs."

Although concrete thinkers are capable of reasoning from the general to the specific (deductive reasoning), and as well, from the specific to the general (inductive reasoning), their power of logical analysis remains weak because they do not assemble evidence impartially. They arrange evidence in order to confirm their premises. When data support their hypotheses, concrete thinkers show a good deal of "objectivity" – or so it may appear to an outside observer. As soon as the evidence goes against the premise, however, concrete thinkers may reject it. During adolescence, with the advent of formal thought, the individual finally accepts the maxim of all scientific thought: evidence determines the validity of a hypothesis. When evidence does not support the hypothesis, only two options are open: (1) reject the hypothesis or (2) test new evidence.

In middle childhood students are first introduced to philosophical ideas, and to scientific procedures; however, these advanced thought modes are rarely deployed with much effectiveness in childhood. They become an integral part of the thought process during adolescence and adulthood. As the toddler struggles with logic, so does the ten-year-old with philosophy. Time and development will eventually rescue the child from this intellectual ineptitude, but it will take several years, and conditions must be favorable.

In summary, despite great advances, the middle child's thought remains limited by the following features:

1. thought is primarily directed toward the real and overlooks the ideal,

2. thought is primarily directed toward the present; the long range implications of ideas are not given thorough consideration,

3. thought is directed more toward organizing facts than toward discerning where facts come from; little mental energy is spent validating the origins of information; the concrete child is greatly influenced by authority

and uses it to authenticate information,

4. thought lacks comprehensiveness; the child rarely formulates alternate hypotheses, and

5. thought is rigid because the child is not able to double check the process by which he derived a conclusion.

The limitations of thought during this stage of mental development provide clues to the improvements that will occur during adolescence; after all, these traits would not be referred to as "limitations" if they were not eventually overcome.

The Growth of General Mental Abilities

Environment and maturation work together in all facets of human growth and development. At times, however, environment exerts minimal impact because the person is not maturationally ready to benefit from experience. Infants do not benefit from attempts to teach them to walk before they are maturationally ready; toddlers do not learn to speak before they are maturationally ready, no matter how much teaching or coaching they receive. In this section we shall investigate the mental abilities significantly influenced by maturation during middle childhood.

Memory – The middle child remembers greater quantities of information and retrieves information with greater accuracy than during any previous developmental stage.

Between six and ten the child becomes more adept at short-term as well as long-term memory. Memory is less scattered than during the preschool years, when the child was as likely to remember irrelevant trivia as important information. Five-year-olds can recall, on average, about four numbers read at one-second intervals; ten-year-olds can recall six or seven. Some ten-year-olds commit to memory a dozen or more telephone numbers, the averages of the top ten batters in each division of the major leagues, the name of every classmate, and numerous chemistry formulas. Inconsistency plagues memory, however, and children of this age may fail to remember the name of last year's teacher or the third of three items on a shopping list.

Some children demonstrate rather impressive number memory but only average or weak concept memory; others have gifted memory for what they have seen (visual memory) but poor memory for what they have heard (auditory memory). For most children, however, memory skills are comparatively uniform; we have little basis for assuming inconsistency in memory function unless it is demonstrated.

If an eight-year-old is given the numbers 4-7-8-9 at one second intervals, he is likely to recall them correctly. However, if the same child is given the numbers 4-7-8-9-1-6-3 (the same sequence, with three extra digits), he may not be able to repeat correctly even the first three numbers of the sequence.

This exemplifies an important principle: when taxed beyond its limits, memory works less effectively than when working slightly below its limits. Adults who recall numbers given at one-second intervals experience similar results, the only difference being that a greater number of digits is required to overload the memory.

Abstraction – Preschoolers have difficulty understanding facts for which they have no first-hand experience; they have even more difficulty with qualities or abstractions that do not relate to a specific object. Ideas such as honesty, purity, and ethnicity are, for the most part, beyond the preschooler's range. During middle childhood the ability to comprehend abstract concepts and the capacity to effectively engineer them improves markedly. Seven-year-olds, for example, are able to provide reasons why wood and coal are alike, pointing out that they come from the ground and are used for heat. They also can explain in what way a baseball and an orange are alike, indicating that each is round. In both of these examples the youngster is able to formulate a generalization, or an abstraction, which links these tangible objects. Quite obviously, they do have limitations. For example, very few seven-year-olds (or eight-year-olds) are able to explain how snakes, cows, and sparrows are alike (they are all life forms, require air, reproduce, etc.). This question requires a higher level of abstraction, and its solution depends on greater mental maturity than is possessed by the average seven- or eight-year-old.

As the ability to deal with abstract ideas improves, the child better understands *relational* terms and ideas. The middle child understands that the strength of one person is relative to the strength of another – that a particular man is strong when compared with one person but weak when compared with another. The preschooler usually does not make comparisons such as this. The discovery that father is not the strongest person in town is a genuine insight, because the preschooler equates strongest in the house with strongest anywhere. The middle child employs relativity where the preschooler uses absolutes. The ability to classify in a relational context, or to perceive the relative nature of the qualities of objects, is dependent on brain development and rarely appears before middle childhood, no matter how rich the environment. For this reason these abilities are thought of as part of the maturational unfolding of the intellect.

Selective Perception – The ability to concentrate on one part of the environment and exclude everything else is referred to as *selective perception*. As the child ages, the capacity for selective perception increases. The six-year-old has difficulty attending to schoolwork when disruption strikes the classroom, because he reflexively turns around to investigate. Rarely before the third or fourth grade does the child concentrate without distraction in the midst of a social disturbance.

Without selective perception the child has difficulty mastering skills that require concentrated attention. (One of the most consistent traits of low academic achievers is their inability to concentrate on schoolwork for long periods; the opposite is true of high achievers.)

The Child's Understanding of Death

Death is an abstraction the preschool mind has difficulty assimilating. Children under the age of five demonstrate little understanding of death as a phenomenon, whereas children seven and older have a fairly good grasp of it by adult standards.

Research on children's understanding of the concept of death tends to focus on three major points: (1) death is irreversible, (2) there are no life functions after death, and (3) death is universal, all living creatures die. Data suggest that preschool children don't effectively grasp these three features of death. Some kids see death as a temporary state, thinking that a dead person might wake up, or come to life. They tend not to believe that all life functions cease; they might accept that a dead person cannot walk around, but at the same time believe that dead people can dream. In addition, preschoolers sometimes conclude that people can avoid death if everything goes right (Craig, 1989, p. 247).

Seven and eight-year-olds, on the other hand, possess a greater comprehension of the differences between life and death. They know that all life runs its course and terminates in death, even the life of plants and insects.

Not infrequently, seven-year-olds will invoke a supernatural concept in order to make death less emotionally painful ("Gramma has gone to heaven"), but while doing so they possess a hazy realization that supernatural beliefs are not bound to the laws of nature.

Here we have been addressing only the intellectual components of the child's understanding of death. Quite obviously, youngsters require emotional reassurance and confidence-bolstering on this topic. When a family member, or a friend dies, death should be presented to the child as an event which holds some promise, or reverence, or integrity.

During the preschool years academic learning takes place best when learning is so interesting and stimulating that it naturally absorbs attention. If the learning task does not hold the child's interest, he has only a limited ability to focus. The middle-years child, on the other hand, is better able to focus mental energy and to deploy selective perception.

Word Games, Thought Games, and the Advancing Intellect

As the mind becomes more complex and powerful it permits more expanded types of word play. During middle childhood this is manifested in a fascination with riddles. A riddle is a problem or puzzle so formulated that some ingenuity is required to answer or solve it; often it is posed as an apparently inexplicable problem. Its answer usually startles us because it is founded upon a double-meaning, a sound which can mean two or more things, or some such word confusion.

Riddles first gather audience among six- and seven-year-olds because preschoolers are not attuned to the subtle differences between word appearance and word meaning; thus they are confused by, rather than intrigued with, riddles. As the intellect expands, however, the child develops a fascination with riddles, and as thinking skills continue to advance progressively more complex riddles are entertained.

Research by Schultz (1974) suggests that the following sequence of riddle sophistication is typical among children aged 6-11:

1. *Riddles with double meaning of a single word.* For example:

Why did the farmer name his hog Ink?

Because he kept running out of the pen.

Understanding this riddle depends upon knowing that "pen" can be used in at least two ways, one of which refers to where a pig lives. First graders are likely to find this riddle understandable and amusing.

2. *Riddles where sounds can be interpreted in two ways.*

Why did the cookie cry?

Because its mother had been a wafer so long.

Here "wafer" and "away for" sound alike but carry totally different meanings. Second graders are likely to find this riddle understandable and amusing. (Of course, everything is lost if "wafer" is not in the child's vocabulary.)

3. *Riddles in which a key word could be the subject, verb, or object of a sentence.*

Tell me how long cars should be washed?

The same as short cars.

Third graders are likely to understand this riddle and find it cute.

4. *Riddles in which two underlying meanings exist.*

How old do you have to be to jump as high as a tree?

Any age, trees can't jump.

Fourth graders understand this riddle, and though they usually won't laugh out loud upon hearing it, they are captivated by its cleverness. They might even try it out on a five-year-old brother, only to be perplexed by his failure to detect the wizardry of it. "Don't you get it? Trees can't jump."

Children near ages six or seven begin to concern themselves with the underlying meanings of words and gestures. This distinguishes them from 4- and 5-year-olds, who are impressed with observable qualities and objective realities.

Some Unique Features of the Thought Process During Middle Childhood

Everybody is ignorant, only on different topics.
Will Rogers

Middle childhood contains more than its share of perplexity and confusion for the developmental psychologist. In thinking skills, for example, the child undergoes a revolution of thought which not only allows him to think in a new key, but to think with greater power and precision. Despite these breakthroughs, which contribute to the advancement of thought, middle children are prone to use an array of downright dopey habits.

Children of eight, for example, often invent facts to "prove" their beliefs. A debate is one series of invented "facts" after another, backed up by imagined or real authoritative quotes and references. (Stamina is often the deciding factor in arguments.) Logic and consistency win out in the classroom but rarely elsewhere during middle childhood. Many kids possess a gift for compressing the largest number of words into the smallest amount of thought.

Understanding of causality is spiralling upward, but children are so obsessed with finding an answer to every question that they succumb to ridiculous explanations. Superstitious beliefs are epidemic. Nine-year-olds may understand molecular structures but may also be afraid to open an umbrella inside the house. Lack of an explanation for the superstition does not dampen their conviction that the superstition is true.

Youngsters carry an abundance of misinformation gathered from peers. A bright eight-year-old may cling to the belief that some people are able to live for months without eating or that some horses can fly, if this information was provided by an apparently smart friend. Ten-year-olds somehow believe that vacant houses are inhabited by eccentric old-timers who stalk about after midnight. Curiosity generally triumphs over apprehension (as was true in toddlerhood) and eventually a gang will investigate the house, bringing back intellectually disappointing but emotionally consoling information.

Logic is crude, even though more advanced than it was during the preschool years. Children stumble into just about every kind of logical inconsistency imaginable. Aristotle must have winced in agony at their total misuse of syllogism. Children of this age are able to draw a conclusion from premises, but frequently it is a conclusion which makes no sense to an adult.

Middle-years children have a tendency to use their intellect to protect their own feelings. They use others as scapegoats and invent reasons to prove that a disliked classmate is really an unworthwhile person. Not until midadolescence do many youths accept the idea that the powers of the mind should not be used to deny the rights of others.

A final word concerning the paradox of egocentrism. As indicated elsewhere, egocentrism lessens as the child gets older. As the intellect becomes more powerful, egocentrism exerts less influence over it. Even taking this into account, the thinking patterns of middle-children are seriously impeded by egocentrism. To protect his sometimes fragile self, a ten-year-old will deny unpleasant facts, over-emphasize facts which enhance his self-esteem, and simply not acknowledge facts an adult would consider important.

Egocentrism influences how the child interprets facts and ideas that pertain to "me." In matters that do not pertain to oneself, information processing is rather objective and efficient.

How Come Laplander's Don't Get Cold

The following passage is often quoted in university textbooks dealing with communication theory. The quote is a humorous look at the importance of personal frame of reference. Most university students find Postman's idea clever and thought-provoking. Youngsters in the mature years of concrete operational thought (9-11) however, are perplexed by its fluidity and seemingly contradictory use of concepts and numbers.

> To a Laplander, a temperature of fifty-eight degrees may be "hot," to a South African it may be "cold." The statement "It is hot (or cold) is a statement about what is going on inside one's body. The statement "The temperature is now ninety degrees (or fifty-eight degrees)" is a statement about what is going on outside one's body . .
>
> This distinction is by no means trivial . . . I can never prove to a Laplander that fifty-eight degrees is "cool," but I can prove to him that it is fifty-eight degrees. In other words, there is no paradox in two different people's concluding that the weather is both "hot" and "cold" at the same time. As long as they both know that each of them is talking about a different reality, their conversation can proceed in a fairly orderly way.

(Neil Postman, *Crazy Talk, Stupid Talk*)

As one ten-year-old said to me after reading this passage: "I don't get it. How come Laplander's don't get cold?"

Sex Differences in Thinking

Do males and females differ in innate cognitive abilities or are observed differences merely the product of societal stereotyping and differential opportunities to develop skills?

Males and females do not differ consistently on measures of overall intelligence, but small differences are observed if individual subtest scores are examined. In 1974 Maccoby and Jacklin surveyed the relevant research and discovered that during early childhood gender differences are not significant but near adolescence differences become more pronounced and continue through adulthood.

On average, males tend to be better at mathematics and females tend to outperform boys at verbal tasks. However, many scholars believe these variances have a cultural base. With respect to reading skills, the female advantage disappears or is reversed in some cultures where males are expected to be academically superior (Matlin, 1987). In terms of math skills, studies indicate a number of reasons for adolescent males having higher interest and performance expectations than females. Males are more likely to see math as being useful to a future career (e.g., male dominated fields like engineering). Parents and students attribute high math scores for males to ability, but identical scores in females to hard work or good teachers (Meece et al, 1982; Parsons, Adler, and Kaczula, 1982). In addition, math teachers generally spend more time interacting with male students (Meece et al, 1982).

The differences are even more pronounced in spatial abilities (skills such as mentally manipulating objects in space, visualizing three dimensional figures from two dimensional drawings etc.). Males on average perform better at these tasks. Evidence of a biological explanation is found for at least some of the variance. Studies by Waber (1977) comparing early and late maturing boys and girls led her to suggest that the difference in spatial abilities may be due to differing rates of maturation, with late maturation favoring development of spatial abilities. In general, boys mature later than girls; thus, according to this theory, they possess slightly greater spatial abilities. These differing abilities may be based upon sex differences in the organization of the right and left hemispheres of the brain.

The Mind Explores Perspectives Other than its Own

One of the many significant advances of childhood is the ability to think about an idea (or an experience) from the point of view of another person. This sounds easy enough to university students who exercise this ability on a daily basis; for the child, however, it is a slow and deliberate process which is impeded by egocentrism and inexperience. In psychological literature this mental advance is referred to as "perspective-taking."

What is Perspective-Taking?

Taking the viewpoint of another person, or imagining what another person is thinking are the basic ingredients of perspective-taking. This attribute exerts considerable influence on the child's ability to understand other people, their actions and their motivations. It also makes possible the advanced forms of communication in which the speaker analyzes the listener's frame of reference. In essence, perspective-taking is a vital part of the child's unfolding complexity.

The ability to "read" another person, to "walk in their shoes," emerges on a somewhat predictable timetable during childhood. At least that is the point of view of R. L. Selman (1974), who has extensively researched perspective-taking.

Selman's Stages of Perspective-taking

Selman believes that perspective-taking develops through five distinct levels each of which reflects a more advanced understanding of how other people think and feel. Selman also argues that each level of perspective-taking is qualitatively different from the others, that levels develop in an invariant sequence, and that virtually all children mature through these levels in the same general manner.

Level 0: Undifferentiated and egocentric perspective-taking (about 3-6 years)

At this stage children recognize the existence of their own inner thoughts, and as well, the inner thoughts of others; however, these are sometimes confused. In this stage kids rarely think that another person can respond to the same situation differently than they did. Their perceptions are highly egocentric; therefore, their understanding of others is undifferentiated.

Level 1: Differentiated and subjective perspective-taking (about 5-9 years)

At this stage children understand that their interpretations of a social situation may be the same as, or different from, another person's interpretations of the same situation. They are aware that different people process information differently, and therefore, draw different conclusions, which in itself is a considerable childhood achievement. In Level 1 children are able to think from another person's perspective in a very limited fashion. The most significant feature of this stage is the child's recognition that each of us responds to information as it is processed through our own personal uniqueness. Children can't judge their own actions from another's viewpoint.

Level 2: Self-reflective or reciprocal perspective-taking (about 7-10 years)

A further advance in perspective-taking occurs when children attain the ability to see their own feelings and actions from another person's perspective. In essence, this allows them to anticipate other people's judgments of their actions more proficiently than in Level 1.

Level 3: Third-part or mutual perspective-taking (about 10-13 years)

This level witnesses the ability to step outside a two-person exchange and imagine how a third person might perceive the interaction. This extension of perspective-taking permits looking at an interaction from two perspectives simultaneously (my own, and my parents', for example). In essence, Level 3 allows the person to step outside himself and view a given situation from two perspectives simultaneously.

Level 4: In-depth and societal perspective-taking (about 14 years and older)

The distinguishing feature of this stage is the capacity to recognize that mutual perspective-taking is moulded by systems of thought, and by larger societal values. For example, recognizing that a viewpoint is based upon "Judeo-Christian" concepts, or understanding that beliefs are influenced by unacknowledged chauvinisms, indicates in-depth and societal perspective-taking. Recognizing that each of us in our perspective-taking is influenced by larger theoretical and conceptual forces is the advance of level 4.

Selman's classification of perspective-taking describes in rather specific terms the nature of the child's unfolding capacity to understand the world from viewpoints other than his own. As we shall soon note, this ability not only influences mental abilities in a significant and far-reaching manner, but also exerts powerful influence on moral development, empathy and compassion.

The Self Evaluates Itself

Myself and I are on the best of terms.
Ivy Compton-Burnett

The middle child probes the outside world with a relentless daring, sometimes giving parents and other observers the impression that the child can barely keep pace with his own intellect. Outward probes, significant as they are during middle childhood, are not the only kind. The mind literally turns on itself in a flurry of self-analysis. Compared with the anguish of adolescent identity crises, it is not an emotionally profound form of introspection, but for the middle child it is a new and exhilarating experience which constitutes a significant part of his psychology and his intellectualism.

Paradoxically, the child's interest in other people prompts a great deal of inner searching. The needs for acceptance, belonging and recognition are so strong at this age that the child constantly looks at himself from what he thinks is the vantage point of those he is trying to impress – especially at age nine, ten and eleven. He thinks and worries about appearances; he evaluates his social "performance," filtering those behaviors which bring praise from those which do not.

The child is not a slave to the inner self, but he is forced to interact with it in a way incomprehensible (and unachievable) to the preschooler, or the six- and seven-year-old. One of the many outcomes of this new adventure in self-discovery is an "evaluativeness" about one's abilities, and one's worthwhileness.

Self-efficacy

The child's sense that she can accomplish what is required in a specific situation is known as *self-efficacy.* Developmentalists agree that what a youngster thinks about herself affects her achievements, and how she feels about herself affects her interpersonal relationships; therefore, self-efficacy becomes a significant factor in day-to-day behavior.

Self-efficacy tends to be situation-specific rather than constant from situation to situation (Bandura, 1981, 1982). Thus, a child's sense of confidence may be strong in a situation requiring athletic skills and weak in a situation requiring social skills. Bandura suggested that four sources of information form the backbone of the child's sense of efficacy.

1. *Prior experience of mastery (enactive attainments).* Episodes of success instill a sense of confidence and episodes of failure instill feelings of ineptitude. Youngsters who participate in games where they succeed, or achieve the purpose of the game, are likely to approach games with anticipation of success. If their experiences lead to failure, or scolding, they assume the game will result in failure or, even worse, that they themselves are failures.

2. *Vicarious experience.* In the phenomenology of childhood, observing someone succeed who is like me raises my own sense of efficacy. Observing someone like me fail, lowers my self-efficacy. Thus, the performance of those with whom the child identifies influences the child's own feelings of self-confidence.

3. *Verbal persuasion.* Youngsters can be talked into thinking better of themselves. Praise is vital. However, so is objective information. "Susan, that is very good. Your penmanship is superb." Youngsters have few ways of validating themselves, but they respond with increased self-efficacy when validated by others, especially by adults they admire or identify with.

4. *Body experience.* When kids feel anxiety or fearfulness before attempting a task, they often expect failure. If they are excited, or optimistic, they are more likely to expect success. More importantly, children who

are tense in general, or fearful in general, are more likely to have lowered self-efficacy.

As we observed in our investigation of toddlerhood, feelings of competence and confidence greatly determine how hard and how long a child will persist at a challenging activity, especially one that may result in failure. As the demands of childhood increase, as perseverance and fortitude become increasingly necessary to handle the tasks expected of a nine-year-old or a ten-year-old, self-efficacy attains remarkable significance. It brings home a central premise of childhood behavior: if the youngster believes she can achieve, the probability that she will do so is far greater than if she believes she will fail. Belief does not assure success; it simply increases its probability.

Learned helplessness

In Chapter three we discussed how young children possess an inborn desire to master their environment and to develop competence. These traits, though powerful during infancy and toddlerhood, do not necessarily remain throughout childhood. By age eight or nine we observe among many youngsters a tendency to *expect failure,* to believe that they will not succeed at a task even before they try it. This diminished view of one's abilities is known as *learned helplessness.*

Dweck and Elliot (1983) researched this phenomenon and uncovered several trends of interest to the student of child psychology. First, children who display learned helplessness tend to explain their failures as due to their abilities, which they view as fixed and unchanging. They do not think that they will improve with practice; they expect not to succeed, and when they fail, it confirms their lack of ability. Second, youngsters who have acquired this sense of helplessness tend to approach problems with anxiety and fearfulness, which unto itself, lessens performance. Third, these kids choose less demanding tasks for themselves, fearing that if they attempt ordinary tasks they will fail. The net effect of this is that youngsters do not pursue tasks they are capable of mastering, and they do not pursue goals they are capable of attaining.

Dweck's research demonstrated that a significant cause of learned helplessness is the evaluative comments that adults give children. Kids who are told that their failures are due to their lack of ability become discouraged and "surrender" more readily than youngsters who are told their failure is due to lack of effort.

Generally speaking, girls are more prone to reduced expectations and learned helplessness. Girls, more than boys, explain their poor performance as caused by low ability; in addition, they become discouraged more readily after failure. Much of the research on learned helplessness among girls was conducted in the early 70s and, partly as a result of this research, early childhood educators presently combat learned helplessness in both boys and girls. In addition, parenting techniques of the 80s and 90s caution against nurturing this trait. Despite these trends girls seem more susceptible to learned helplessness than boys.

Perceptual Style: How it Impacts What the Child Knows

Quite obviously all children do not process and perceive information in the same ways. In fact, no two people perceive anything in identical fashion. The world simply provides more stimulation than the human mind can process; to survive we focus our perceptions, narrow our input, and censor what our senses deliver to us. Each of us possesses a style of perceiving which can be divided into what psychologists call field-dependence and field independence.

Field Dependence and Independence

Our perceptual style determines whether we focus on stimuli in the "background" or the "foreground" of our perceptual field, whether we focus on objects or people, and whether we perceive specifics or generalities. For example, while watching a hockey game in an arena, one fan might focus almost entirely on the puck, the players, assorted collisions, and occasionally, the referee. His attention is fixed upon the specific events which constitute "the game." Simultaneously, a less "fan-atic" friend also watching the game attends to the noisy crowd, the immense Coliseum, and the friendly aromas emanating from the concession stands. Witkin and his associates (1962) term these differences in perceptual style *field dependent* and *field independent*.

Individuals who focus on the immediate environment while paying little attention to background stimuli are known as *field-independent* because their perceptions are highly focused upon a specific range, and they are somewhat independent of the larger setting. The child transfixed on a computer game in a noisy arcade is field-independent. The fan who attended to the hockey game, the crowd and the food aromas is field-dependent because he is taking in the entire perceptual field.

Of great importance to developmental psychology is the observation made by Witkin (and a host of other researchers since his initial observations) that *some children possess a field-independent perceptual style, whereas others are basically field-dependent in their perceptual style.* This difference results in remarkably dissimilar perceptions being processed in any given situation. Even identical twins, if they differ in field dependence-independence, will see, feel, and react to completely different stimuli in the same environment.

An interesting correlate is that field-*independent* children tend to focus most of their attention on objects and tasks, whereas field-*dependent* kids tend to focus on people and interpersonal skills.

During the past 20 years the accumulated research suggests that few children are *exclusively* field-dependent or field-independent; nevertheless, some youngsters consistently separate the object of their perception from its "field" (field-independent), while others incorporate the background into almost everything they perceive (field-dependent). This perceptual orientation influences what they see, which in turn influences their actions, which in turn influences other people's reaction to them, which in turn influences their self-concept. Thus, a profound chain of events is triggered by whether a child's basic perceptual orientation is field-dependent or field-independent.

The influence of field-dependence and field-independence on classroom learning has been investigated by numerous researchers. (Hale, 1982; Garger & Guild, 1984). Even though few children are exclusively one or the other, several consistent trends appear. Of great interest to school teachers is that field-dependent youngsters tend to think globally, and to interpret ideas in terms of their context, while field-independent kids tend to examine parts more than wholes, and to think in specifics rather than in generalities. Other consistencies are highlighted in the following chart:

Cognitive Learning Styles

Field-Dependent (Relational)	Field-Independent (Analytical)
Thinks globally (concentrates on whole rather than parts)	Thinks analytically (examines parts)
Is interested in general ideas	Concentrates on specifics
Interprets ideas in terms of immediate context	Identifies basic concepts as having meaning within themselves
Has a social orientation	Has a stimulus-centred orientation
Seeks concepts that have special, personal relevance	Is interested in new concepts for their own sake
Sees cognitive relationships as tentative and inferred	Sees cognitive relationships as more established principles
Uses language meanings that are highly affected by context and nonverbal cues	Uses language based more on established verbal meanings
Uses more direct observation for concept attainment	Uses more hypothesis testing to attain concepts

(Sources: Adapted from Hale, 1982, pp. 32-33; Garger and Guild, 1984, p. 10).

In sum, perceptual wiring greatly influences intellectual intake. Quite obviously, all children do not perceive the same phenomena in the same setting; therefore, what they perceive and how they interpret these perceptions is by no means a clear-cut matter. In essence, what is perceived is *determined as much by perceptual style* as by stimuli in the perceptual field.

The Nature of Intelligence

Many psychologists resist the notion that children possess a single "overall" intelligence. These psychologists also disapprove of measuring intelligence with a single IQ score. They reason that if evaluating an automobile with a single rating is simplistic, evaluating human intelligence with a single score is impossible.

Among the more influential contemporary psychologists to argue in favor of a more complex intelligence is Howard Gardner. He believes in *multiple intelligences,* at least five types of which are observable and measurable. The concept of multiple intelligences has been around for a long time, but it fell into disfavor in the 50s and 60s when environmental explanations of intelligence were in the forefront of psychological theory. Recent advances in our understanding of the different functions served by the right and left brain hemispheres has re-ignited interest in the idea that children (and adults) possess a wide range of specific abilities some of which may be highly advanced, others average, and others below average in their power. Gardner reasons that these specific "intelligences" greatly influence not only the inclinations of children, but also their aptitudes. At any rate, the concept of multiple intelligence forces the developmental psychologist to think of intellectual ability as more complex than a single generalized trait. The following represent Gardner's suggested forms of intelligence:

1. *Musical intelligence* depends on the ability to perceive tone and pitch. Although musical intelligence is influenced by learning, such vast differences exist among individuals that hereditary factors are thought to establish its foundation.

2. *Logic-mathematical intelligence* derives from analysis of abstract ideas separated from the every day world. This is the intelligence of theoretical physics.

3. *Spatial intelligence* allows the individual to perceive the objective world with precision, and to reconstruct or modify it. It is the intelligence required of building, designing, and re-arranging.

4. *Personal intelligence* derives from self-analysis and the ability to register and comprehend the motivation of others.

5. *Linguistic intelligence* is what traditional IQ measures refer to as "verbal" intelligence. It manifests itself in precise and economical deployment of language.

Gardner believes that different "intelligences" evolve along different developmental paths. Musical intelligence, for example, tends to emerge early in life (Mozart as a musical child prodigy), while mathematical intelligence blossoms in late-adolescence and early adulthood; linguistic intelligence, on the other hand, may not peak until the 50s or 60s.

Brain Development During Middle Childhood

The thought process in human beings derives from a brain which has no equal in nature. And though it rests at the pinnacle of the natural order, its greatness manifests itself in rhythmic, time-bound episodes. Like every vital organ, the brain develops on a genetically determined timetable, and from its primitive beginnings flow the primitive thoughts of toddlers, and from its majestic maturity flow the thoughts of Einstein and Shakespeare.

Great advances in our knowledge of the human brain have taken place in the past several decades, including what we know about its growth and development during middle childhood. In their overview, Cole and Cole (1989) charted several interesting developments; from their research this segment draws much of its material.

The following changes in brain structure, organization and activity have particular relevance to the intellectual development which typifies the middle childhood years.

1. *Increased lateralization* – The process by which one side of the brain takes control in organizing a particular mental process or behavior is known as *lateralization*. As children mature, one hemisphere attains dominance over the other which permits greater specialization and increased proficiency of psychological functions. Middle childhood is a time of increased brain lateralization, and it is also a time when more complex thought, and more effective coordination of action take place. For example, complex behaviors such as writing with a pencil, and playing soccer are executed far more effectively in middle childhood. In essence, the skills we associate with mid-childhood owe their emergence, in great measure, to increased brain lateralization.

2. *Brain size and activity* – The brain increases in size but also changes its patterns of electrical activity during middle childhood. Between ages five and seven the rate of growth in the surface area of the frontal lobes increases rather sharply. The myelination of the cortex nears completion. The brain wave activity of preschoolers displays more *theta* activity, which typifies adult sleep patterns; between five and seven years occurs an increase in *alpha* activity, which is characteristic of engaged attention in the adult. As middle childhood advances, alpha

activity predominates.

3. *Brain complexity* – By middle childhood the brain has achieved a complexity almost equal to that of adults. The frontal lobes coordinate activity of other brain centres when the child is forming a systematic plan of action. Since middle children attain greater proficiency at systematic planning during the same time as these changes occur in the frontal lobes, some experts (most notably Luria, 1973) infer that brain development is responsible for this improvement. When we suffer damage to the frontal lobes our behavior is characterized by a weakened ability to maintain our goals, we become more easily distracted, and readily lose our concentration. In many regards, our behavior and our intellectual functioning resembles that of the preschool child who has not experienced frontal lobe maturity.

Near the end of middle childhood the brain has had dramatic growth, having attained about 90 percent of its adult weight. Continued growth in the area of the brain associated with foresightful activity permits more effective transaction of rule-bound games and projects. In addition, the right and left sides of the brain are bridged by neural connections in the corpus callosum. This linkage brings language and thought into closer working units and, in general, engenders more effective classroom learning.

Brain centres which monitor muscle development and coordination also grow at this age, producing a more capable body. Without question, the unfolding of intellectual abilities is anchored in the nature of brain development.

Moral Development During Middle Childhood

> *To make children capable of honesty*
> *is the beginning of education.*
> John Ruskin

Investigating the mental processes of children is essentially a study of abilities, processes and skills. The ways in which these are applied to moral issues is an area of concern for developmentalists because mental abilities are the foundation for all concepts and abstractions, including morality. Of special concern is the child's understanding of justice, fairness, punishment and equality.

All children learn moral codes and beliefs which render less powerful their propensity for egotistic self centredness and render more powerful impulses for sharing, cooperation and other altruistic behavior.

Most developmentalists agree that in their beginnings the moral beliefs of children are learned, acquired, or imitated from others. Eventually, however, they become internalized both cognitively and emotionally, and mean more to the child than mere parroting. The process by which moral codes become internalized is the pressing issue, and like all detective stories, piecing together the threads of evidence into a verifiable link is the heart of the challenge.

Although mental development influences moral beliefs and attitudes we must bear in mind that it doesn't determine moral *behavior*. The fact that a child believes something is morally right does not mean he will act upon it, nor does the belief that something is morally wrong guarantee he will avoid it.

Two conditions inherent to the topic cloud our understanding of moral development. First, moral behavior is difficult to define. Even the experts do not agree on what it is. Second, moral action is more abstract and ambiguous than mere physical action, since it considers consequences, motives, and purposes. The study of moral development abounds with philosophical issues that rarely spring to the front in other areas of human development. Scientific research is confounded by such complexity; therefore, it is a topic for which little certainty or clarity exists.

Two scholars of moral development, Jean Piaget and Lawrence Kohlberg, have contributed what is generally thought to be the most important data and theory on the topic of childhood moral development. Although neither of these renowned scholars is able to answer all questions pertinent to childhood morality, their concepts remain the most widely recognized and accepted.

Here the main points of Piaget and Kohlberg are overviewed in order to put moral growth into developmental perspective. Piaget's writings deal, for the most part, with moral development in children, whereas Kohlberg's research deals with "levels" of moral development through early adulthood. Piaget and Kohlberg believe (and provide evidence to support the belief) that *moral growth develops in general stages,* with each stage influenced by experience gathered in the previous stages.

Piaget's Theory of Moral Development

Piaget believed that the capacity to make moral judgments comes about primarily from interaction with peers and from increasing cognitive maturity. During the childhood years two fairly distinct stages of moral development are noted: (1) the *heteronomous stage* (heteronomous means under the authority of another) and (2) the *autonomous stage.*

The heteronomous stage is characterized by belief in rigid, inflexible sets of rules taken from others, usually parents. Moral judgment is based on narrow concepts and egocentric motives. The child thinks of moral rules as physical facts that have their own existence, much as adults think of the law of gravity or other laws of nature. As mental ability matures and as a wider range of social interaction takes place, the child moves gradually toward a more expansive morality.

The autonomous stage is marked by the child's recognition that moral goodness or badness is based on something more than violation of rules. Motives become important considerations. At the autonomous stage of moral development the child is likely to recommend clemency for a wrongdoing committed unintentionally. (In criminal law this viewpoint is embodied in the distinction between murder and accidental manslaughter.) During the earlier stage of moral development the child gauged the appropriateness of punishment purely on the act itself, without considering the intentions of the person who committed the act. In the autonomous stage the child accepts the idea that good and bad depend on *motives* as well as *consequences*. During this stage, cooperation, respect for others, and tolerance of the rights of others limber up the child's moral character.

Several important differences exist between the heteronomous stage and the autonomous stage of moral development, and these differences exert considerable influence on childhood morality. In the heteronomous stage the child thinks that actions are either totally right or totally wrong; children in this stage do not take into account individual motives; rather they focus on consequences; they think that rules are inflexible and unchangeable, like natural laws; they believe that moral wrong-doing always warrants punishment. In essence, their moral outlook is action-centred, authority-based, punitive and inflexible. The "enlightened" morality of the autonomous stage is more humane and less punitive. Specifically, it places greater emphasis on cooperation, and it is less absolutist; it takes into account intentions and motivations as well as consequences; it also recognizes that rules can be altered to fit the situation (sometimes); the limitations of punishment as a behavior modifier are seen more clearly, and the concept of rehabilitation takes hold; finally, the child recognizes the role of the person in formulating a personal morality.

According to Piaget, moral development should be understood as part of the total development of the person, not as an incidental adjunct to the personality, attached by training. Moral growth is contingent on mental growth, social interaction, and personal introspection.

Enduring Piagetian Concepts of Childhood Morality

Not all of Piaget's ideas concerning moral development have been supported by research. The concepts that have best survived the test of time, and the rigor of cross-examination, include the following:

Intentionality in judgment – Young children tend to evaluate the goodness or badness of an act in terms of the consequences that derive from the act; older children consider consequences but also give weight to intent. To demonstrate this point, children were asked who was worse – a child who broke five cups while helping his mother set the table or a boy who broke one cup while stealing some jam. Four-year-olds generally consider the child who broke the most cups guilty of the greater crime; nine-year-olds, however, charge the thief with the greater wrongdoing. During the middle-childhood years intention becomes a consideration in moral judgment.

Relativism in judgment – Young children tend to view behavior as being completely right or completely wrong. They also assume that everyone interprets moral behavior the same way as they; they do not consider that someone might disagree about whether a certain act is right or wrong. As thought becomes less rigid, allowing the child to understand that actions are not absolutely right or wrong, a certain relativism evolves in matters of good and bad.

Independence of sanctions – Children believe an act is wrong if it elicits punishment and right if it elicits praise. Upon witnessing a parent spank a youngster, the young child almost always infers that the youngster *must* have done something wrong, or the spanking would not have occurred. (Their thinking is similar to the transductive logic of the toddler.) The older child investigates further before passing judgment, recognizing that it is the act, not the response it elicits, that authenticates moral behavior.

Use of reciprocity – As noted earlier, egocentrism impedes the ability to view a situation from another's perspective. As this limitation is outgrown, children acquire greater intellectual understanding and greater moral tolerance. Advancing age invariably brings greater awareness of the subjective personhood of others, and with it comes a "moral generosity" not typical in younger years.

Use of punishment as restitution and reform – Younger children believe in direct, severe punishment for wrongdoers; as adolescence nears, greater emphasis is placed on treating "bad" behavior in such a way that it is less likely to occur in the future. The trend is toward rehabilitation rather than punishment.

Naturalistic views of misfortune – As children approach adolescence they drop the tendency to perceive accidental misfortune as a form of punishment for previously committed "sins." They accept the idea that personal catastrophes do not represent punishment for previous misdeeds.

Kohlberg's Theory of Moral Development

Lawrence Kohlberg believed that moral judgment develops through a series of stages. As a result of his long-range studies with a group of 75 boys, Kohlberg has differentiated three levels of moral judgment. These levels are greatly influenced by cognitive development, social interaction, and personal growth.

Kohlberg's three levels of moral development are (1) the premoral level, (2) the conventional level, and (3) the principled level. Each level has two stages. In outline form, his model of moral development looks like this:

Level I: Premoral (ages 4 to 10, approximately)

Stage 1 – Punishment and obedience orientation

Stage 2 – Naive instrumental hedonism

Level II: Conventional Role-Conformity (ages 10 to 13, approximately)

Stage 3 – Maintaining good relations and the approval of others

Stage 4 – Authority maintaining morality

Level III – Morality of Self-Accepted Moral Principles (ages 13 and older, for some individuals, never)

Stage 5 – Morality of contract and democratically-accepted law

Stage 6 – Morality of individual principles of conscience

Premoral Level

At this level morality is governed by external factors – the standards are those of others. Children at the premoral level are aware of social rules, of right and wrong, of good and bad; however, these are perceived only in terms of the pleasure or pain associated with them. Children recognize that obeying rules may lead to praise and that breaking rules may lead to punishment; their concern is not with the rightness of the rule, but with behavior.

The first stage in the premoral level of moral judgment is the *punishment and obedience orientation.* The child measures the goodness of an act in terms of the consequences that accrue from it. If the consequences are bad, so is the act; if no consequences follow the act is neither right nor wrong. The child obeys to avoid punishment, not because of respect for the rules. The child's primary concern is "What will happen to me?" The second stage is the *instrumental-hedonism orientation.* Proper behavior is that which satisfies personal needs. The rightness or wrongness of action is assessed in terms of how it benefits "me." At this stage the child has no reason to behave in a manner that brings negative consequences. In the adult sense of the word, morality really does not exist at the premoral level.

Conventional Level

At the conventional level of moral development, following the codes of the family, group, or nation is perceived as proper behavior. This represents an advance over the premoral level, because the child recognizes that consequences are not the only basis for proper action; it is an immature morality in that the individual has not developed personal guidelines for moral conduct but rather, simply conforms to family or social expectation. The child wants to be thought of as "good." At this level loyalty exists; children cannot be swayed from their posture merely by punishment or removal of rewards. They actively support what they believe is right.

As with each level there are two stages. The first is the *interpersonal relations orientation*. At this stage good behavior is that which pleases others or is considered good by others. Behavior is highlighted not only by conformity but also by the *desire* to conform. At this stage behavior is assessed in terms of intention; in other words, rightness or wrongness is partly determined by personal motives. The second stage is *authority-based morality*. Orientation here is toward authority, rules, regulations, and maintenance of social order. Unconventional behavior is viewed skeptically and dealt with harshly; duty, loyalty, and allegiance are viewed positively and rewarded highly. This level of morality, common to children in the early grades of school, remains strong even through junior and senior high school. For this reason, children at this stage of moral development are extremely susceptible to teachings of nationalism and ethnocentrism. Peers who like to dominate have no trouble finding followers, and children who like to be dominated have no trouble finding leaders. This morality contributes to the gang mentality so typical of late childhood.

Principled Level

At the principled level, a genuine attempt is made to formulate moral values and principles that are validated by objective, impersonal, and ideal criteria. Moral judgment is no longer based primarily on social convention, authority, and loyalty; it becomes more autonomous and less the result of conformity. It is a genuine morality in that it acknowledges that socially accepted standards can conflict with one another and the individual must ultimately arbitrate them. Kohlberg considered this the highest of the three levels of moral development because it represents commitment to moral concepts on grounds other than the utilitarian or authoritarian.

The first stage of the principled level is *morality of contract*. Right action is here determined by the rights of the individual as a member of society. Each person has the right to certain freedoms by virtue of being a person; because people are different, values take on different emphases. However, all individual rights exist within the larger context of the global community. This is the "official" morality of the Canadian government and Constitution. The second stage at this level is *morality of personal conscience*. In this stage of moral development the individual judges between right and wrong on the basis of personal conscience, which in turn, is based on self-chosen ethical principles thought to be universally valid. These principles tend to be abstract, like the Golden Rule, rather than concrete, like the Ten Commandments. The concept of justice is the dominant principle around which rules of this stage are formulated.

The cognitive, emotional, and value components of morality change during each stage of moral development. For example, the reasons that children obey rules seem to change with their level of morality. Kohlberg (1964) described the motivation for obedience at each stage:

Stage 1 – Obey rules to avoid punishment.

Stage 2 – Conform to obtain rewards, have favors returned.

Stage 3 – Conform to avoid disapproval of others.

Stage 4 – Conform to avoid censure from legitimate authorities and the guilt that comes from defying authority.

Stage 5 – Conform to maintain the respect of the impartial spectator judging in terms of community welfare.

Stage 6 – Conform to avoid self-condemnation.

The value of human life is also understood differently in succeeding moral stages; therefore, its moral significance attains different qualities at each moral stage:

Stage 1 – The value of a human life is confused with the value of physical objects and is based on the social status or physical attributes of its possessor.

Stage 2 – The value of a human life is seen as instrumental to the satisfaction of the needs of its possessor or of other persons.

Stage 3 – The value of a human life is based on the empathy and affection of family members and others toward its possessor.

Stage 4 – Life is conceived as sacred in terms of its place in a categorical moral or religious order of rights and duties.

Stage 5 – Life is valued both in terms of its relation to community welfare and in terms of life being a universal right.

Stage 6 – Belief in the sacredness of human life as representing a universal human value of respect for the individual.

Kohlberg did not believe that children function at only one moral stage at any given moment in their development. A ten-year-old, for example, may demonstrate behavior that corresponds with the third stage, but elements of the moral outlook of stages two and four may also be present. Moral growth progresses from stage to stage, but it does not do so in a single bound; rather, it moves in gradual steps, some large and some small. Kohlberg claims that each stage is reached as a result of the attainment of the preceding stage – a notion he shares with other stage theorists, including Piaget. The important point is that Kohlberg does not view moral development as an automatic progression through stages; rather, stages represent the combined effects of mental and social maturity on the capacity for moral judgment.

The Connective Links between Mental Development and Moral Development

Winston Churchill expressed the link about as well as anyone when he stated: "It is a fine thing to be honest but it is also very important to be right." In matters of morality, justifying behavior is as important as the behavior itself. Morality must be conceptualized and explained; it is, therefore, in very significant measure, an intellectual enterprise.

Mental development does not cause moral *development* even though it greatly influences its content; and mental development does not cause moral *behavior* even though it greatly influences the ability to inhibit or exhibit personal desires. Without question, moral development and mental development are linked in numerous significant ways, and the link connects a great deal of every child's behavior.

In this chapter we have looked at Piaget's concepts of cognitive development, Selman's concepts of perspective-taking and Kohlberg's ideas about moral stages. All three of these important subsets of child development interrelate with and lend substance to each other.

In Piaget's *Preoperational stage of cognitive development* (overviewed in Chapter seven) the child uses symbolic representation, but overall mental abilities are weakened by centration and irreversibility. At the same age, according to Selman, the child understands the subjectivity of others but doesn't recognize very well that people can actually think about each other. Simultaneously, in Kohlberg's scheme the child's moral conduct is most influenced by the rules of authorities and by the consequences of actions.

In Piaget's *Concrete Operations stage of cognitive development,* the characteristics of an object are separated from action relating to it, conservation skills evolve, and the ability to deal with abstractions increases. As far as perspective-taking is concerned, the child comes to realize that people can evaluate each other's subjectivity. To Kohlberg, in this stage of moral development right is understood in limited and egocentric terms, and personal interests greatly influence moral conduct.

Pertaining to the foregoing, it is clear that thinking skills create the framework for moral rules, and establish the foundation for perspective-taking. The overlap of intellectual abilities, perspective-taking and moral development forms the basis for profound connective links which integrate and unify the flow of child development.

The Major Concepts of this Chapter

1. The mid-years children have considerably better intellectual skills than preschoolers and are less egocentric both intellectually and emotionally. Their thought is concrete in nature (Piaget's term) and they learn to deal with classes, relations, quantities, mental representations, and serialization.

2. Thought in mid-childhood is primarily directed toward the real and present, is concerned with organizing facts, lacks comprehensiveness and is somewhat rigid. Memory skills improve, concentration and selective perception improve, and thought becomes more abstract. Relational terms and ideas are then better understood.

3. Sex differences in mental abilities include the better performance of boys on visual-spatial tasks and mathematics, while girls perform better on reading and tasks of a verbal nature. Differences on academic tasks in the main are thought to be environmentally determined, while there is some evidence for a biological basis for boys' better performance on spatial tasks.

4. The mid-years child becomes capable of self-evaluation. Four sources of a sense of self-efficacy are prior experience, vicarious experience, verbal persuasion, and body experience. If a child learns to expect failure learned helplessness may result.

5. Perceptual style (field-dependence, field-independence) affects the way children perceive, think and learn. Other forms of cognitive style, such as global or analytical thought, are also important to the overall learning style of the child.

6. Theories of intelligence range in their emphasis from those which stress a global intellectual capacity to those which state that intelligence is a function of multiple intelligences which develop along different paths.

7. Brain development in mid-childhood is characterized by increased lateralization, increased brain size and activity and increased brain complexity. By the end of mid-childhood the brain has reached about 90 percent of its adult weight.

8. Moral development is influenced by mental development. Preoperational thought usually accompanies the earlier stages of moral development while advancement in concrete operational thought is concomitant with higher levels of moral development.

9. Piaget proposed two stages of moral development (heteronomous and autonomous) which influence mid-childhood. Important Piagetian concepts of moral development include intentionality in judgment, relativism in judgment, independence of sanctions, use of reciprocity, use of punishment as restitution and reform, and naturalistic views of misfortune.

10. Kohlberg outlined a theory of moral development broken down into three levels, each consisting of two stages.

10

Middle Childhood:
The Physical Body and the Social Being

The childhood shows the man,
As the morning shows the day.
John Milton

The child continues to mature physically during middle childhood, but physical growth is less spectacular than social or cognitive growth. Middle-years children, unlike body-conscious adolescents, take their bodies for granted because growth is stable, consistent, and it does not strain their emotional fabric. Except during the sixth year when illness and body disruption are fairly common, body functions run smoothly during the entire course of middle childhood. The child's laissez-faire attitude toward physical development will change markedly during early adolescence, when virtually every phase of development will be affected by the disruptive changes of the puberty growth spurt. But for now, physical development is really the least of the growing person's problems.

On the other hand, social development is flamboyant and adventurous. The social world expands even more dramatically than during the preschool years when the child first ventured alone into the outside world. New friendships are formed, but more importantly, they are characterized by genuine emotional attachment. For the first time in the life cycle the child forms deep bonds of relatedness outside the family unit. In great measure this migration away from the confines of the household toward the world of peers highlights middle childhood. During these years the groundwork is laid for the emotional and social richness of adolescence, which looms closer with each birthday.

Physical Growth during the Middle-Childhood Years

The Significance of Physical Growth on the Child's Psychology

The unfolding body is, of course, a vital fact unto itself, but it is also a catalyst for other significant dimensions of child growth. Firstly, physical growth makes new behaviors possible (crawling, walking, speaking) which become critical facts in the child's daily routine. As well, physical development sets the upper limits of behavior and thus determines what the child cannot do. Therefore, preschoolers do not play Little League baseball (effectively) no matter what the expectations of their father-coach. In addition, the child's physical abilities greatly affect how other people respond to him. The child who can look you in the eye, shake your hand, and say "Good morning," elicits a maturity of response that a younger, less able child simply can not.

Secondly, adult expectations are directly influenced by the child's physical development. A five-year-old is expected to climb on a jungle gym without assistance while a two-year-old requires prompting and encouragement. Five-year-olds are expected to remain still where a two-year-old is allowed to roam at will.

Thirdly, physical growth has a profound effect on the child's self-esteem, especially during middle childhood where peer and adult reactions are influenced by size, mobility and appearance (Bee, 1989). In essence, physical development triggers social and psychological reactions which permeate the entire range of childhood growth.

General Trends in Physical Growth

For the most part, growth during these years is regular and consistent. The average North American six-year-old stands about 117 centimetres (4 feet) tall and has a mass of about 23 kilograms (50 pounds). Height increases at the rate of approximately six percent per year during middle childhood, while mass increases about ten percent per year. During the tenth year girls begin to have slightly more mass and stand slightly taller than boys of the same age, but this is a difference that doesn't make much of a difference. The trend is toward similarity in height and weight and it continues until about age 13 or 14, after which boys, as a group, mature into greater height and mass.

The gangly, gawky look of middle childhood comes about because of continued lengthening of the skeleton and the loss of fatty tissue. Eight- and nine-year-olds often display a lean, hungry look, which will be outgrown when body mass catches up with skeletal length. A streamlined body profile, however, although common, is not universal. Some boys break from the general trend by going through a period of plumpness between early childhood and early adolescence. Even more commonly girls of this age acquire a good deal of fatty tissue, thus developing a roly-poly silhouette.

Eight-year-old girls with closely cropped hair (or boys of the same age with long, flowing hair) are difficult to distinguish from members of the opposite sex. Female breasts are not noticeable as such; male shoulders are no broader than female shoulders; and the hourglass profile is rare among girls of this age. The physical appearances by which we distinguish male from female are strikingly absent during middle childhood.

The middle-childhood years are spent readying the body for the massive growth of early adolescence, something of a calm before the storm. Not by accident is middle childhood a period of relative emotional tranquility. Growth is primarily social and cognitive rather than anatomical; hence, the child is relatively free of the psychological strain that accompanies physical growth.

The classroom is an ideal laboratory for observing the progress of physical control and motor maturity during the middle-childhood years. A classroom of first graders is oceanic: everything and everyone seems to move and sway constantly. As Elkind put it, "Looking in on a first-grade class with the constant motion, jiggling, shoving, pushing and talking can give the observer a distinct experience of seasickness" (1971, p. 65). The six-year-old gathering is an anthill of action interrupted only when youngsters are sidetracked by an interest such as coloring or when they grow tired and rest to rebuild energy reserves. A second-grade classroom is less frenzied, because action is more purposive and less random. Seven-year-olds demonstrate more self-control and physical discipline than six-year-olds. Seven can sit for a length of time without giving the impression that another minute of sitting will result in insanity. Eight-year olds bring a modest degree of what adults consider decorum to the classroom. The classroom is neater and tidier than during the first or the second grade, with considerably less helter-skelter activity, less jumping in and out of seats, less scurrying about. More concentration of attention, restraint of limb movement, and general composure are evident. Fourth and fifth graders show even greater constraint. The frequency of impulsive action continues to decrease, while the frequency of purposive, goal-directed action continues to increase. Students may remain seated for up to an hour if engrossed in their work. Classrooms of nine- and ten-year-olds often exude a businesslike atmosphere because their movement is economical, even parsimonious.

Many psychologists believe that mid-childhood is the most placid and predictable period of the entire growth cycle. Although the terms "placid" and "predictable" may lure one into a false sense of security, the middle-childhood years are indeed less dramatic and less traumatic than any other period of child or adolescent development. Glandular development is in the same general balance at the end of the period as it was at the beginning. Disease is less prevalent than at any other period in the growth cycle. Skeletal growth is consistent but not spectacular.

The outstanding physical developments of this age are (1) increased manual dexterity, (2) increased strength, (3) increased resistance to fatigue, and (4) increased overall body coordination. Refinements in muscular and motor coordination allow greater freedom of play and work and greater endurance. Games last longer and fatigue comes later. Like children at all developmental ages, the middle child has an impulse to exercise newly emerging skills; therefore, the middle-childhood years are filled with exercise and practice ranging from the helter-skelter to the disciplined.

The Latency Period

Two general usages of the term "latency" are encountered. One use is in Freud's theory of psychosexual development; there the term refers to the period, between the ages of six and eleven, when children have little interest in sexual gratification and undergo increased identification with the like-sex parent. A second usage of the term refers to a period of slow, comparatively uneventful growth just prior to the pubescent growth spurt. I will use the term in the second way. To prevent confusion the aspect of latency we are concerned with will be referred to as *growth latency*.

During growth latency the body experiences a considerable degree of physical equilibrium. The child gains, on the average, only a couple of kilograms (4 to 5 pounds) per year and grows approximately 2 to 4 centimetres (1 to 2 inches) in height. The latency period comes to an end with the surge of growth that takes place about a year before the onset of sexual maturity. This period of rapid growth is sometimes referred to as the *maximum growth age*.

In the latency period children are spared the problems that accompany fast growth. Muscles cause little difficulty; complexion is smooth; and the great intake of calcium, protein, phosphorus, and other elements that is required during major growth spurts is not necessary. Neither is psychological life excessively troubled by the emotional difficulties that typically accompany rapid growth of muscle, bone, genitalia, and internal organs. Latency is indeed the calm before the storm – nature's attempt to build reserves for the taxing growth spurt that we know as adolescence.

Body Types

Humans come in assorted shapes and sizes, and by no stretch of the imagination do middle children bear exception to this rule. We see as many different body shapes as people, but it is nevertheless possible to formulate general classifications of body shapes. Primarily because of the pioneer research of Sheldon (1940), body types have come to be classified as *endomorphic, ectomorphic,* and *mesomorphic*.

Chronological Age Versus Maturational Age

A frequently used index for determining the extent to which biological (or maturational) age coincides with chronological age was devised by Bayley and Pinneau (1952). Their classification scheme makes use of three categories:

1. Average: when maturation age is within one calender year (plus or minus) of the chronological age.
2. Accelerated: when maturation age is more than one year advanced over chronological age.
3. Retarded: when maturation age is more than one year behind chronological age.

Thus, a girl who is eight years old and whose maturation age is between seven and nine would be in the average range. An eight-year-old whose maturation age is nine years, six months would be considered accelerated, whereas an eight-year-old whose maturation age is six years, six months would be considered retarded by this classification scheme. As a general rule (taking exception for early and later maturers), individuals tend to remain in the same classification throughout childhood.

The child with an ectomorphic body type has a lean, almost stringy build. Very little body fat surrounds the skeleton, and the outline of the rib cage is visible. The label "skinny" inevitably becomes affixed to ectomorphic types because, no matter how extensive one's vocabulary, it is the most descriptive term available. Limbs tend to be long and thin, the chest flat and underdeveloped; the shoulders are contoured and sloping rather than straight and stout; and hands usually are long and thin, as if fitted by nature for the piano. Muscle tissue and fatty tissue are present in only a limited degree. One should not, however, be deceived by the ectomorphic profile. The ectomorph may be as rough and rugged as more muscular people; many first-rate basketball and volleyball players possess ectomorphic body builds. (In fairness, however, it must be conceded that athletic events tend to be dominated by mesomorphs.) During the late-childhood years many youngsters appear to be ectomorphic who, when they have finished growing, will more closely resemble the mesomorph or endomorph. This is because a sudden increase in height without a corresponding increase in mass results in a scarecrowlike physique, with bony protrusions here and there. When mass increases the drawn out, impoverished look disappears, and a new body presents itself.

The mesomorphic body type is characterized by well-developed musculature, broad shoulders, expanded chest cavity, narrow (compared with the shoulders) pelvis, and strong legs and arms. Facial bones are prominent, and the head rests on a sturdy neck. The forearms, wrists, and ankles are larger than those of ectomorphs and afford greater strength and stamina. The mesomorphic body is well suited for combative activities, as the Greeks long ago discovered. Cinema Tarzans and running backs in professional football are invariably of this body type. The classic masculine mesomorph profile is presented in Michelangelo's "David." Since the Golden Age of Pericles (the art of which inspired Michelangelo) the mesomorphic body type has been the prototype of robust masculinity.

The endomorph is considerably different from the slender ectomorph or the athletic mesomorph. The endomorphic body is round and smooth, because it harbors more body fat. The trunk is round and thick, and the head is large and rather rounded – in striking contrast to the long, thin, projectile head of the ectomorph. Arms and legs are large but do not have the muscular definition of the mesomorph's; hands and feet are best described as pudgy. The bony protrusions of leaner types are nonexistent in the plump endomorph. The most famous of all endomorphs is Santa Claus.

A few further comments about body types are in order. All three body types are found in both males and females. Males are more commonly associated with the mesomorphic body type than females, but this is because the type is unfairly equated with bulging muscles. *Skeletal profile* is the most important component of body type, and the mesomorphic skeletal outline exists for males and females alike when allowance is made for the expanded pelvic girdle natural to women. Very few individuals are "pure" mesomorphs, endomorphs, or ectomorphs; a mixture of types is the rule.

The consistency of body proportions during the first 20 years of life has been convincingly supported by Broverman and associates (Broverman, 1964). Their research indicates that preadolescent body proportions are highly correlated with postadolescent body proportions. Thus, endomorphic children usually mature into endomorphic adults, mesomorphic children into mesomorphic adults, and so it is also with ectomorphic children. Endomorphs tend to begin their growth spurt sooner than ectomorphs and thus they generally are the largest members of the preadolescent community.

Although not all mesomorphs are inclined toward sports, they are physically better suited to excellence in athletics than the other body types. Endomorphs, male and female alike, are considered less physically attractive by children (and adults); consequently they learn to live with crude witticisms about being overweight. Ectomorphs can disguise their body type with shrewd deployment of clothing, but nevertheless they usually feel self-conscious about their slender profile even though (particularly among females) many of their friends would love to have such a problem.

Children's Understanding of their Bodies and their Body Parts

Despite the fact that they know the names of their visible body parts, few children in the early years of middle childhood (six through eight) attain a very sophisticated understanding of internal anatomy. Crider's research on how youngsters understand their inner workings is instructive (1981). Children know that swallowed food ends up in their stomach, probably from being told so rather than from the sensation of eating. This differs from knowing the location of the heart which pounds after exercise, or bones, which can be grasped and squeezed. The brain perplexes them, although they accept that it somehow produces thought.

Their understanding of anatomical function is poor unless they have received accurate information from parent or teacher. Kids in Grade Two claim that "Blood is what makes everything work." "Your brain is what makes your eyes see." "The liver doesn't really do anything. It's just there, like a cow's liver."

Advanced understanding is not the hallmark of the concrete thinker, and comprehension of human anatomy is no exception to this rule. For the most part, children learn how their bodies work (much as they learn how cars work) from parents, teachers, books, and TV. What they know is directly proportional to what they have been taught.

Obesity in Childhood

Being obese is not the same as being overweight. Obesity refers to the amount of adiposity (fat cells) in the body. Researchers estimate that 5-15 percent of all North American children are considered obese.

Hormone problems account for only a small percentage of child obesity in North America. Nutritionists believes that overfeeding leads to multiplication of fat cells, which in turn increases susceptibility to becoming fat during later childhood or adolescence.

Obesity occurs more frequently in low-income families. Poor dietary habits and the overeating of "junk food" (high in calories and low in nutrients), are considered major factors in this phenomenon.

Fat cells are manufactured during three basic periods: 1) the prenatal period, 2) the first 24 months after birth, and 3) during puberty. Youngsters who produce excess fat cells during these periods have difficulty maintaining weight which is appropriate for their height (Fogel, 1988).

Research indicates that overweight toddlers are also likely to be overweight during Grades 1, 2, and 3. In addition, obesity at age six is predictive of adolescent obesity. Since correlation between weight in childhood and weight at a later age is not perfect, many overweight youngsters do not become obese teenagers. The consistency is sufficient, however, to merit attention.

The genetic component to obesity is suggested by twin studies. Identical twins are far more similar to one another as far as body fat is concerned than are fraternal twins. Research with adopted children also shows higher correlations of body fat with biological parents than with adoptive parents.

Generally speaking, obese children are more sedentary than ordinary youngsters; most experts believe that inactivity plays an important role in childhood obesity.

Sex Differences in Physical Growth

As mentioned earlier in this chapter, the differences between the sexes during middle childhood are not significant when body height, weight, depth, strength, and mobility are compared. In fact, throughout the childhood period the sexes are more similar than different in virtually all hereditary traits. However, as a few important differences exist, a brief overview will prove instructive.

To appreciate growth differences between males and females, one must note that girls mature at a faster rate than boys during the first 10 or 12 years of life. At birth girls are slightly more advanced in both skeletal and muscle development; they reach important junctures of development sooner than boys and experience fewer developmental abnormalities. Girls begin their adolescent growth spurt sooner than boys, reach sexual maturity sooner, and finish their pubertal growth at an earlier age. Girls are less likely to experience radical growth spurts; their development is steadier and more predictable than that of boys. Strength, and strength in proportion to body mass, are fairly similar for boys and girls during the childhood years but shift in favor of boys during the adolescent period. By midadolescence boys undergo dramatic increases in physical strength because they develop more muscle tissue, larger lungs and heart, and the ability to carry a greater amount of oxygen in the blood. By late adolescence boys are superior to girls in physical skills requiring raw strength, respiratory endurance, and muscular velocity. Boys are not necessarily more developed than girls with regard to agility, body coordination, rhythmic control, balance, or timing. Finally, throughout the pre-adult life cycle girls possess a greater percentage of fatty tissue, which prevents the skeleton from protruding through the skin and which contributes to a rounder, more contoured appearance. Boys, who have less fat, are more angular and solid.

During childhood the sexes are similar in physical growth, with female development being somewhat smoother. During adolescence, however, boys become considerably larger, stronger, and quicker than girls.

General Athletic Abilities

Athletic skills increase with each year during middle childhood. Ten-year-olds invariably are stronger, quicker, and smoother than eight-year-olds, and eight-year-olds show a similar superiority over six-year-olds. Unquestionably age is positively correlated with athletic abilities during all periods of childhood.

Summary of Sex Differences in Physical Growth

Characteristic	Nature of Difference
Rate of maturation	Girls are on a faster timetable throughout development; this difference amounts to about two to four weeks at birth and about two years at adolescence. Girls tend to begin puberty sooner, and finalize it sooner than boys.
Predictability or regularity of maturation	Girls' physical growth is more regular and predictable. The final height of a girl, for example, is easier to predict than that of a boy. Growth tends to be less turbulent for girls, whereas growth spurts are more noticeable for boys.
Strength and speed	Little difference appears in childhood, but after puberty boys are stronger and faster. In grade three, for example, a mixed track meet will yield a fairly equal number of girl and boy winners.
Heart and circulation	With puberty, boys develop a larger heart and lungs and a greater capacity for carrying oxygen in the blood than do girls. In most activities requiring endurance or velocity boys begin to demonstrate considerable superiorty.
Fat tissue	Girls from birth onward have a thicker layer of fat tissue just below the surface of the skin, and after puberty a larger percentage of their body weight is composed of fat. In childhood, however, to determine gender by roundness is difficult.
Motor skills	In the preschool years, girls are better at tasks requiring jumping, hopping, rhythmic movement, and balance. In elementary school and later, boys are better at activities requiring running, jumping, and throwing, while girls are better at hopping. These differences are difficult to evaluate, however, because from the beginning boys have more encouragement and better coaching than girls in most physical activities.

(Based upon Bee, 1989)

Children who excel in one athletic ability tend to be good in others . The fastest runners in the third or fourth grade also tend to be good jumpers and rope skippers. Thus, a general-abilities factor (G-factor) is observed in athletic skills. Boys tend to be slightly superior in many athletic skills although this difference between the sexes is not universal. Performance differences are greatly influenced by practice and coaching; even the most physically advanced ten-year-old boy cannot begin to match the achievements of girls the same age who have undergone a couple of years of gymnastic training if the boy has received no training.

The Social World of Middle Childhood

The social world of middle childhood is exceptionally fluid and flexible; it twists and bends to suit the ever-changing needs and impulses of its constituents. The internal operations of a gang can change completely because the kingpin has departed for dinner. More commonly than believed by adults, a gang member will show up for a meeting only to discover that she was expelled during a meeting that she missed. Again, to the surprise of adults who do not understand youth power-politics, the same youngster may win back the good will of the pack by buying them each a milkshake or by threatening to kick the bejabers out of them if they don't reconsider their action. The social world of middle childhood is a milieu of codes, rules, impulses, and experiments. This is the age when children first seriously attempt to get along with one another without adult supervision and when they undertake their first adventure in self-government. In the society of children, one hurriedly learns to take care of oneself and to become proficient at social survival.

One task of these years is to establish a sense of identity that is not based solely on adult evaluation. As children move away from the emotional security of the home, they acquire new labels and identities. They may learn that they are fat or skinny; ugly or attractive; black, yellow, white, brown, or red; and dependable or untrustworthy (or maybe a little of each, depending on the situation).

The child lives in several different cultures that do not share the same values. The school, the home, and the peer group each has unique rules and regulations, and not infrequently the rules of one conflict with the rules of another. The middle child learns that other people do not automatically think kindly of him the way they do at home, and he now tries to adjust to others rather than demanding egocentrically that they make the adjustment. The child is less candid with parents because he is living a small but increasingly private life away from the household.

Groups tend to become separated by age as well as by sex: ten-year-olds do not mix with seven-year-olds (except in special circumstances), and boys do not generally mix with girls, although exceptions to both of these generalizations are fairly easy to find.

Beginning at age seven or eight children begin to associate primarily with same-sex peers. Boys chase and tease girls rather than play with them. Boys seek out other boys and are likely to be embarrassed if found alone with a group of girls. From age 9 through 11 some boys experience anxiety over their associations with girls, and they are confused about whether they are supposed to be interested in them.

Children join peer groups for many reasons. Among the most important are (1) to establish an identity that it not based on the family, (2) to share time with other children who have similar social-psychological problems, and (3) to acquire greater social competence.

Children of the same age are drawn together by merit of their similar maturation and shared experiences. They oppose one another, on occasion, because of their many differences, but the magnetism of similarity pulls them together. Many family outings are bearable only when the child brings along a friend to provide the unique companionship born of juvenile homogeneity.

Conformity

With regard to conformity middle-childhood is a mixed bag. In some ways youngsters are rugged individualists who resist demands for conformity. Some of their idiosyncrasies are remarkably resistant to extinction; consider the fourth-grade boy who insisted on taking a nap after lunch and did so sprawled between the desks of the classroom. After several weeks of resisting this habit, the teacher finally gave up and brought a blanket to class so that the after lunch nap would be a bit more comfortable. This habit lasted for over a year before the youngster conformed to the norm of classroom behavior. On the other hand, some children stifle every trace of personal eccentricity if it interferes with acceptance. Middle children can be talked into many behaviors they would never do on their own if pressure from friends is strong enough. They are especially prone to follow in grey areas where they sense what they are doing is wrong but have never been explicitly told not to engage in the behavior.

In other ways, however, they are conformists in the tradition of Rotarians and Legionnaires.

Peer pressure

That middle-years children are more susceptible than younger children to peer manipulation is well documented. Hartup (1970), reporting on peer interaction and social organization, concludes that preschool children are comparatively immune to peer pressure and rarely change their perceptions to conform with someone else's. Hunt and Synnerdale (1959) report that only about 10 to 15 percent of kindergarten-age children modify their outlooks; however, children in the middle years are more inclined to follow their peers in experiments of this nature.

For most youngsters the ability to resist peer pressure is underdeveloped for the following reasons: (1) all children possess a strong desire to be accepted by their peers and are reluctant to jeopardize good standing; (2) children are prone to accept naive stereotypes about good and bad, right and wrong; therefore, they usually find the narrow outlook of their peers acceptable (nothing contributes more to conformity than narrowness of outlook); and (3) most children are not sufficiently confident in themselves or in their sense of what is improper to oppose the group.

Popularity

Studies of school-age children indicate that popular children are attractive, friendly, and good sports. Good-looking girls (if they are not overly impressed with their own beauty) tend to be more popular among both boys and girls than girls of average attractiveness. In general, bigger and stronger boys are more widely accepted than less physically developed kids. The most talented, creative, and intelligent children are more widely accepted than slow learners or retarded children.

Traits that discourage popularity include anxiety, uncertainty, indifference, aggressiveness, hostility, and unattractive physical attributes, such as obesity or a limb handicap. These are not absolute indicators of unpopularity, but they are highly correlated with it during middle childhood. (The personality features in this list are similar to those that correlate with unpopularity during adolescence, namely anxious dependency on others, the desire always to please others, and preoccupation with the reactions and praise of others.)

The topic of childhood popularity is not the easiest to investigate because kids often do not themselves know with certainty why they like or dislike another child. In some research, for example, the psychologists must provide a series of reasons why some kids are liked or disliked and ask the youngster to choose the most appropriate reason for his particular likes and dislikes. Despite this, a considerable amount of information has been gathered on this topic, much of which is consistent and insightful. A composite summary of this research is presented in the following chart:

Reasons for Liking	Reasons for Disliking
Is helpful, friendly, cooperative	Is aggressive or hostile
Is able to give desired kinds of attention and approval	Takes things away from others
Shares common interests	Violates rules or does forbidden activities
Possesses desirable material goods	Disrupts ongoing activities
Lives close by	Ridicules peers
Is able to manage conflicts successfully	Ignores others or withdraws
	Exhibits behavior that is considered by the group as "strange"
Accommodates to activity flow	Is a "cry baby"

Langlois (1977, 1979), who has researched this topic as thoroughly as anyone, believes that in the preschool years physically attractive children are more popular with their peers, and better received by adults. Even teachers, who are trained to treat children impartially, rate physically attractive youngsters more favorably than less attractive kids.

The relationship between childhood popularity and physical attractiveness is not easy to understand. Many researchers accept the following suggestion:

> Expectations for attractive and unattractive children may set a self-fulfilling prophecy into motion: unattractive children may be labeled as such and learn over time the stereotypes and behaviors associated with unattractiveness. Consequently, older children may exhibit aggressive behaviors consistent with this labeling and behave in accordance with others' expectations of them. (Langlois & Downs, 1979, p. 416)

The quality of the child's relationship with parents exerts some influence on their popularity. The findings on this topic are mixed, but a number of general trends present themselves. First, parents who like their children and who openly show their affection toward them tend to have children who get along with their peers. Second, parents who discourage aggression and who attempt to correct antisocial behavior have children with fewer acting-out problems and more social acceptability. Third, parents who do not create an atmosphere of excess frustration tend to have children who get along well with peers. These parental correlates of child popularity should not be surprising, because interaction with parents is the single most important factor in the child's emotional life. The peer group is a monumental reality, but success in it is largely determined by what has gone on in the home long before it became an important territory in the child's social world.

Youngest children tend to be more popular than oldest children. The most accepted explanation for this maintains that younger siblings benefit from the responsibility (and effort) of older brothers and sisters who inherited most of the household chores, thus liberating younger family members for social activities. Some psychologists, however, do not feel compelled to account for this phenomenon because it is a loose trend (rather than a solid pattern) which has *many* exceptions.

The Unpopular Child

Not all children are popular, but reasons for unpopularity vary. When children are asked to name their best friends, or even the "kids that you like," about 10 percent of the members in any group are not named at all (Asher & Renshaw, 1981). These kids are not necessarily outcasts (although some of them are), but they do not have friends and, therefore, are isolated from their peer group.

Two factors are of importance here. The first is *rejection*. Youngsters rejected by other kids are usually rejected for reasons important to the childhood community. Among six-to-ten-year-old boys, for example, reasons for rejection include: anti-social behavior, excessive aggressiveness, or, at the other end of the continuum, wimpy, crybaby behavior. A second factor associated with non-popularity is *neglect*. Some kids are simply neglected. They are not disliked, they are not rejected, they simply are overlooked. These children tend to be shy, under assertive, or less attractive than other kids. Of the two types, the neglected child is the more likely to become accepted eventually because other children in time come to recognize their likable qualities, even if they are not presented assertively. Rejected kids are less likely to eventually be accepted because their non-acceptance is based upon traits and behaviors other children find unlikable; therefore acceptance is not likely to take place until the behavior changes.

In the social world of childhood acceptance is based upon specifics more than generalities. The unpopular child is not so merely because of an aura, or a general demeanor; usually specific behaviors are the issue. For example, unpopular kids usually lack skills for starting conversations, for complimenting other kids, or for making clever jokes about their own failings. Scarr's comments on this topic are quite insightful:

> Unpopular children lack social skills for initiating contact with peers, maintaining relationships, and resolving conflicts. When unpopular children attempt to join an ongoing activity, they tend to make critical comments, state their own opinions, ask questions, and otherwise call attention to themselves. Popular children wait for a break in the conversation or action, then edge in by focusing on the activity rather than on themselves. In about two out of three cases, a child's attempt to join a group fails. Popular children try another strategy; unpopular children either persist in their ineffective attempts to get attention or give up. (1986, p. 430).

Furthermore, unpopular children (like unpopular adolescents) tend to perceive their problems as something unsolvable ("I can't make anybody like me"), or as a fixed condition ("Nobody will ever like me").

School teachers, coaches and others who work with large numbers of children note that unpopular kids seem more likely than popular kids to develop emotional problems and anti-social behavior. The evidence supporting this observation, however, is not straight forward because so little controlled research has focused on these children. *Ex post facto* (after the fact) research indicates that delinquent and anti-social adolescents often were disliked and rejected as children, but this does not mean that all rejected and disliked children become anti-social or delinquent.

Friends and Friendship

During middle childhood both a narrowing and a widening of social interaction takes place. The widening involves an increased outgoingness, a lowering of barriers, and an expansion of interests. The narrowing involves the tendency to become more discriminating in the selection of friends and playmates. We see a tendency to choose a best friend with whom free time is shared. Especially in the latter half of middle childhood, comradeship flourishes. These pairings demonstrate striking durability, sometimes lasting into and even through adolescence. Exchanges of ideas, outlooks, and impressions are central to these relationships but are not the only reason for them. Usually best friends are of the same sex, but this trend has exceptions.

Close friends are valued because so much of the world is distant and impersonal. Middle childhood is an age for inquisitiveness about human relationships, and these inquiries are better explored in tandem than in isolation. All in all, the social needs of this age are more completely met when one has a best friend and, as in so many matters of social necessity, kids seek out best friends as if responding to impulses etched in their social program.

Same-Sex Friendships

Middle childhood is not a time for excessive mingling of boys with girls. As a rule, boys stick with boys and girls with girls. As well, most evidence indicates that boys prefer boys and girls prefer girls. This proclivity for sex-segregation is not typical of earlier childhood stages. Preschoolers, for example, rarely draw sex lines and when they do, the lines tend to involve games thought to be gender-specific, such as playing with dolls, or playing football. Toddlers, being the impervious souls they are, draw almost no lines on boy-girl interchange.

Same-sex relationships are not the only kind; they are simply the most prevalent. Outright rejection of the opposite sex is rare at this age: *intentional avoidance* is more descriptive. Boy-girl relationships, when they exist, are less durable than girl-girl or boy-boy relationships.

Why then are same-sex friendships so universal in middle childhood? Explanations focus on *social learning* (almost no developmental psychologists accept the Freudian viewpoint that rejection of opposite sex members is the child's attempt to resolve the Oedipal complex). Boys by age eight or ten accept matter-of-factly that girls cannot play their games or that they don't want to play them; girls of this age usually avoid activities generally associated with boys – especially rowdy activities and collision sports. Boys invariably ridicule what they consider effeminate, although girls are not as disdainful of that considered masculine. Boy-girl relationships are usually taunted by both sexes at this age because everyone knows that togetherness is the first step in the formation of sexual liaisons (although not much more is known).

If youngsters are required to intermingle they usually can do so effectively, especially if they have a competent adult supervisor. However, when left to their own inclinations and the cluster of social reflexes peculiar to their age, they consistently form same-sex rather than mixed-sex friendships and gangs.

Aggression: Darwin Rules the Playground

Aggression and hostility are significant forces in childhood. For many youngsters kicking or hitting is a "natural" reaction to frustration. Most children, especially those subject only to weak adult supervision, can be taunted into physical fights, although youths who consistently win fights tend to start them. (Some psychologists believe that the superiority with words of the late-developing boy arises from his learning to settle arguments with words rather than fists. Early-developing boys, holding a commanding edge in height and mass, have less need for words.)

Even at this early age, boys show more anger and aggression than girls. Research suggests that boys are more aggressive than girls in virtually all cultures and that male primates, in general, are more aggressive than females. (In no way is masculine aggression a humanly unique phenomenon!) Boys also begin aggression at a younger age, and are more likely to retaliate when they are offended. Many boys, by middle childhood, have acquired a generally hostile attitude and interpret the actions of others as hostile and aggressive even when they are not, setting the stage for an ongoing pattern of aggression and retaliation.

Investigations into the hormonal and biological basis of aggression have not yielded clear-cut data on sex differences, but this is partly due to the fact that research instrumentation is imprecise and ambiguous. Most developmentalists believe that biological and endocrinological factors contribute to masculine aggressiveness, but it simply is not known precisely what they are or how they work.

Numerous factors contribute to childhood aggression, including frustration, fatigue, general coping skills, and the ability of adults to anticipate and prevent conditions that lead to frustration and anger. (This cluster of variables parents, teachers, and other adults entrusted with children try to engineer in order to lessen the incidence of aggression.)

Finally, research indicates that children judged most aggressive by their classmates at age eight turned into the most aggressive adults. As well, the most aggressive children are more likely to have parents who punished them harshly than least aggressive children. Perhaps the most disappointing finding of all: once aggression is established as a way of solving problems it becomes a self-perpetuating behavior that is resistant to control (Pines, 1985).

Competition

Competition during middle childhood, especially among boys, can be fierce. Some youngsters are obsessed with winning at any cost, whether in the athletic arena or playing checkers with mother. As a rule, highly competitive children are poor losers and totally without grace after defeat. They often pout or throw temper tantrums. This fierce competitiveness does not indicate a fundamental defect in their personality but it certainly taxes everyone who must deal with it.

Boys tend to be more competitive than girls; at least they are more flamboyant and demonstrative. Girls are also competitive, and it is naive to think they are not. Like boys, they take defeat seriously; being "number one" is too powerful in our society for girls to be exempt from it. In terms of behavior, however, noticeable differences do exist between the sexes. Boys tend to be more aggressive in competitive settings, and, in general, more outrageous. They are more likely to throw tantrums after defeat, and they are more likely than girls to disparage themselves when they lose. The egocentric tendency to overestimate one's own abilities and underestimate the abilities of competitors is a middle-childhood trademark which makes defeat not only frustrating but also incomprehensible.

Prejudice

By the time children reach Grade one they have acquired a considerable number of society's prejudices; by mid-childhood they have acquired even more. Children absorb societal prejudices because (1) they imitate what they see and hear, and (2) they are not gifted at analyzing prejudiced ideas and concepts. Childhood prejudices are rarely based on negative personal experiences with other minority groups; rather, they are usually grounded in socialization, imitation, or simply in compliance.

Frenkel-Brunswick (1958), in a classic study of prejudice in children, found that several personality trends characterize prejudiced children. Such children tend to reject individuals considered weak or "different," while admiring the strong and powerful. They hold rigid views about proper "masculine" and "feminine" behavior and dislike variation from these rigid prescriptions. Prejudiced children tend to be more fearful and insecure and to feel more helpless than less prejudiced children. Interestingly, children with abundant prejudices tend to mention punishment and lack of affection when asked to describe their parents, whereas low-prejudice children tend to mention affection and cooperation.

Prejudice is reinforced in the community of children when powerful peer-group members manifest it or when discriminatory actions bring laughter or approval. Children (unless taught otherwise) are usually not aware of the impact prejudice registers on its victims, although when they become the target they protest. The surface nature of middle-children's thought process is reflected in the substance of their prejudice. Interestingly, even though the ability to analyze prejudicial ideas greatly improves after middle childhood, this mental advance does not result in the elimination of prejudiced beliefs among adolescents – a fact that intrigues clinical psychologists.

The Role of the Parent

Children frequently find one parent easier than the other to deal with. Boys who like roughhouse, usually do so with their father. (Some 11-year-old boys are almost as strong as their mothers.) During middle childhood father may have more say than mother in family discipline, especially if the household condones physical punishment such as spanking.

Around nine and ten some girls exhibit a fascination with father. At the same age, boys are known to become quite unfascinated with mother. They resent her insistence on hygiene and cleanliness, considering it somewhat ridiculous to wash off elbow dirt that will simply reappear tomorrow. They consider manners stupid and cannot comprehend why a younger sibling should be tolerated. Despite these domestic squabbles, the household actually survives rather well; in fact, things are calm compared with the domestic strife that invades many households during the adolescent years.

Parent-child interactions are not always wholesome, especially in households where parents are overly protective or overly rejecting. Children who are overprotected receive excessive parenting (usually mothering) and are not given the opportunity to develop personal independence or to learn the ropes of childhood in an open environment. Overprotective parents spend too much time with their child, and the quality of the interaction is often stifling rather than liberating. They tend to think that their child is ill when he is not. When illness does strike, they believe it more serious than it is. Overprotective parents take their kids to the doctor's office three or four times more often than ordinary parents. Overprotected kids do not cope well with peers, because they have been so sheltered that they possess weak interpersonal skills.

Rejected children are a different matter altogether. They are punished more than other children, and they rarely receive the affection every kid needs to handle the strain of childhood life. The rejected child holds a low self-concept, which manifests itself in self pity, in hostile aggression, or in fighting and quarreling.

The Downside of TV Viewing

Hundreds of research studies have investigated the effects of TV viewing on children. Remarkably, most of them yield similar findings, which in the world of social science research, is a bit unusual. The following findings, submitted by The American Academy of Pediatrics Task Force on Children and Television (1985), typify general findings uncovered in a variety of different research settings throughout the 80s.

Negative Consequences of Daily TV Viewing Repeated exposure to televised violence promotes a proclivity to violence and a passive response to its practice.

Television viewing increases consumption of high caloric density snacks and increases the prevalence of obesity.

Learning from TV is passive rather than active, and detracts from time spent reading or using active learning skills.

Television conveys unrealistic messages regarding drugs, alcohol and tobacco, and indirectly encourages their use.

The portrayal of sex roles and sexuality on TV is unrealistic and misleading: sexual relationships develop rapidly; the risk of pregnancy is rarely considered; adolescence is portrayed as a constant state of sexual crisis. These characteristics may contribute to adolescent pregnancy. Pornography on cable TV is an important concern.

TV promotes ethnic and racial stereotypes and does little to promote a sympathetic understanding of handicapped people.

Television conveys an unrealistic view of problem solving or conflict resolution.

Year by Year Growth Profiles

Since 'tis Nature's law to change,
Constancy alone is strange.

John Wilmot

As we mentioned in Chapter Eight, growth profiles describe and isolate some of the consistently recurring traits of children during specific calendar years. Like most investigations in developmental psychology, growth profiles rely upon averages and norms; therefore, they are descriptions of how children behave not prescriptions about how they should behave.

Children develop in a moderately predictable sequence, and children of similar age manifest a wide range of similarities in their physiology, psychology and morality. Growth profiles attempt to summarize these similarities of action born of age and experience.

The Six-Year-Old

Physical development is the source of numerous difficulties for the six-year-old. The first molars are emerging; the body is more susceptible to infection than it was during the preschool years; nose and throat problems increase; vision may show the first signs of strain; and gastrointestinal symptoms sometimes become manifest. Parent-child relationships are frequently stormy, because of the child's tendency to bossiness and impudence. For most children the year between the sixth and seventh birthdays is transitional, and the strain of transition is felt by the child and everyone who shares his or her world.

As a rule, the first year of school requires more adjustment for children who have not undertaken a year of preschool, but rare is the child for whom the first grade is a totally pleasant experience. Upon entering school the child leaves behind the protection and security of home. Although children are not anonymous in school, this is the closest most of them have come to the experience of anonymity. The quandary is a bit like that of the university freshman, far from home, uprooted, and convinced that everyone else is completely at home in this foreign den of learning. School stresses *group* rules, *group* participation, and *group rights;* this orientation does not mesh with the child's self-oriented and egocentric nature. School stresses timetables, schedules, and readiness; these constraints do not mesh with the child's impulsive nature. School requires a revised understanding of self, with greater emphasis on interpersonal expertise; the extent to which the youngster accommodates to these facts determines in large measure how well the first year of school goes.

A growing awareness of personal limitations looms in the consciousness of six-year-olds. Exposed to the world of numbers, letters, and sentences, children quickly sense a body of thought beyond their resources. By comparing their talents with those of classmates, the children assess their own strengths and weaknesses. The tendency of most six-year-olds to be more impressed with their strengths than their weaknesses assists them immeasurably in coping with a strenuous year. This "divine imperiousness" does not contribute to a completely honest self-evaluation but it does enhance self-esteem at a time when it is needed.

Six enjoys a certain amount of structure, convention, and routine in day-to-day living. He may want the table set just so, the bedroom precisely arranged, and a story told with the expected intonation and ending. In the 50s Arnold Gesell suggested that the predominant traits of the six-year-old are impulsiveness, dogmatism, excitability, compulsiveness, and affection. And, in fairness to Gesell and his research staff at Yale University, few scholars in the past four decades have much altered his description.

Sixes like to touch, handle, grab, mix, and manipulate. They do not merely inspect an object visually; they must touch it, as though the other senses would not operate unless triggered by messages from the fingertips. The craving for tactile stimulation brings about renewed interest in the sense-pleasure play of the toddler: clay, mud, sand, and dirt are rediscovered.

Gifted at starting projects but a dunce at finishing them, Six might be happier if life were a continual series of beginnings. If Sixes were to follow their inclinations, little would ever be finished, but a great deal would be started.

Ruled while at home and school, many six-year-olds assume the role of ruler when the social climate permits. (They never suffer a shortage of followers.) Six is inexpert at handling complex interpersonal relationships and therefore simplifies matters whenever possible. Part of the simplification involves reducing social relationships to governor and governed. Despite this tendency, social play among six-year-olds is often so diffuse and unstructured that participants can wander in and out almost at will without significantly altering the course of play. In play, sex lines are not sharply drawn, and whether a youngster is a boy or a girl does not appreciably influence anyone's expectations. This gender obliviousness will soon disappear, to be sure.

The ability to pretend is perhaps at its lifetime zenith. Six- year-olds can be anything they want to be: butterflies, flags, falling leaves, or punitive police officers. They lapse unannounced into and out of various roles. Interestingly, the six-year-old is often most organized when assuming the role of someone else. Sixes are more aware than Fives of the difference between role-playing and real life; yet one wonders just how completely differentiated things are within their fluid personality.

One can easily think of six-year-olds as hypochondriacs. They complain of ailments with greater regularity than they did during the preschool years. Muscles frequently ache, especially those of the arms and legs; mucous membranes inflame more readily than usual; and sties often develop. Throat infections frequently spread to the ears or lungs. Otitis media (inflammation of the middle ear) is at its greatest incidence since mid-toddlerhood. Allergic responses are high, aggravated by the sensitivity and ease of congestion of the mucous membranes of the nose. Girls may complain that their urine burns because of reddened genitalia – a condition that requires care. Boils may appear on the face, neck, or arms. Tension mounts to a peak in the sixth year, sometimes generating outbursts of screaming, violent temper tantrums, or even striking out physically at parents or peers.

Six-year-olds are active. Even while sitting they squirm, fidget, slide to and fro, and lean backward. Six-year-olds are not ready to sit quietly in the classroom for long periods, as will be expected in a few years. They learn best when they act out or fantasize, when they see tangible benefits of work, when their work brings praise and enthusiasm from the teacher, and when they have the freedom to flit about and check out the work of other students in the classroom. Learning and movement are part of the same process for the six-year-old.

The Seven-Year-Old

Seven is perhaps the first age at which the child is likely to show signs of genuine pensiveness and "deep" thought. Seven have a great deal to think about. Their transition from a "home child" to a "school child" required adjustments in lifestyle as well as cognitive patterns. Seven synthesizes and pieces together the fragments of what was, a year before, an unsolvable puzzle.

A kind of quieting down comes at seven. Six-year-oldness tended to produce brash reactions and bursts of activity. The seven-year-old goes into lengthening periods of calm and of self-absorption during which he works his impressions over and over, oblivious to the outer world. It is an assimilative age, seven is a time for salting down accumulated experience and for relating new experiences to the old.

Seven is more organized than Six; less energy is consumed in aimless wandering, and this parsimony of action has its equivalent in the child's questions, which become surprisingly clear and cerebral. The child relies less on authority for solutions. "Because I said so" does not have nearly the effectiveness at seven that it formerly had. Seven does not reason well, by adult standards, but at this age reason is used more adroitly and meaningfully than before. Inasmuch as seven-year-olds are more impressed than before by physical explanations, they demand that answers have a certain logic as well as overall sensibility. Seven usually does not perceive exactly what is wrong about an illogical statement but may nevertheless reject outright an illogical statement or a half-baked explanation. Rays of critical light shine from the horizon, but at seven, it remains a distant horizon.

Behavior is regulated with greater facility than a year ago; therefore, fewer impulsive bursts appear. Temper tantrums for most children are disappearing at seven – a further indication of enhanced self-control. The pronoun "I" is being replaced with "we" because Seven occasionally identifies in terms of a group; the preschooler rarely does. As Seven is remarkably advanced socially in contrast to the five-year-old, even adults who don't like kids often find them interesting and fun to visit with at this age.

Ethical sense remains immature and rigid, but personal behavior is definitely evaluated in terms of criteria beyond the person. Although seven-year-olds respond more favorably to praise than punishment, their embryonic sense of ethics leads them to conclude that punishment is the best deterrent to inappropriate behavior. This viewpoint remains firm throughout childhood; even in grades seven, eight, and nine, school principals dare not let students determine the punishment for those who break rules, because of the tendency of these students to be ruthless in dishing it out.

Seven learns to accommodate to the expectations of the teacher and eagerly anticipates the teacher's evaluations and appraisals. The child perceives the teacher's word as infallible and gives it priority when it conflicts with other sources of information. Scepticism of teacher's omniscience will emerge during later childhood years, but for the seven-year-old teacher remains as close to truth as adults can hope to be.

Most seven-year-olds are adept with cultural tools that facilitate time/space orientation, such as clocks and calendars. The seasons of the year usually are known by their correct name rather than as hunting season, basketball season, or swimming season. Many seven-year-olds accurately differentiate 30 minutes from an hour, a distinction found rather difficult the year before.

Sevens can be described not only in terms of what they are but also in terms of what they are not. They are not as flighty, assertive, and impulsive as they were at six but rather more reflective and thoughtful. They are more aware of others and capable of social politeness, although it frequently fails them. They are sampling various strategies for coping with school and schoolmates and incorporating ethics into their life-style. They are taking the first significant steps away from mother and father and, in virtually every facet of social and emotional development, evidencing growth. They teeter on the boundary between childhood innocence and the social pragmatism of later childhood.

The Eight-Year-Old

Commanding attention is the outgoing, forthright, almost aggressive nature of the eight-year-old. Eights can be viewed as miniature exponents of the Protestant Ethic because they believe that discipline, hard work, and talent will solve most problems. Although periodically admitting that they do not possess the skills required to solve a particular dilemma, Eights will in the same breath assure us that, if they did, the problem would be conquered in no time at all. The belief that human skills can solve all problems leads Eight to idolize and glorify figures who are the best at what they do, including sports heroes, movie or television stars, scientists, and doctors. Eight's glorification of these idols is not total, however, because she is also developing insight into the limitations of adults, especially teachers and parents.

Most children are more outgoing at eight than they were at seven. Play is gregarious and boisterous; the give-and-take of childhood hassle is accepted, and it inflicts less psychological hurt than it did the year before. Entrepreneurship, encouraged by the eight-year-old's growing awareness of money, manifests itself in paper delivering, pop-bottle hunting, and other activities that yield financial return.

Teachers and parents agree that Eight is less "childish" than Seven. In almost all areas of life the eight-year-old deals more effectively with adults; he responds to their communication and even learns to assume their frame of reference once in a while. Because Eights are proud of their growth, acknowledgment of it at the proper time is a prized reward. Many eight-year-olds are *unquenchable* talkers who delight in presenting theories as to why such-and-such occurred or failed to occur, sometimes giving the impression that they are more interested in hearing themselves talk than in the accuracy of the narration.

Intellectual curiosity is at its loftiest peak since toddlerhood. Social relationships, international events, astronomy, and the inner workings of automobile engines occupy the eight-year-old mentality. General ideas about electricity, democratic rule, football formations, and marital strife are assimilated, although not completely understood. Eights are not emotionally overwhelmed by what they cannot fathom; they had enough of that when they were seven. The eight-year-old sometimes conjures up memories in the adult mind of the small-town, good-natured young man depicted in 1930 movies who comes to the city expecting everyone to be as wholesome and agreeable as he is. Many parents find their child more congenial than at any time during the preceding several years.

Body proportions are shifting away from unisex shapelessness and beginning to assume some adolescent features. Arms are more elongated and the hands enlarged. Boys are fond of rough play and less vulnerable to fatigue than at seven. Segregated sex gatherings are more frequent, and the perverse habit of attracting the attention of an opposite sex member by shouting a derisive or insulting term begins, although it is infantile compared with the barbaric extremes it reaches in 11- and 12-year-olds.

Although eight-year-olds have a definite interest in sexual behavior, their interest is quite different from that of the adolescent. The interest of the eight-year-old is based more on curiosity than on sexual impulses per se.

Boys of this age enjoy hanging around older boys who talk about the wonders of sexual play. Eight will inspect pictures of nudes with interest but not enthusiasm, with curiosity but not desire, with a sense of daring but not guilt. Some eight-year-olds have experimented with the genitals of either same- or opposite-sex friends, but the motivation for this behavior is not sexual in the adolescent or adult sense. Curiosity and adventurousness better explain the sexual play of eight-year-olds.

The Nine-Year-Old

The nine-year-old is not easy to understand, because this age straddles two different worlds: that of the child and that of the preadolescent. Most Nines feel completely comfortable in neither, being too immature for the social complexity of the preadolescent and too elderly for the innocent goings-on of six- or seven-year-olds. Despite this delicate balance, emotional life is comparatively free of serious conflict; hence, day-to-day behavior is rarely characterized by social rebellion or psychological turmoil.

Many nine-year-olds are characterized by an intellectual attitude of realism, a social attitude of reasonableness, and a psychological attitude of self-motivation. No longer do they categorically reject an idea merely because it contradicts their own; nor do they refuse to listen to an argument simply because they dislike the person from whom it emanates. The nine-year-old is more self-motivated than the eight-year-old and less dependent on the praise and approval of adults. Parents cannot escape the realization that their child is gradually phasing out of childhood, because the social, intellectual, and psychological traits of preadolescence are undeniably budding.

Eight-year-olds enjoy collecting; however, the spirit of Nine leans toward classifying and planning. Nine is addicted to minutiae; a favorite pleasure is to educate parents or teacher about news gleaned from television or newspaper. Sports heroes are classified into top ten hitters and pointmakers; hobbies are sorted into special shelves and alcoves. Nine is a year of expansion, but with it comes the need to contain by ordering and classifying.

Emotional life is deepening, with finer discriminations of feeling being registered. New emotions are rocking the personality; although they are not as devastating as those encountered during adolescence, they are powerful on occasion. The child at this age may respond tearfully to a touching movie scene, indignantly to the story of a wrongdoing, or empathetically to news of a disaster. Nine is not a victim of emotions, but a new world of deeper emotion, closer in breadth and openness to that of the adolescent, is beginning to grip the personality. Many parents report that their nine-year-olds display affection more openly and convincingly than they did at eight.

Nine likes to be trusted, to be given responsibility, and to sample special freedoms, and as a rule these duties are honored. Nine-year-olds are capable of assuming considerable household responsibility when the occasion demands. During family illness, for example, they may take over management of the household for days or weeks at a time. In low income families children of this age may feed and dress younger siblings and get them off to school each morning. Nine is a good protector. She will stand up to another kid who pushes a younger sibling or defames the family name; nine is an age for bloody noses, scratched faces, and injured pride.

The facts of life are still rather abstract for both boys and girls. Nine assimilates facts about sexual intercourse and reproduction but frequently overlooks the emotional or subjective dimension of human sexuality. Ethical beliefs about sexual behavior can be discussed with the nine-year-old in a fairly straightforward manner.

Nine is open to instruction and is able to put up with a teacher he does not like. Evaluations reflect cool detachment: "I don't like old man Fisher, but he's not a bad teacher." Nine-year-olds are chatty talkers because they have a good deal to talk about; they often greet one another with a fact rather than "hello."

Nine-year-olds tend to get along well with parents for at least two basic reasons: (1) they appreciate the responsibilities of mother and father; and (2) they are not strongly attracted to behavior parents oppose. The parent-child chaos of the teen years is in large part due to the reversal of these conditions.

Distinct feelings of right and wrong emerge; as a result guilt feelings are common at this age. However, for some nine-year-olds nothing bothers the conscience. To tell a lie without batting an eye is quite possible for many youngsters, as is stealing without a pang of guilt. When angered to the point of fist fighting, nine-year-olds may fly into a rage; if they were more proficient with their fists they would maim an opponent. Nine sometimes demonstrates a callous disregard for the feelings of others, especially if such behavior has the backing of an older person, if it brings praise, or as seems so frequently the case, if the child feels he has elevated himself by debasing another.

The Ten-Year-Old

For many children the year that produces the least difficulty of the entire childhood era is that of the ten-year-old. On the whole, Ten is rather well-adjusted to the family and the community. This equilibrium can be attributed to four conditions. (1) Social demands are coped with fairly easily because they are not strenuous and because the child's increasing social facility eases interpersonal interaction. (2) Biological impulses are in check. Most ten-year-olds are at least two years away from the wholesale changes that will transform them into adolescents. (3) Ten is admired by younger children, and their respect reinforces Ten's sense of growth and maturity. (4) Ten believes in the future and is eager to venture into it. These are the ingredients of confident optimism.

Ten is easy to reason with because attitudes are flexible rather than rigid, and the mind is "open" rather than "closed." Tens like to hear alternate ideas and arguments, although they remain highly partial to their own. The child of ten is more skilled at criticizing the nature of personal thought than ever before, grasping the idea that conclusions derive from processed information. Ten-year-olds frequently are fascinated with themselves and their ideas, and enjoy hearing themselves talk about various topics. They remind us of George Bernard Shaw's comment: "I often quote myself; it adds spice to the conversation." Ten distinguishes between public and private knowledge, having outgrown the preschool belief that one's private thoughts can be read by others. The flourishing clubs and secret organizations attest to the fondness of Tens for private information not shared with parents. Privacy bolsters their sense of self-possession and independence.

Ten is increasingly aware of the gang, the clique, and the "in" crowd. Most gangs have a leader of sorts but fluidity is the norm. Few ten-year-olds have the social skills or the psychological fortitude to directly oppose the group, yet peer pressure is not overpowering as it frequently is during early adolescence.

Personal and social harmony are trademarks of ten-year-olds, as are self-acceptance and self-confidence. Here is how one expert puts it:

> In general the ten-year-old is self accepting. He likes his body and his looks, he likes what he can do in the way of sports – which is considerable – and what he can do academically. His own self-acceptance is heightened by the acceptance accorded him by peers, by family, and by school. There is a sort of mutual admiration society between the ten-year-old and his social world, which supports and reinforces his positive self-image, his self-confidence and his self acceptance. (Elkind, 1971, p. 83)

The Eleven-Year-Old

Eleven is the age of transition. Physical growth inches closer to puberty; social transitions move toward the outer circle of teen society; personal transitions engender greater richness and depth of emotion. Not all changes are exclusively toward new realities; some are away from old ones. The unisex appearance of late childhood is disappearing; dependence upon parental bonds is lessening; shallowness of childhood introspection is giving way to more pensive depths.

Boys are less developed physically than girls at 11; the most advanced girls are noticeably different from the least advanced; among boys these developmental differences are less dramatic. The average girl has achieved about 90 percent of her adult stature and about 60 percent of her adult weight. The tremendous energy consumed at this age requires increased caloric intake and Eleven eats habitually in order to keep the body furnace fueled. The edginess of physical activity often laps over onto emotional stability, resulting in peaks of intensity and outbursts of temper. Eleven rarely displays the evenness of temperment so commonly observed during the previous year when she was more of a child and less an adolescent.

Numerous social events work their way into the life of the 11-year-old. Each day is filled with new exposures; each new exposure requires some adjustment, bending, and blending. To cope with the expanding social universe, new social skills are invented and old ones refined. Eleven becomes more skilled than ever in communicating with adults in the style to which *they* are accustomed. In many regards, the rapid outward expansion of this year reminds us of the similar social explosion encountered by the six-year-old during the first grade of school. Rarely, however, is Eleven as difficult as Six. The skills of nonverbal communication are increasing. The youngster learns to measure acceptance from peers as well as from adults by their gestures, mannerisms, and glances. He does not require explicit words to receive and an explicit message. This skill greatly facilitates his ability to deal with adults who are not gifted in dealing with pesky early adolescents. (It also fosters an infatuation with mockery based upon facial expressions and other "in" modes of communication.)

The first gestures of genuine psychological emancipation commonly begin at age 11, and although the need for independence is embryonic at this stage it is unmistakably present. Independence, as a genuine psychological need of adolescence, eventually blossoms full strength during the middle teens, affording the major impetus for individuation from the biological family. Because the world of childhood is blending gradually with that of adolescence, most growth impulses at age 11 are not firm or unequivocal. Often they are weak, almost distant. They become stronger, however, with time; to this generalization there are virtually no exceptions.

The tribulations which accompany growth from one stage to another are easily noticed in the 11-year-old. Temper explosions, mood swings, fist fights, and sorrow tears are some of the tension outlets common for this age. Most growth during this year, despite the aggravations, is fairly stable and consistent. Numerous growth changes take place, but sometimes so harmoniously that they escape the notice of the very person in whom they are occurring.

The 11-year-old is no moral philosopher. Feelings about right or wrong are intense but shallow; she usually cannot be bribed (as can the preschooler) but she can be brought to admit to the ambiguity or inconsistency of her beliefs, especially if she somehow benefits from such "insight." Paucity of moral substance makes Eleven a potential victim of group pressure and, in large measure, contributes to a capacity for social cruelty.

In many instances the eleventh year marks an all-time high in the separation of the sexes. Females are typically more socially mature and this actually complicates their lives because for some inexplicable reason boys at this age become fixated upon a rather diminished interpretation of what constitutes masculine behavior. They tend to mask their interest in females behind obnoxious behavioral assertions which other equally stunned boys consider "manly." Eventually, however, (usually by age 14) the entire charade is foiled by the biology of puberty and the chemical sexuality it nurtures. Because nature bestows puberty on boys about 18 months later than upon girls, physical and social interests between the sexes are temporarily thrown off balance. Eleven is the intersection through which this biologically-induced social anomaly passes. The 11-year-old youngster is the person who experiences the sensations, bewilderments, and pleasures of living at such a crossroad.

Developmental Tasks of Middle Childhood

As the child ages, social demands increase, expectations for maturity of conduct increase, and self-imposed demands for excellence and mastery increase. Therefore, the most significant developmental tasks of this period are interpersonal and skill-based.

Learning to Establish an Independent Identity

During middle-childhood personal identity is not solely based upon family relationships. A broader self-concept evolves: friends and playmates figure prominently in daily life, and most children want to be thought well of by them. Middle children do not wish to be known only as the children of their parents, preferring to be identified by their own uniqueness. Because children are in the process of sampling new identities, they need constant feedback and reassurance. Since this surge of independence marks the first significant split in parent-child bonds, to parents it brings the inevitable realization that their child is growing beyond the physical confines of the house and the emotional confines of the family.

Even though the child is searching and exploring, he requires a stable base of security to return to after ventures into the expanded social world. Children work hard to establish an identity away from the household but parents are still the most important people in their lives. Expansion of the circle of social acquaintances does not signal the loss of parental importance; it merely reflects the need to share life and growth with more people.

Learning Group Skills

Youngsters cannot effectively establish their childhood identity unless they interact with peers according to the unwritten but real rules of childhood society. These rules, informal though they may be, require the ability: (1) to "give and take," to compromise and negotiate with other group members; (2) to participate in group events; (3) to attain social consistency and predictability, and; (4) to keep secret information private.

These skills are easily learned by most children, but every child has some difficulty along the way because of conflicting rules and expectations. Rules regulating the society of children do not always jibe with those of adult society, and to complicate matters, children's rules frequently contradict one another, stressing subservience to the group rather than the rights of the individual. The ability to cope with other children is a major test of interpersonal skills, and when conflict becomes too strenuous, children usually return home, mull it over, then drift back to the world of peers.

Parents who are over-protective may prevent their child from learning group skills that develop only at a personal price. For the toddler the price of learning to walk is hundreds of spills and falls; for the preschooler the price of learning the rights of others is hours of bickering and squabbling; and for many middle-years children the price of learning about group life is ridicule, periodic ostracism, and a good deal of thinking about what makes other kids tick. For North American children, learning appropriate group skills is an important developmental task because personal identity in adolescence and adulthood is greatly influenced by effective survival within a variety of groups. Thus, learning group social skills in middle childhood is a stepping stone to future identity.

Learning to Satisfy Needs in a Peer Context

All children possess psychological needs that must be satisfied if growth is to be continuous and complete. These include needs for security, achievement, recognition, order, and independence. These needs are important during all childhood stages, but it is during middle childhood that a major shift occurs in the means by which they are gratified. In virtually every realm the child becomes progressively more involved with peers and less involved with family. The need for recognition, which through the preschool years is almost exclusively gratified by parents, now shifts more toward the peer group. The need for acceptance, perhaps more than any other, reflects this trend away from family. The family continues to exert great influence, of course, but the child is now acted on by forces outside the family with greater impact. Because adjusting to new ways of satisfying psychological needs is sometimes emotionally difficult (for both child and parent), the middle childhood years are not without their share of hurt. However, most children handle these difficulties without excessive ego injury and without long-term distress.

Learning Appropriate Sex Roles

In the past two decades a loosening of rigid beliefs about appropriate male and female behavior has taken place in North America. As a result, less emphasis is now set on acquiring *precise* sex roles. Certain traits do, however, influence children's judgments of the masculinity or femininity of an individual. Youngsters today are not likely to think a boy masculine merely because he can kick a football farther than anyone else in the class, although this probably will help his masculine image. Among boys of this age, masculinity is an attitude rather than a series of roles or behaviors. The attitude is similar to that held by "society-at-large," although more exaggerated. For young boys masculinity generally implies (1) standing up for one's rights (however "rights" are defined), (2) not being dominated except by consent, (3) proficiency at masculine skills (however these skills are defined), and (4) excellence at any skill, except those specifically designated as feminine.

For young girls, femininity is less precisely defined, with several factors contributing to its ambiguity: (1) our society does not overtly praise feminine roles as highly as masculine roles; (2) one of the most highly prized feminine roles is adaptability; therefore, specific patterns are less common; and (3) even during childhood, girls in our society are taught the importance of accommodating to masculine activities and roles. For all of these reasons, girls hold fewer clearly defined ideas about what is feminine than boys do about what is masculine.

Learning Cognitive Maps

Many of the beliefs and attitudes that guided the child through toddlerhood and the preschool years are now obsolete. A more sophisticated understanding of the world is required if the child is to cope adequately with the magnified demands of maturity. The child develops new tools that allow a more complete understanding of the workings of the universe, the inner secrets of the personality, and the underpinnings of social interchange. Magical explanations do not suffice as they did during the preschool years; neither does parental say-so. The middle-years child needs to learn how mysteries can be solved, and how questions can be answered; he must learn to compile and evaluate information. All children require explanations, but during middle childhood not any explanation will suffice; to be accepted, an explanation must meet the standards imposed by advancing mental maturity.

The Impact of Heredity on Human Development: Identical Twins during Middle Childhood

With advancing years identical twins manifest increasing differences in temperament and personal outlook but nevertheless remain similar in important heredity-linked variables, such as height, weight, body type, and intelligence. More than during any of the previous developmental ages, identical twins choose separate paths even though they walk them with extremely similar abilities.

Of the major areas of growth described in this chapter, in physical and mental growth identical twins show the greatest similarity. They exhibit markedly similar physical patterns; they enter growth latency and spurt out of it at about the same age. Their body types will also be closely matched;

thus, if one twin is mesomorphic, the chances are excellent that the other also will be. Skeletal growth will be extremely similar as it is one of nature's most governed qualities; skeletal information about one twin will tell a great deal about skeletal growth in the other.

The striking similarity of physical measurements does not guarantee identical *abilities*. For example, one twin may have begun competitive gymnastics at age seven and, as a result, by age ten possess more developed musculature, greater flexibility, and greater stamina than her twin. The inherited physical potential of these girls is identical; however, potential is profoundly influenced by training and by middle childhood, training is as important in the emergence of abilities as is hereditary potential.

Identical twins run abreast in their mental development, passing important landmarks (such as mastering conservation tasks) at about the same age; their IQs, if measured by the best intelligence tests, will be very close. If the IQ score of one twin is 100, the chances are about 90 percent that the IQ of the other will be within 5 points of 100, if the girls are raised in the same household.

The mental advances associated with the stage of concrete thought will occur for both girls during middle childhood, although there is no assurance that the changes will appear at the same time or in exactly the same sequence. The aspects of mental development influenced by maturation (such as memory) will exhibit parity. But mental abilities are greatly influenced by coaching and practice; so, even though identical twins have similar potential, one twin may have *actualized* potential far more than the other. The *deficiencies* of thought also show many parallels in the two girls; however, this is an area infused with tremendous individual differences.

The *social world* of identical twins is another ball game altogether, because social development is minimally regulated by maturation and maximally influenced by temperament, learning, and the unique configurations of personality. Maturational factors dictate some general tendencies, but social development is more influenced by environment than by any innate trait. One twin may hold a high self-concept and the other a poor self-concept; one may be popular with the peer group and the other unpopular. Aggression and competitiveness may differ considerably, because of differing responses to pressure and frustration.

Our twins may demonstrate similarity with regard to popularity, self-concept, and aggression, but we should not attribute this similarity to hereditary factors. If our twins' parents are overly protective, or punitively rejecting, each girl might respond differently to this faulty treatment, one perhaps becoming aggressive and the other passive. However, both girls likely would suffer some adverse effects from parental mistreatment.

Similarities between identical and fraternal twins on a variety of characteristics and diseases		
	Identical	Fraternal
Hair Color	88%	22%
Eye Color	99%	28%
Blood Pressure	63%	36%
Pulse Rate	56%	34%
Clubfoot	32%	3%
Diabetes Mellitus	84%	37%
Tuberculosis	74%	28%
Epilepsy (idiopathic)	72%	15%
Scarlet Fever	64%	47%
Stomach Cancer	27%	4%
Smoking Habit	91%	65%
Alcohol Drinking	100%	86%
Coffee Drinking	94%	79%
Feeblemindedness	94%	47%
Schizophrenia	80%	13%
Manic-depressive Psychosis	77%	19%
Mongolism	89%	7%

(based upon M.W. Strickberger, 1968)

Moral development, like social development, is highly individualized, and maturation does not influence it as much as do social factors. Nevertheless, mental maturity does influence moral judgments. Therefore, one can safely predict that neither twin will function consistently at Kohlberg's Level III, because neither possesses the ability to think about issues in the complex manner required for Level-III judgment. The thought process is colored by egocentrism during middle childhood, and when solving moral puzzles twins both operate under this constraint; to this extent they are similar. However, with regard to the specific conclusions they will draw, or the particular moral decisions they will make, one can only guess at how similar they will be.

Thus, having grown through childhood, our imaginary identical twins are now ready to phase into early adolescence, where they will continue to grow in their unique personalities and to mature in independent directions. Their physical growth and their mental abilities, however, will continue to bear a striking resemblance because the genetic blueprints that regulate human growth and development continue to exert powerful influence through the adolescent years.

Overview

During the middle-childhood years the youngster moves from the baby-ishness of the preschooler to the composure and matter-of-factness of the schoolchild. Middle children interact with adults in a fluid and versatile manner completely beyond the expectations of a preschooler and, because of increases in their range of emotion, understand aspects of adult experience heretofore out of their reach. All of these advances subtly shape the middle child in annual increments.

Middle childhood is, in some respects, nature's moment for taking a breath. The hectic pace of earlier childhood growth lets up (although certainly growth does not grind to a halt), and, all things taken into account, the middle child grows in a more uniform manner than during earlier years when the uncompromising guidelines of heredity ruled development.

Physical growth proceeds at a fairly uniform pace. Although each individual grows at a personal rate, the tendency is for growth to be smooth rather than turbulent and consistent rather than sporadic. The body becomes stronger, thicker, and wider, and its owner acquires greater coordination of movement. The latency period precedes the major sexual transformations of puberty; therefore, in middle childhood the sexes are not radically different on most important biological dimensions. The three dominant body types (endomorphic, mesomorphic, and ectomorphic) are easily observed among middle children, and the ability to accurately predict the future body build of a given child increases as baby fat disappears and the skeleton moves toward its adult configuration.

The social world mushrooms into prominence during middle childhood. Social involvements deepen, friendships strengthen, and interaction with the clique is elevated to an art form. The need to belong acquires a nonfamilial dimension – a childhood first. Aggression and competition become integrated into the personality, and their effective socialization is a major challenge to parents, schools and the child himself.

Canadian Youth and Fear of Nuclear Threat

Between 1984 and 1989, 8,000 Canadian junior and senior high students had their thoughts on the future polled in the *Canadian Children's Concerns about the Future* (CCCAF) survey (Lewis, Goldberg and Parker, 1989). The results of this study show remarkable consistency with other national surveys. For example, the most frequent response to the question, "When you think of your future, what three things do you worry about the most?," was fear of war (nuclear or otherwise). Similar results were reported by Solantus, Rimpela, and Taipale (1984) in their survey of Finnish youth.

From a list of nine "possible worries," 65 percent of the Canadian students ranked nuclear war as "very important," second only to "parent's death." This result concurred with the attitudes of California youth reported in 1983 (Doctor, et al, 1983).

The CCCAF study allows professionals to consider adolescent fear of the nuclear threat in comparison to other common preoccupations of youth. For example, when asked whether thoughts of their job plans had led to feelings of anxiety, 63 percent of the students agreed that this had occurred at least a few times in the past month. On the other hand, 59 percent reported similar unemployment-inspired anxiety and 57 percent reported similar nuclear war inspired anxiety. Furthermore, 23 percent of the students surveyed reported that thinking of nuclear war had a) affected their future plans to marry and have children, or b) caused them to "live for today and forget about the future."

Although 47 percent of the respondents had talked about nuclear issues in the home, school, or with peers at least once in the last month, their primary source of information was television. The media (TV and print) were the primary sources of "nuclear education," followed by books, family, school, and friends.

More research is required to determine whether "living in the nuclear shadow" will have detrimental effects on the mental health of today's youth. However, current research suggests that young people:

a) have access to information on the nuclear threat,

b) have a fear of nuclear war that affects their view of the future.

Major Concepts of this Chapter

1. Physical growth during these years is regular and consistent. Outstanding physical developments include increased manual dexterity, increased strength, increased resistance to fatigue, and increased coordination.

2. Comparing chronological age with maturational age allows for classification into "average," "accelerated" and "retarded" rates of development.

3. Body types are classified as endomorphic (lean build), mesomorphic (athletic, well developed musculature) and ectomorphic (rounded body, greater body fat).

4. Sex differences in mid-childhood include the following: girls mature faster than boys, reach puberty earlier, and their development tends to be more regular and predictable. Additionally, girls tend to have a greater percentage of body fat than boys. Athletic skills of boys and girls increase during the childhood years.

5. Social development is marked by the formation of peer groups and peer relationships beyond the family. Conformity, dealing with peer pressure, and popularity are important to the mid-years child.

6. Aggression during the mid-years is more evident in boys than in girls. The relative influence of biological and environmental causes for this are unclear.

7. By the time children reach Grade one they may have acquired many societal prejudices. These prejudices are usually based on "differences" reinforced within the community of children.

8. Major developmental tasks of the mid-childhood years include learning to establish an independent identity, learning group skills, learning to satisfy needs in a social context, learning appropriate sex roles, and learning cognitive maps.

9. Identical twins manifest increasing differences in temperament and personal outlook during the childhood years but show much similarity in physical and intellectual growth. Although physical development tends to be parallel, physical abilities may be quite different as the result of different interests and training. Social development may show marked differences as this is guided more by temperamental and environmental influences.

References

Ainsworth, M. (1973). The development of infant-mother attachment. In B. Caldwell (Ed.) *Review of child developmental research, 3*. University of Chicago Press.

Aleksandrowicz, M., & Aleksandrowicz, D.R. (1974). Obstetrical pain-relieving drugs as predictors of infant variability. *Child Development, 45,* 935-945.

American Academy of Pediatrics. (1978). Juice in ready to use bottles and nursing bottle caries. *News and Comment, 29,* 1.

Asher, S.R., & Renshaw, P.B. (1981). Children without friends. In S.R. Asher and J.M. Gottman (Eds.) *The Development of Children's Friendships* (pp. 273-296). New York: Cambridge University Press.

Avery, M., Aylward, G., Creasy, R., Little, A., & Stripp, B. (1986). Update on prenatal steroid for prevention of respiratory distress: report of a conference. *American Journal of Obstetrics and Gynecology, 155,* 2-5.

Bandura, A. (1982). Self-efficacy mechanism in human agency. *American Psychologist, 37,* 122-147.

Bandura, A., & Schunck, D.H. (1981). Cultivating competence, self-efficacy, and intrinsic interest through proximal self-motivation. *Journal of Personality and Social Development, 41,* 586-598.

Bandura, A., & Walters. R.H.(1963). *Social Learning and Personality.* New York: Holt, Rinehart & Winston.

Baumrind, D. (1972). Socialization and instrumental competence in young children. In W.W. Hartup (Ed.), *The Young Child: Reviews of Research (Vol. 2),* 202-224. Washington, D.C.: National Association for the Education of Young Children.

Bayley, N. (1969). *Manual for the Bayley Scales of Infant Development.* New York: Psychological Corporation,

Bayley, N., & Pinneau, S.R. (1952). Tables for predicting adult height from skeletal age: Revised for use with the Greulich-Pyle Hand Standards. *Journal of Pediatrics, 46*(4), 423-41.

Bee, H. (1989). *The Developing Child.* New York: Harper & Row, Publishers.

Behrman, S., Kistner, R., and Patton, G. (Eds.). (1988). *Progress in Infertility.* Boston: Little, Brown & Co.

Belkin, G.S., & Gray, J.L. (1977). *Educational Psychology: An Introduction.* Dubuque, Iowa: Wm. C. Brown.

Bell, R.Q. (1968). A reinterpretation of the direction of effects in studies of socialization. *Psychological Review, 75,* 84-88.

Bettelheim, B. (1987). *A Good Enough Parent.* New York: Alfred A. Knopf.

Blackman, L. (1985). Chlamydial infection in early infancy. In N.M. Nelson (Ed.) *Current Therapy in Neonatal-Perinatal Medicine 1985-1986.* (pp. 156-158). Burlington, Ont.: B.C. Decker.

Blau, T.H. (1974). Sinister psychology. *Science News,* 106(14).

Bloom, B. (1965).*Compensatory Education for Cultural Deprivation.* New York: Holt, Rinehart & Winston.

Bower, T.G.R. (1975). Infant perception of the third dimension and object concept development, in L.B. Cohen and P. Salapatek (Eds.) *Infant Perception: From Sensation to Cognition.* New York: Academic Press.

Bower, T.G.R. (1979). *Human Development.* San Francisco: Freeman.

Bowlby, J. (1952). *Maternal Care and Mental Health.* World Health Organization.

Brophy, J.E. (1977). *Child Development and Socialization.* Chicago: SRA.

Broverman, D.M. (1964). Physique and growth in adolescence. *Child Development, 35,* 857-70.

Bruner, J.S. (1966). *Toward a Theory of Instruction.* Cambridge, Mass.: Belknap Press of Harvard University Press.

Cairns, R.B. (1979). *Social Development: The Origins and Plasticity of Interchanges.* San Francisco: Freeman.

Caplan, F. (Ed.). (1973). *The First Twelve Months of Life: Your Baby's Growth Month by Month.* New York: Grosset & Dunlap.

Caplan, F., & Caplan, T. (1977). *The Second Twelve Months of Life* Toronto: Bantam Books.

Chasnof, I. (Ed.). (1986). *Drug Use in Pregnancy: Mother and Child.* Lancaster: MTP Press.

Chukovsky, K. (1963). *From two to five.* Berkeley: University of California Press.

Church, J. (1966). *Language and the Discovery of Reality.* New York: Vintage Books, Random House.

Clarke-Stewart, A., & Friedman, S. (1987). *Child Development: Infancy Through Adolescence.* New York: John Wiley & Sons.

Clarke-Stewart, K. (1973). Interactions between mothers and their young children. *Monographs of the Society for Research in Child Development, 38,* (Nos. 6-7).

Cole, M., & Cole, S. (1989). *The Development of Children.* New York: Scientific American Books.

Corrigan, G. (1976). The fetal alcohol syndrome. *Texas Medicine, 72,* 72-74.

Cratty, B.J. (1970). *Perceptual and Motor Development in Infants and Children.* London: Macmillan.

Craig, G.J. (1989). *Human Development, 5th Ed.,* Englewood Cliffs, N.J.: Prentice Hall.

Crider, C. (1981). Children's conception of body interior. In R. Bibace and M.E. Walsh (Eds.) *Children's Conception of Health, Illness and Bodily Functions.* San Francisco: Jossey-Bass.

DeCasper, A., & Fifer, W. (1980). Of human bonding: newborns prefer their mother's voices. *Science, 208,* 1174-1176.

DeCasper, A., & Prescott, P. (1984). Human newborn's perception of male voices: preference, discrimination and reinforcing value. *Developmental Psychobiology, 17,* 481-491.

Dennis, W. (1940). The effect of cradling practices upon the onset of walking of Hopi children. *Journal of Genetic Psychology, 56,* 77-86.

Doctor, R., Shoumaker, W., Powell, A., Creaner, L., & Cohen, K. (1983). *Nuclear War: A Study of Concerns of Adolescents About this Threat.* Paper presented at the International Society of Political Psychologists Meeting, Oxford, England.

Dodson, F. (1970). *How to Parent.* New York: Signet.

Dweck, C.S., & Elliott, E.S. (1983). Achievement motivation. In P. Mussen (Ed.), *Handbook of Child Psychology: Vol. 4. Socialization and Personality Development.* New York: Wiley.

Elkind, D. (1971). *Sympathetic Understanding of the Child: Six to Sixteen.* Boston: Allyn & Bacon.

Erikson, E. (1950). *Childhood and Society.* New York: Norton.

Ernhart, C., Sokal, R., Martier, S., Moron, P., Nadler, D. Ager, J., & Wolf, A. (1987). Alcohol teratogenicity in the human: A detailed assessment of specificity, critical period, and threshold. *American Journal of Obstetrics and Gynecology, 156,* 33-39.

Espenschade, A. (1960). Motor development. In W. R. Johnson (Ed.), *Science and Medicine of Exercise and Sports.* New York: Harper & Row.

Flavell, J.H. (1963). *The Developmental Psychology of Jean Piaget.* Princeton, N.J.: Van Nostrand Reinhold.

Fogel, A., & Melson, G.F. (1988). *Child Development: Individual, Family, and Society.* St. Paul, Minnesota: West Publishing Co.

Fraiberg, S. (1959). *The Magic Years.* New York: Scribners.

Frenkel-Brunswick, E. (1958). A study of prejudice in children. *Human Relations, 1,* 295-306.

Galinsky, E. (1986). *Between generations: The six stages of parenthood.* New York: Times Books.

Gardner, H.O. (1983). *Frames of Mind.* New York: Norton.

Garger, S., & Guild, P. (1984). Learning styles: The crucial differences. *Curriculum Review, 23,* 24-27.

Gesell, A. (1940). *The First Five Years of Life: The Preschool Years.* New York: Harper & Row.

Gesell, A., et al. (1940). *The First Five Years of Life: A Guide to the Study of the Preschool Child.* New York: Harper & Brothers.

Gesell, A., & Ilg, F.L. (1943). *Infant and Child in the Culture of Today.* New York: Harper & Brothers.

Gesell, A., & Ilg, F.L. (1946). *The Child from Five to Ten.* New York: Harper & Brothers.

Goldfarb, W. (1947). Variations in adolescent adjustment of institutionally reared children. *American Journal of Orthopsychiatry, 17,* 449-457.

Gordon, I.J. (1969). *Human Development.* New York: Harper & Row.

Goleman, S. (1984). Studies of children as witnesses find surprising accuracy. *New York Times, November 6,* Section C, p.4.

Gottlieb, M.I., & Williams, J.E. (1987). *Textbook of Developmental Pediatrics.* New York: Plenum.

Gray, G.W. (1967). Human growth. In W.S. Laughlin (Ed.), *Human Variations and Origins.* San Francisco: Freemans.

Green, M. (1989). *Theories of Human Development.* Englewood Cliffs, N.J.: Prentice Hall.

Guinan, M., & Hardy, A. (1987). Epidemiology of AIDS in women in the United States: 1981 through 1986. *Journal of the American Medical Association, 257,* 2039-2042.

Hacker, N., & Moore, J. (1986). *Essentials of Obstetrics and Gynecology.* Philadelphia: W.B. Saunders.

Hale, J.E. (1982). *Black Children: Their Roots, Culture and Learning Styles.* Provo, Utah: Brigham Young University.

Harlow, H.F., & Zimmerman, R.R. (1959). Affectional responses in the infant monkey. *Science, 130,* 430.

Hartup, W.W. (1970). Peer interaction and social organization. In P.H. Mussen (Ed.), *Carmichael's Manual of Child Psychology (3rd ed.; Vol. 2)*, 457-558. New York: Wiley.

Hobel, C., Medearis, A., & Oakes, G. (1985). Assessment of fetal health. In N.M. Nelson (Ed.), *Current Therapy in Neonatal-Perinatal Medicine 1985-1986*. 1-6. Burlington, Ont.: B.C. Decker Inc.

Hunt, R.G., & Synnerdale, V. (1959). Social influences among kindergarten children. *Sociology and Social Research, 43*, 171-174.

Ichinoe, K., Wake, N., Shinkai, N., Shiina, Y., Miyazaki, Y., & Tanaka, T. (1987). Nonsurgical therapy to preserve oviduct function in patients with tubal pregnancies. *American Journal of Obstetrics and Gynecology, 156*, 484-487.

Kagan, J. (1970). On class differences and early development. In V.H. Denenberg (Ed.), *Education of the Infant and Young Child*. New York: Academic Press.

Kagan, J. (1981). *The Second Year: The Emergence of Self-Awareness*. Cambridge, MA.: Harvard University Press.

Kagan, J. (1984). *The Nature of the Child*. New York: Basic Books.

Kagan, J., & Klein, R.E. (1973). Cross-cultural perspectives on early development. *American Psychologist, 28*, 947-961.

Kallman, F.J. (1946). The genetic theory of schizophrenia. *American Journal of Psychiatry, 103*, 309-322.

Kaplan, H., & Sadock, B. (1988). *Synopsis of Psychiatry*. Baltimore: Williams & Wilkins.

Keeling, J. (Ed.). (1987). *Fetal and Neonatal Pathology*. New York: Springer-Verlag.

Koch, H.L. (1966). *Twins*. Chicago: University of Chicago Press.

Kohlberg, L. (1964). Development of moral character and moral ideology. *Review of Child Development Research, 1*, 383-431.

Krogman, W.M. (1972). *Child Growth*. Ann Arbor: University of Michigan Press.

Lange, D.L., Baker, R.K., & Ball, S.J. (1969). *Mass Media and Violence: A Report to the National Commission on the Causes and Prevention of Violence (Vol. 2)*. Washington, D.C.: Government Printing Office.

Langlois, J., & Downs, C. (1979). Peer relations as a function of physical attractiveness: the eye of the beholder or behavioural reality? *Child Development, 50*, 409-418.

Langlois, J., & Stephan, C. (1977). The effects of physical attraction and ethnicity on children's behavioural attributions and peer preferences. *Child Development, 48*, 1694-1698.

Leboyer, F. (1975). *Birth Without Violence*. New York: Knopf.

Lefrancois, G.R. (1974). *Of Humans: Introductory Psychology by Kongor*. Monterey: Brooks/Cole.

Lenneberg, E.H. (1966). The natural history of language. In F. Smith and G.A. Miller (Eds.), *The Genesis of Language*. Cambridge, Mass.: M.l.T. Press.

Lenneberg, E. (1967). *Biological Foundations of Language*. New York: Wiley.

Liebert, R.M., & Baron, R. (1972). Some immediate effects of televised violence on children's behavior. *Developmental Psychology, 6*, 469-475.

Lewis, R.C.B., Goldberg, S., & Parker, K.R. (1989). Nuclear worries of Canadian youth: replication and extension. *American Journal of Orthopsychiatry*.

Luke, C. (1988). *Television and Your Child.* Toronto: Kagan & Wood Ltd.

Luria, A.R. (1973). *The Working Brain.* New York: Basic Books.

Maccoby, E.E., & Jacklin, C.N. (1974). *The Psychology of Sex Differences.* Stanford, CA: Stanford University Press.

Maccoby, E.E. (1980). *Social Development: Psychological Growth and the Parent-Child Relationship.* New York: Harcourt Brace Jovanovich.

Maccoby, E.E. (1974). Middle childhood in the context of the family. In W.A. Collins (Ed.), *Development During Middle Childhood: The Years from Six to Twelve.* Washington D.C. National Academy Press.

Malina, R.M. (1979). Secular changes in size and maturity: Causes and effects. In A.L. Roche (Ed.), Secular Trends in Human Growth, Maturation and Development. Monographs of the Society for Research. In *Child Development, 44*(3-4, Serial No. 179).

McGraw, M. (1940). Neural maturation as exemplified by achievement of bladder control. *Journal of Pediatrics, 16,* 580-590.

Meece, J.L., Parsons, J.E., Kaczola, C.M., Goff, S.B., & Futterman, R. (1982). Sex differences in math achievement: Toward a model of academic choice. *Psychological Bulletin, 91,* 324-348.

Merritt, T., Hallman, M., Bloom, B., Berry, C., Benirschke, K., Sahn, D., Key, T., Edwards, D., Jarvenpaa, A., Pohjavuori, M., Kankaanpaa, K., Kunnas, M., Paatero, H., Rapola, J., & Jaaskelainen, J. (1986). Prophylactic treatment of very premature infants with human surfactant. *New England Journal of Medicine, 315,* 785-790.

Mishell, D., Kirschbaum, T., & Morrow, C. (Eds.), (1988). *1988 Year Book of Obstetrics and Gynecology.* Chicago: Year Book Medical Publishers.

Mitchell, J.J. (1973). *Human Life: The First Ten Years.* Toronto: Holt, Rinehart & Winston.

Mitchell, J.J. (1975). *The Adolescent Predicament.* Toronto: Holt, Rinehart & Winston.

Mitchell, J.J. (1978). *Adolescent Psychology.* Toronto: Holt, Rinehart & Winston.

Mitchell, J.J. (1980). *Child Development.* Toronto: Holt, Rinehart & Winston.

Mitchell, J.J. (1986). *The Nature of Adolescence.* Calgary: Detselig Enterprises.

Mittler, P. (1971). *The Study of Twins.* Harmondsworth, Mddx., England: Penguin.

Moshman, D., Glover, J.A., & Bruning, R.H. (1987). *Developmental Psychology.* Boston: Little, Brown & Co.

Mussen, P.H. (1963). *Psychological Development of the Child.* Englewood Cliffs, N.J.: Prentice-Hall.

Mussen, P.H., Conger, J.J., & Kagan, J. (1979). *Child Development and Personality (5th ed.).* New York: Harper & Row.

Naeye, R.L. (1980). Sudden infant death. *Scientific American, 242,* 56-62.

Nelson, N. (Ed.). (1985). *Current Therapy in Neonatal-Perinatal Medicine 1985-1986.* Toronto: B.C. Decker.

Newman, B.M., & Newman, P.R. (1978). *Infancy and Childhood.* New York: Wiley.

Newman, Freeman, F. N., & Holzinger, K. J. (1937). *Twins: A Study of Heredity and Environment.* Chicago: University of Chicago Press.

Nilson, L., Furuhjelm, M., Ingelman-Sundberg, A., & Wirsen, C. (1976). *A Child is Born.* New York: Delacourte Press.

Papousek, H. (1967). Experimental studies of appetitional behaviour in human newborns. In H. W. Stevenson (Ed.), *Early Behavior: Comparative and Developmental Approaches*. New York: Wiley.

Parson, J.E., Adler, T.F., & Kaczala, C.M. (1982). Socialization of achievement attitudes and beliefs: Parental influences. *Child Development, 53,* 310-321.

Paton, T., & Yacoub, W. (1987). *The Risk Register Approach to the Observation of Children's Development*. Edmonton: Edmonton Board of Health.

Persaud, T., Chaudley, A., & Skalko, R. (Eds.). (1985). *Basic Concepts in Teratology*. New York: Alan R. Liss.

Piaget, J. (1932). *The Moral Judgment of the Child*. Boston: Routledge & Kegan Paul.

Piaget, J. (1951). *Play, Dreams and Imitation in Childhood*. New York: Norton.

Piaget, J. (1952). *The Origins of Intelligence in Children*. New York: International Universities Press.

Pines, M. (1970). Infants are smarter than anybody thinks. *New York Times Magazine,* November 29.

Pines, M. (1985). *Science Digest, 68,* 36-39.

Pribam, K.H., & Luria, A.R. (Eds.). (1973). *Psychophysiology of the Frontal Lobes*. New York: Academic Press.

Provence, S., & Lipton R.C. (1962). *Infants in Institutions*. New York: International Universities Press.

Robichaux, A., & Grossman, J. (1985). Obstetric management of herpes simplex infections. In N.M. Nelson (Ed.) *Current Therapy in Neonatal-Perinatal Medicine 1985-1986*. (pp. 54-56). Burlington, Ont.: B.C. Decker.

Rodeck, C. (1985). Fetoscopy and chorion biopsy. In N.M. Nelson (Ed.) *Current Therapy in Neonatal-Perinatal Medicine 1985-1986*. (pp. 84-89). Burlington, Ont.: B.C. Decker.

Rosenberg, M. (Ed.). (1987). *Smoking and Reproductive Health*. Littleton: PSG Publishing.

Rovee, C.K., & Rovee, D.T. (1969). Conjugate reinforcement of infant exploratory behavior. *Journal of Experimental Child Psychology, 8,* 33-39.

Rudd, P., & Peckham, C. (1988). Infection of the fetus and the newborn: prevention, treatment and related handicap. *Bailliere's Clinical Obstetrics and Gynecology, 2,* 55-69.

Rutter, M. (1983). School effects on pupil progress: Research findings and policy implications. *Child Development, 54,* 1-29.

Sadler, T. (1985). *Langman's Medical Embryology*. Baltimore: Williams & Wilkins.

Sadovsky, E., Samualoff, A., Sadovsky, Y., & Ohel, G. (1986). Incidence of spontaneous and evoked fetal movements. *Gynecological and Obstetrics Investigation, 21,* 177-181.

Scarr, S. (1983). An evolutionary perspective on infant intelligence. In M. Lewis (Ed.) *Origins of intelligence: Infancy and early childhood. (2nd ed.)*. New York: Plenum.

Scarr, S. (1986). *Understanding Development*. New York: Harcourt, Brace & Jovanovich.

Schaffer, H. (1966). The onset of fear of strangers and the incongruity hypothesis. *Child Psychologist,* 96-106.

Scheinfeld, A. (1957). *Twins and Supertwins.* New York: Lippincott.

Schell, R.E., & Hall, E. (1979). *Developmental Psychology Today.* New York: CRM/Random House.

Sears, R.R. (1957). *Patterns of Child Rearing.* New York: Harper & Row.

Sears, W. (1989). Wearing your baby. *Mothering,* Winter. Santa Fe, New Mexico.

Selman, R.L., & Byrne, D.F. (1974). A structural developmental analysis of levels of role taking in middle childhood. *Child Development, 55,* 288-304.

Sheldon, W. (1940). *The Varieties of Human Physique.* New York: Harper & Brothers.

Shultz, T.R. (1974). Development of the appreciation of riddles. *Child Development, 45,* 100-105.

Shultz, T.R., & Horibe, F. (1974). Development of the appreciation of verbal jokes. *Developmental Psychology, 10,* 13-20.

Skeels, H.M. (1939). A study of the effects of differential stimulation on mentally retarded children. *Proceedings Addresses of the American Association on Mental Deficiency, 44,* 114-136.

Smith, A. (1960). A further note on mongolism in twins. *British Journal of Social and Preventive Medicine, 14,* 27.

Smith, P., Wait, R., & Mumford, D. (1985). Teenage pregnancy. In N.M. Nelson (Ed.) *Current Therapy in Neonatal-Perinatal Medicine 1985-1986.* (pp. 28-33). Burlington, Ont.: B.C. Decker.

Solantus, T., Rimpela, M., & Taipale, V. (1984). The threat of war in the minds of 12-18 year olds in Finland. *The Lancet, 8380,*(1), 784-785.

Spitz, R. (1965). *The First Year of Life.* New York: International Universities Press.

Spock, B. (1957). *Baby and Child Care.* New York: Pocket Books.

Sroufe, L.A., & Cooper, R.G. (1988). *Child Development.* New York: Alfred A. Knopf.

Stern, C. (1973). *Principles of human genetics.* San Francisco: W.H. Freeman.

Strickberg, M.W. (1968). *Genetics.* New York: Macmillan Pub. Co.

Stone, J, & Church, J. (1968). *Childhood and adolescence* (2nd ed.). New York: Random House.

Sunley, R. (1968). Early nineteenth century American literature on childrearing. In E.D. Evans (Ed.), *Children: Readings in Behavior and Development.* (pp. 2-18). New York: Holt, Rinehart & Winston.

Tanner, J.M. (1963). The regulation of human growth. *Child Development, 34,* 817-847.

Thomas, A., & Chess, S. (1977). *Temperament and Development.* New York: Brunner/Mazel.

Thomas, A., & Chess, S. (1986). The New York Longitudinal Study: From infancy to early adult life. In R. Plomin and J. Dunn (Eds.) *The Study of Temperament: Changes Continuities and Challenges.* Hillsdale, N.J.: Earlbaum.

Thomas, J.R., & French, K.E. (1985). Gender differences across age in motor performance: A meta-analysis. *Psychological Bulletin, 98,* 260-282.

Trotter, R.J. (1987). *Psychology Today,* 32-38.

Waber, D.P. (1977). Sex differences in mental abilities, hemispheric lateralization, and rate of physical growth at adolescence. *Developmental Psychology, 13,* 29-38.

Watson, E.H., & Lowrey, G.H. (1962). *Growth and Development of Children* (4th ed.). Chicago: Year Book Medical Publishers.

Watson, J.B. (1924). *Behaviorism.* Chicago: University of Chicago Press.

Webb, P.K. (1989). *The Emerging Child: Development Through Age Twelve.* New York: MacMillan Publishing Company.

White, B.L. (1971). *Human Infants: Experience and Psychological Development.* Englewood Cliffs, N.J.: Prentice-Hall.

White, S.H. (1969). Some general outlines of the matrix developmental changes between five and seven years. Paper presented at the International Congress of Psychology, London.

Woodward, M.A. (1966). *The Earliest Years: Growth and Development of Children Under Five.* Oxford: Pergamon Press.

Yussen, S.R., & Santrock, J.W. (1978). *Child Development.* Dubuque, Iowa: Wm. C. Brown.

Zajonc, R.B. (1975). Birth order and intellectual development. *Psychological Review, 82,* 74-88.

Index